Consuming Female Beauty:
British Literature and Periodicals, 1840–1914

Gender and the Body in Literature and Culture
Series editors: Ruth Heholt and Joanne Parsons

Recent books in the series:
Consuming Female Beauty: British Literature and Periodicals, 1840–1914
Michelle J. Smith

Forthcoming
Vladimir Mayakovsky, Poetics of Virility and Masculine Style
Connor Doak

The Drunkard in Victorian Fiction and Culture: From Conviviality to Cursed Thirst
Pam Lock

Consuming Female Beauty: British Literature and Periodicals, 1840–1914

Michelle J. Smith

EDINBURGH
University Press

Edinburgh University Press is one of the leading university presses in the UK. We publish academic books and journals in our selected subject areas across the humanities and social sciences, combining cutting-edge scholarship with high editorial and production values to produce academic works of lasting importance. For more information visit our website: edinburghuniversitypress.com

© Michelle J. Smith 2022, 2024

First published in hardback by Edinburgh University Press 2022

Edinburgh University Press Ltd
The Tun – Holyrood Road
12(2f) Jackson's Entry
Edinburgh EH8 8PJ

Typeset in 11/13 Adobe Sabon by
by Cheshire Typesetting Ltd, Cuddington, Cheshire, and
printed and bound by CPI Group (UK) Ltd,
Croydon, CR0 4YY

A CIP record for this book is available from the British Library

ISBN 978 1 4744 7009 4 (hardback)
ISBN 978 1 4744 7010 0 (paperback)
ISBN 978 1 4744 7011 7 (webready PDF)
ISBN 978 1 4744 7012 4 (epub)

The right of Michelle J. Smith to be identified as the author of this work has been asserted in accordance with the Copyright, Designs and Patents Act 1988, and the Copyright and Related Rights Regulations 2003 (SI No. 2498).

Contents

List of Figures vi
Acknowledgements viii

Introduction 1

Part I: Nature vs Artifice
1. The Impossible Ideal: Beauty, Health and Character 29
2. The Dark Side of Beauty: Cosmetics, Artifice and Danger 54

Part II: Youth and Ageing
3. Beauty and Girlhood 83
4. Beauty and Ageing 109

Part III: Reshaping Female Beauty
5. The Celebrity as Beauty Icon 135
6. Embracing the Beauty Regimen in British and American Women's Magazines 159

Conclusion 184

Bibliography 189
Index 200

Figures

0.1	Alexander Walker, Three Types of Beauty. *Beauty*. 1836. New York: Henry G. Langley, 1845.	15
2.1	'The Celebrated American Specialist', advertisement. *Queen* 3 December 1892: n.p. Bodleian Library.	68
3.1	Sydney Cowell, 'They Had the Beauty of Youth and Health'. *Girl's Own Paper* July 1896: 632.	84
3.2	Rowlands' Kalydor advertisement, *Girl's Own Paper*, 'Lily Leaves'. Extra Summer Number 1886: n.p.	91
3.3	Illus. Mrs W. Allingham, *Six to Sixteen*. London: George Bell and Sons, 1886.	100
4.1	Undated advertising brochure for Plantol soap. John Johnston Collection of Printed Ephemera, Bodleian Library.	112
4.2	Blackham's hair products, pamphlet. John Johnson Collection of Printed Ephemera, 1895. Bodleian Library.	113
4.3	Pears' Soap advertisement. *Myra's Journal of Dress and Fashion* 1 June 1888: 325.	115
4.4	Camelline advertisement. *Woman* 15 April 1896: iii. Bodleian Library.	116
4.5	Illustration of Mrs Skewton, 'Phiz'. *Dombey and Son*, 1848.	126
5.1	Diaphane advertisement. *Queen* 4 June 1892: xxx. Bodleian Library.	138
5.2	Pears' Soap Advertisement. *Sketch* 3 January 1894: 552.	140
5.3	'Our Ladies Pages'. *Sketch* 16 January 1895: 590.	142

5.4	Frederick Dolman. 'Madame Marie Roze at Home'. *Myra's Journal of Dress and Fashion* 1 June 1891: 1.	143
5.5	Géraudel's Pastilles advertisement. *Sketch* 28 November 1894: 243.	147
5.6	Hilder and Godbold advertisement. *Myra's Journal of Dress and Fashion* 1 July 1879: n.p.	150
5.7	Neigeline advertisement. *Sketch* 10 October 1894: 611.	151
5.8	Rimmel's Specialties for the Complexion advertisement. *Myra's Journal of Dress and Fashion* 1 July 1880: 222.	153
5.9	Pomeroy Skin Food advertisement. *Sketch* 12 January 1910: vi.	154
6.1	'Beth'. 'The Diary of an Ugly Duckling'. *Delineator* January 1908: 117.	169
6.2	La Blanche face powder advertisement. *Delineator* August 1905: 297.	171
6.3	Grace Peckham Murray. 'The Fountain of Youth. First Paper: The Face'. *Delineator* January 1904: 92.	173
6.4	Grace Peckham Murray. 'The Fountain of Youth. First Paper: The Face'. *Delineator* January 1904: 95.	173
6.5	Dr Edison's Obesity Pills advertisement. *Delineator* July 1896: 12.	176

Acknowledgements

With copious thanks to Kristine Moruzi for her encouragement throughout the drafting of this monograph, and for her rigorous feedback on the full manuscript. I'm also grateful to Victoria Tedeschi for performing research assistance in the early stages of the project and to Deakin University for funding this work and my archival research. Todd Manion has lived with this book intruding upon our evenings ever since we met and has provided the support and motivation that made it possible to research and write, even while we grappled with a newborn baby on our own in lockdown.

Dedication

For my beautiful daughter, Wendy, and beautiful mother, Julie.

Introduction

> Now let us see how far we can cultivate physical charm. Very few are strictly beautiful, very few strictly ugly; all the debateable ground that lies between these extremes can be claimed and held by judicious effort. I wish all women would look at such effort in the light of a simple and imperative duty.
>
> 'The Service of Beauty. Personal Beauty', *Girl's Own Paper*, 9 February 1889, p. 299.

This excerpt from one of many articles published in the *Girl's Own Paper* on the subject of girls' appearance embodies several of the major transformations in how female beauty was understood in the Victorian period. First, it proclaims that beauty is 'never a "fixed quantity"', something a woman is either born with or permanently lacks (299). The permeability of a girl's or woman's appearance depends on numerous factors, including 'the variable spirit within, on expression, on setting, on an infinite amount of things that change it as we look' (299). Second, the anonymous author takes the malleable nature of beauty to mean that women owe it to themselves and others to improve their appearance. The author identifies attention to 'health, manner, and dress' as the means to make 'all the difference between plainness and good looks' (299). The idea that sustained attention to health, character and clothing could produce beauty helped to create a new industry and the new expectation for women to perform a daily beauty regimen.

Nevertheless, the trajectory of beauty and consumer culture is not nearly as straightforward as this might suggest. This article from the *Girl's Own Paper* identifies one of the prime complicating factors to the idea that female beauty could be created by a woman who had been born, or who had become through age or illness, unattractive. The author describes the 'Professional Beauty' – personalities who obtained celebrity status primarily for their appearance – as 'a reproach to English womanhood' for her perversion of a 'good and sacred gift' (299). The notion that beauty could be used by women 'as a key to open forbidden doors' and 'turned into a power for evil' speaks to the sensitivity of the subject of artifice and the association of beauty with danger in certain circumstances (299). At once it is a girl's or woman's 'duty' to cultivate her 'charm' or ability to fascinate others, but similarly only a thin line separates this requirement from unnatural and corrupting practices. This near impossible demand lies at the core of the chapters that follow, as I interrogate how conceptions of female beauty in print culture were informed and transformed by the burgeoning consumer culture of the period.

Consuming Female Beauty connects the emergence of consumer culture in the second half of the nineteenth century with the development of new models of beauty to demonstrate how beauty ideals for girls and women were substantially reshaped in British print culture from 1840 to 1914. It analyses how physical beauty appeared in fiction, periodicals and their advertising, and beauty manuals to produce the first comprehensive history of how female beauty ideals were radically transformed in and through mass print culture. Underlying this discussion is an attempt to chart how female beauty shifts from an innate or 'natural' attribute to become a quality produced through the consumption of images and goods in order to transform the self. This examination demonstrates how the commercialisation of beauty practices became integral to the socialisation of young women. It aims to develop knowledge of how beauty ideals were constructed and circulated to readers during a period in which consumer culture began to thrive, revealing both the origins of contemporary standards of beauty and how the association between female beauty and appropriate consumption was formulated. Moreover, as both cosmetic usage and beauty in general were largely associated with women, they are also important factors in broader changes in gender roles (Martin 3).

This monograph addresses the period between 1840 and 1914 to construct a narrative of the interrelationship of female beauty with the development of the modern, female consumer. It commences in 1840 because in the subsequent decades the modern fashion and retail industries began to evolve. The book concludes in 1914 as the shifts in beauty ideals I examine, such as more commonplace use and acceptance of coloured cosmetics, were largely complete by this era. The emergence of the modern fashion industry was enabled by the mass production and reproductions that the sewing machine and paper patterns made possible. As Rosy Aindow observes, these changes transformed how British people understood dress, with major implications for those with lower incomes, who could more readily emulate fashions that were once the preserve of wealthier people (1). Class is also significant in that during this period the growth of the urban middle class encouraged the pleasure of display, consumption and female visibility in the public sphere (Black 25). The middle of the nineteenth century also marks the beginning of the technological and economic changes that enabled periodicals to include high-quality illustrations, fashion plates and dress patterns, and saw an increasing focus on beauty and fashion in girls' and women's magazines. Moreover, the period witnessed transformations in transport, communications and trade that encouraged commerce, which had impacts upon the beauty industry and the transatlantic circulation of beauty ideals (Jones 33).

This monograph draws on a range of print materials, including popular fiction, the periodical press (including advice columns and advertisements), and advice and manuals read by girls and women that contain substantial engagement with fashion, beauty and health. It considers both literary and genre fiction, focusing on key Victorian novels whose authors are preoccupied with beautiful or inappropriately artificial women, such as Charles Dickens's *Dombey and Son* (1848) and George Eliot's *Adam Bede* (1859), as well as sensation, crime and girls' fiction. From the 1850s, the number of books that sought to define or advise women about the cultivation of beauty increased in number (Ribeiro 239). Advice books were a crucial source of promotion for beauty culturists (beauticians or cosmeticians), establishing the idea that beauty could be cultivated, and helping to 'legitimate[e] the pursuit of beauty as a worthy task of self-improvement and feminine duty' (J. Clark 143). The periodicals chosen for analysis show how girls and women from a range of social spheres were encouraged to think about beauty and the use of beauty products and regimens, as well as providing examples from various decades throughout the second half of the nineteenth century and into the twentieth. For example, the *Queen* (1861–1958), a high-quality publication that included hand-coloured fashion plates and which was aimed at a privileged readership, and *Woman* (1890–1912), a conservative penny weekly with significantly lower production values, both presented remarkably consistent ideas about female beauty. The examination of female beauty across a broad range of Victorian print culture extends upon existing scholarship that either focuses on the visual arts or on discrete aspects of women's appearance within fiction.

Aileen Ribeiro's *Facing Beauty: Painted Women & Cosmetic Art* (2011), for example, works through transforming beauty ideals from the sixteenth century to the twentieth century by tracing depictions of women in paintings. Several studies of specific aspects of women's appearance in nineteenth-century fiction, such as clothing and hair, emphasise the empowering or transformative potential of enhancing the face and body. Kristine Bayles Kortsch examines women's literacy in 'dress culture', including wearing, producing, buying and interpreting the meaning of clothing, as a 'type of feminine knowledge in Victorian social practice' (4) while Rosy Aindow's account of clothing during this period connects the emergence of modern fashion with increasing scrutiny of the 'relationship between clothing and social identity', namely with respect to class (16). The heavy scrutiny and regulation of aspects of women's appearance was tied to anxieties about wider changes, such as those of class, but also, most significantly of 'changing power relations between the sexes' (Ofek x). Within fiction, specific bodily features, such as hair, 'were an expression or encoding of femininity' (Ofek x). As Galia Ofek demonstrates, depictions of elements of appearance not only mirrored models of womanhood 'but also questioned, revised and redefined assumptions about the nature and making of femininity, they were also a means to create conditions for social and political changes' (x).

The last crucial shift that contributes to the transformation of beauty ideals and practices during the second half of the nineteenth century is the growth of the consumption of commercially manufactured beauty products and treatments. Brands of consumer products more widely became household names that 'entered the ready vocabulary of fiction', while beauty products such as Rowland's Kalydor were regularly advertised in the part issues of novels (Altick 214, 230). Especially from the 1880s, beauty culturists utilised advertisements and promotional tools to target women readers and, by the First World War, '[t]he body had become the prevailing icon of commodity culture' (Richards 205). Elizabeth Carolyn Miller suggests that consumerist rhetoric encouraged late-Victorian women to understand being looked at as a way to 'exercise power', particularly 'if one vigorously consumes in order to construct the image that affords the most power and control' (70). Yet she also acknowledges differing critical stances on consumer culture, particularly from a Marxist perspective, which view the consumer realm as a site of oppression. Lori Ann Loeb's description of the repeated Victorian advertising motif of the woman looking into a mirror pinpoints these competing tensions at the core of women's consumption. The ideal 'commercial woman' gazing at her reflection in a mirror takes pleasure in her appearance and her beautification (Loeb 42). While she evidently has money and time available for leisure, as Loeb points out, she also 'reinforce[s] a commercial ideal of the Victorian woman as an ornament' (42), situating her in opposition to any figuration as powerful and in control.

My study is primarily interested in how consumer culture plays an integral role in the shift in the female beauty ideal, becoming an essential component of what would become the 'work' of beauty. It is a contested point as to whether buying and applying skin creams, hair products and cosmetics constitutes exploitation or empowerment. I suggest, however, that there was a degree of freedom entailed in the departure from the natural, healthy and God-given as qualities that determined female beauty throughout much of the nineteenth century. While any modern ideal of feminine appearance requires disposable money and steals time from other tasks that women might perform or enjoy, the eventual incorporation of beauty products into a daily regimen also marked the end of long-standing connections between appearance and character and morality. The ongoing fiction of natural and healthful beauty placed many women in the position of using cosmetics secretively – whether commercially produced or concocted at home via published recipes – while others whose appearance had declined due to illness or ageing were condemned to ill judgement, rendered invisible or mocked for attempting to ameliorate their looks. Indeed, by the early twentieth century, women over the age of 35 became the target market for the beauty industry, given the promise of youth held by hair dyes, skin creams, and salon treatments (Jones 60).

The expansion in print culture was accompanied by changing ways of viewing the self and others, which complicates any account of beauty derived solely from fiction in the same way as attention to print culture complicates ideas about beauty derived solely from paintings of the period. Images became central to the enlarging realm of print, especially as engravings and chromolithographs were supplemented with photographs as the century progressed. In *The Victorians and the Visual Imagination* (2000), Kate Flint describes how the lowered cost of newsprint and printing technologies combined with the growth of the press enabled the widespread dissemination of images (3). She points to the new kinds of visual information that came with the flourishing of the illustrated press, such as details about nation, culture and the unfamiliar; however, perhaps the largest impact of the proliferation of circulating images came in knowledge about, and influence upon, ideas about personal appearance and beauty. Ofek identifies the visuals that began to circulate through paintings, descriptions of hair in novels, illustrations in magazines and instructions for grooming in etiquette manuals as 'formative images of femininity' that 'originated, reflected, or responded to Victorian models of womanhood' (x). Women's magazines were especially rich sources of images of attractive and stylish women. Not only did fashion plates provide full-page coloured representations of fashionably dressed women, but advertisements for clothing and a variety of beauty products also became larger in size and strikingly illustrated, particularly in the final decades of the century (28). In her study of advertising and Victorian women, Lori Anne Loeb suggests that the increasing glamour of fashion advertisements points to 'heightened consumer interest in the pleasures of personal ornament and in the pleasures of the social use of the middle-class figure, especially the female figure for display and status enhancement' (28). One important development in female display was the circulation of beauty ideals through repeated publication of photographs and illustrations of certain beautiful women.

While most of the images of beautiful women included in Victorian print culture were nameless, illustrated figures who adorned advertisements or modelled clothing styles in fashion plates, photography enabled the images of a small number of society or 'professional' beauties, actresses, and singers to become widely known. As Geoffrey Jones observes, the prevalence of photography by the late nineteenth century meant 'one could study, preserve, and distribute one's own image anywhere' and correspondingly '[v]isual self-awareness' intensified and promoted the growth of new industries to cater to people's new-found aesthetic self-consciousness (44). The combination of changes in visual and print technologies and culture meant that there were not only ways to create detailed images of the self, but affordable and widespread means for them to be circulated nationally and even internationally. The female celebrity's image and personal mystique became ubiquitous in images and editorials in women's magazines. Beautiful women themselves became commodities as periodicals used their images 'as an eye-catching marketing device on increasingly crowded newspaper stalls' (Easley 149). Those who reached a high level of public recognition, such as actresses Sarah Bernhardt, Ellen Terry and Lillie Langtry, 'exploited the mechanisms available for creating and marketing a celebrity persona', including opportunities to be featured in articles, interviews, profiles and photographs in print (Eltis 170). Kathy Peiss explains that new visual technologies had the effect of standardising female appearance, but more than this, these 'standards became increasingly defined by actresses and professional beauties' who became celebrities and 'stars' rather than women of dubious morals, as they had once been understood (48). Beauty standards were gradually solidified through a process of negotiation and feedback between what would become celebrity women, print culture and readerships of women consumers.

What is beauty and why female beauty?

Defining the essence of female beauty is a slippery endeavour. Indeed, there are numerous books wholly devoted to the subject, including several nineteenth-century texts that I discuss in this introduction. Most of these contemporary discussions of beauty focus on women. As Robyn Cooper suggests, the term 'beauty' was problematic in its application to male appearance, with 'handsome' a more common descriptor. Even more significant, however, is her identification of differing relationships to beauty for men and women. While it may have been a desirable attribute for men to be aesthetically pleasing, 'for women it was bound up with their identity and purpose' (Cooper 34). The defining nature of beauty for women is also reflected in the way in which the periodical press and advertising 'prioritised women's relationship with fashion over that of men's' (Aindow 3).

The most pertinent foundational question to be asked about female beauty is whether it is an enduring ideal or changeable according to historical period and location. Most scholars emphasise its variability. Valerie Steele, for example, explains that beauty cannot be equated with sexual attraction, otherwise it would not be changeable. Instead of a 'physical given', she suggests beauty is 'an artificial construct that varies from culture to culture' (Steele, *Fashion* 41). Jones similarly suggests that regardless of evidence that some facial features may be regarded as universally attractive, the variability of beauty reflects 'inherited differences' in features such as skin colour, hair texture, cultural and religious practices, combined with the impact of different diets and climates (6). While art historian Aileen Ribeiro acknowledges that most writers believe that beauty is 'created out of a specific culture', she favours a combination of universalist and relativist perspectives (25–6). She maintains that Western art is consistent in its representation of certain features as beautiful, such as clear skin, large eyes, straight nose, and a long neck. These enduringly beautiful features, she suggests, are 'retained in images of female beauty but set within the prevailing fashions (such as clothes and body shapes) [. . .] and heightened by the use of cosmetics' (26).

There are broad qualities that tend to be prerequisites for beauty, such as unblemished skin and the absence of disease or deformity. Indeed, early cosmetic surgery performed by barber-surgeons from the sixteenth century – prior to the advent of anaesthesia and antiseptic – most often treated facial injuries and disfigurements caused to the nose by epidemic syphilis (Gilman 10). Beyond these absences, the ideal size and shape of facial and bodily features are in a continual process of flux, influenced by 'the morality and body image of the dominant class' (Thesander 11). As Steele observes, there were changes in the ideal nineteenth-century beauty from the pretty and 'sylph-like' early Victorian woman, to the voluptuous mid-Victorian woman, the 'Gibson Girl' from the 1890s, and the 'slender Poiret "flapper"' of the 1920s (6).[1] This book considers some of the reasons for changes in female beauty ideals as the century progressed with respect to the acceptance of artificial methods of improving the face, skin and hair including cosmetics and dyes, complementing existing accounts of changing expectations of female bodies at the turn of the century as outlined in histories such as Ina Zweiniger-Bargielowska's *Managing the Body: Beauty, Health, and Fitness in Britain, 1880–1939* (2010).

Beauty does not straightforwardly equate with sexual attractiveness; however, many facets of beauty and fashion were readily connected with sexuality. The sexual resonances of cosmetics fuelled debate about the propriety of their use and judgement of women who transgressed complex – and changeable – rules surrounding their use. Coloured cosmetics mimic the physiological changes that occur during sex, for example, such as reddened cheeks and glowing skin, and their use 'could be seen as preparation for a sexual encounter' (Ribeiro 16). Fashionable clothing also drew attention to the body and signalled for male attention, with such allusions to sexual desire constituting '[w]hat is so problematic about fashionable dress' (Aindow 87). Individual aspects of a woman's face and body, such as flowing hair, were linked with 'growing cultural, political and personal concerns with the difficulties of controlling, managing or channeling women's vigour' (Ofek: x). Particularly by the end of the century, women's increasing public presence and movement ensured their external appearance took on a new importance, and unsurprisingly they embraced beauty products and practices in response (J. Clark 172).

Women's bodies and clothing are an integral part of their appearance upon which they can be judged, however the face is the locus of female beauty. Ribeiro describes how 'the constant scrutiny of the female face is a fact of western culture; it is the most naked (in the sense of vulnerable) part of the body and the signifier of identity' (36). The importance of the face as the encapsulation of the self underscores several arguments opposing cosmetic use in the period, such as the belief that covering or enhancing features constituted deception that might mislead potential suitors. Jessica Clark's *The Business of Beauty: Gender and the Body in Modern London* (2020) provides a comprehensive history of the rise of 'complexion specialists' in London at the *fin de siècle*, with almost twenty – primarily women – located around Bond Street by 1908 (172). However, prior to the rise of the reputable brand-name cosmetics industry – and even still judgements lingered, as they continue to do today – women both criticised artifice at the same time as engaging in beauty practices overtly and covertly (Clark 3).

While Peiss suggests that prior to the First World War visibly painted women in the United States 'remained spectacles to a certain extent' (55), coloured cosmetics had not always been off-limits for respectable women in Western cultures, as they were for most of the nineteenth century. Indeed, cycles of acceptability and rejection, and a preference for artifice replaced by a natural look, repeat across the centuries. The earliest cosmetics were perfumes produced in ancient Egypt and Greece, and it was the revival of perfumery in Europe in the sixteenth century that fostered the development of other products such as rouge and face paint (Martin 13). Before their commercialisation in Italy in the eighteenth century, most cosmetics were made by women at home, based on recipes obtained by word of mouth or published in advice books that were popularised alongside the growth in cosmetic usage in the sixteenth century (Martin 19). Morag Martin's *Selling Beauty: Cosmetics, Commerce, and French Society, 1750–1830* (2009) examines changing make-up trends that demonstrate shifting attitudes to artifice over time. With the reign of Louis XIV (1643–1715), new practices that produced severe white skin, bright red checks and involved the application of black silk patches (*mouches*) were popularised, but this look was eventually 'replaced by naturally flushed skin and an open, honest countenance free of artifice' (Martin 1). Nevertheless, the subsequent rejection of artifice – as occurs in Britain during the Victorian period – did not curtail the trade in cosmetics during the eighteenth century; Martin explains that by the French Revolution cosmetics retreated from public view but remained 'a private and necessary part of many women's toilettes' (2). This points to an earlier and internationalised history of women consuming cosmetics despite exhortations to do otherwise and in contravention of prevailing ideas of what constituted beauty.

As this monograph explores, fundamental contradictions surrounded expectations of female beauty in Victorian Britain, such as the opposition between the natural and the artificial, at least in terms of the detectability of any methods of improving the appearance. In addition, long-standing mythologies surrounding women's vanity informed negative judgements of women who adorned themselves to excess, or who sought to retain a youthful appearance as they aged. The natural was itself a constructed category, which demanded the unobtrusive and secretive use of beauty products. Jessica Clark describes one beauty culturist as promoting 'an "artificial naturalness"' that posed no threat to Victorian values (125). The rhetoric of the natural beauty that permeates print culture of the period does not align with likely – and in some instances, recorded – practices of girls and women, and even of the men who produced images of female beauty. In relation to the expected look of a woman's face, Pamela K. Gilbert observes that Victorian women were 'expected to be lighter – and brighter – in color than men' and that the 'contrast of blushing cheeks against white skin was highly valued' (296).² The idealisation of this contrast was promoted in portraiture, with a guide to such paintings of the period suggesting that brilliancy of colour was crucial for portraits of women, regardless of the true colour of their own skin and lips (Gilbert 296). The ideal woman's face in reality, then, comprised pale skin with blushing cheeks that appeared 'natural', something which posed a 'marketing challenge' for coloured cosmetics given their visible effects and moral questionability (Jones 62–3).

At this point in the discussion of the preference for skin whiteness, it is necessary to address the relationship of female beauty to race. Most British representations of idealised beauty within the vast body of nineteenth-century print culture presume or depict white women. Authors of beauty treatises and manuals, such as Alexander Walker and Eliza Haweis, both of whom I discuss in the following section, refer to racial differences in relation to beauty, but primarily to reaffirm the superiority of the aesthetics of a white, Western appearance. Discussions, or actual depictions, of beautiful women who were not white were rare, particularly in women's magazines, which helps to clarify the focus on the predominant white beauty ideal in the chapters that follow. The society magazine the *Queen* (1861–1958, for instance, stands out for its occasional exoticised advertisements or cover illustrations featuring veiled 'middle eastern' or 'eastern' women who otherwise conformed to white, Western ideals. British perfumers and purveyors of beauty products, including Eugène Rimmel, promoted a racialised beauty through the 'alabaster complexion of an "English Rose"' (J. Clark 122). Whiteness of the skin was an ideal promised by numerous cosmetic creams and powders, which signalled 'freedom from hard outdoor labour and racial purity' (Matthews David 21).

In Peiss's social history of beauty, she notes the presumed superiority of white racial beauty and the association of fair skin with Anglo-Saxon virtue and civilisation, which had particular implications for white supremacy in the American context (31). Fair skin was not only viewed as desirable, but was linked with 'purity, goodness, and upper-class status' (Gilbert 283). These associations ensured that cosmetic usage also worked to make distinctions based on both class and race (Peiss 31), with coexisting apprehension about the possibility of cosmetics enabling their transgression. Various factors, then, associated white skin with the ideal woman. In her study of Victorian skin, Gilbert draws attention to the feminine gendering of fairness as 'aligned with purity', in contrast with the sexualisation of darkness (282). Nevertheless, artificially white skin not only had racialised, classist and sexual meanings, but, in practical terms, could conceal signs of ageing and disease, as well as blemishes. As Martin notes in the eighteenth-century French context, white skin was equated with respectability and the use of heavy white make-up at one stage came to connote a greater degree of respectability than naturally pale skin, suggesting meanings that also extend beyond race (13).

A similar movement from the overwhelming valorisation of 'natural' and 'healthy' beauty towards the acceptance and eventual embrace of the full array of cosmetics products and practices in Victorian Britain is a key concern of this monograph. In the first section of this introduction, I have focused on the ways in which contemporary scholars understand nineteenth-century beauty in retrospect. In the following section, I engage at length with works by two nineteenth-century writers who espouse their own understandings of the foundations of human beauty, particularly beauty in women. The two books, one by a male author with a medical background published just prior to mid-century, and the other by a woman who wrote on personal and domestic style on the cusp of the embrace of the beauty regimen and cosmetics, illustrate the shift from beauty as innate and indicative of character to a quality that women should cultivate and improve, particularly as they aged.

Conceptualising beauty in the nineteenth century: Contrasting perspectives, Part I, Alexander Walker

Increasingly sophisticated knowledge of medicine and anatomy and the strong associations of beauty with health saw numerous physicians postulate on the subject for a professional readership. Alexander Walker's *Beauty, Illustrated Chiefly by an Analysis and Classification of Beauty in Women* (1836) is an early example of a male authority utilising biological science to speculate on the physiological differences of women. While he claims to be focusing on classical aesthetic ideals, *Beauty* helped to circulate influential ideas about female beauty that drew on the quasi-scientific concept of physiognomy and which elevated 'natural' beauty to pre-eminence. Walker studied at the Edinburgh medical school and wrote a series of three books on the subject of 'Woman', the first of which was *Beauty*.[3] The book was relatively popular with a general male, middle-class readership and went into numerous British and American editions throughout the century, with a fifth edition published in 1892 in Glasgow and Edinburgh showing its longevity throughout the nineteenth century.[4]

The 1845 American edition contains a preliminary essay by the unnamed editor, who emphasises the importance of the topic given that 'men are moved by nothing more generally and certainly than by the power of Beauty – particularly Beauty in Woman' (ix). The editor's reference to the 'monarch power' of women's beauty alludes to a danger and power imbalance for men who must bow down to it (Walker xii). The presumably male editor refers to 'necromance' in relation to the threatening aspect of female beauty's 'command', not only referencing the supernatural but also the assumed hierarchy of beings with 'the poor mass of mortals, stricken and panting like cornered deer [vulnerable men] before the inexorable hunter [beautiful woman]' (Walker xii). Beauty is conceived of as a deadly and unnatural power that can upend the patriarchal order, hence making Walker's study crucial for the implied general male readership who must act in response to female attraction (Cooper 35). As Robyn Cooper notes in her account of Walker's works, the 'language of desire' evident in *Beauty* indicates that it 'is very much a man's book', rather than one that women might also be expected to read (46). In its focus on the assessment and judgement of female beauty, his texts connect with similar titles that purported to classify and thus contain the 'power' of beauty for a primarily male readership (Hartley, 'A Science' 22).

Walker offers several reasons for his focus on female beauty. First, *Beauty* contains an inherent presumption that men are the human default; women present 'peculiar modifications' of 'the form of the species' (21). Second, women's beauty is 'best calculated to ensure attention from men', and men solely exercise the power of sexual selection and thus have the ability 'to ensure individual happiness, and to ameliorate the species' (21). Female beauty is therefore not a frivolous topic relating to adornment and aesthetic pleasure, but one bound up with the development of humanity given its capacity to signal a woman's fertility. Walker nevertheless attempts to distinguish between 'male beauty' as a 'grand or sublime beauty' and 'female beauty', which is 'minor or subordinate' (47, 94). The gendered inflection of minor beauty or 'prettiness' (female beauty) is evident in humans in the characteristics of 'smallness, subordination, and subjection', while male beauty is related to the qualities of 'greatness, superordination, and power' (47). While there are evident physiological differences in average male and female body sizes that influence the gendered separation of smallness and greatness, the terminology relating to power and dominance is laced with patriarchal conceptions of male superiority. Walker makes an explicit connection between the sublime and 'physical and moral superiority' (94), which accords with the tendency to distinguish the 'beautiful female and the sublime male' (Balfour 327). Walker's reference to sublime beauty draws on Edmund Burke, whose aesthetic treatise *A Philosophical Enquiry into the Origin of Our Ideas of the Sublime and Beautiful* (1757) distinguished the two categories based on emotional response, with the sublime evoking fear. While Burke identifies smallness as the first quality of beauty, Walker comments that Burke 'confusedly thought' that this was the only kind of beauty to reiterate his model of minor and grand types and refute a feminised conception of beauty (49).

Despite the superior qualities inherent in grand beauty, which is unique to men, further elaboration by Walker on sub-types of beauty is reserved for women. Walker conceives of three types or 'species' of female beauty: locomotive, nutritive and thinking (Fig. 0.1). His frequent use of the word 'species' to refer to the types of beauty has obvious dehumanising connotations and is reflective of an era in which the classification of plants, animals and people was a scientific preoccupation. As Dana Mount and Susie O'Brien observe, this 'hyper-categorisation' saw an overlap between botanical classification and 'racist categorisation of human difference/race' (523). Walker explains that any one woman usually only exhibits one of these types and that men generally prefer one type or another, which allows for differing perceptions of whether a woman is beautiful or not. Walker's types purport to derive from a knowledge of anatomy, and each type is grounded in one of the bodily 'systems' he identifies. For Walker, as Lucy Hartley observes, beauty is a 'physical index of excellence of the internal state' (*Physiognomy* 120). The locomotive or mechanical

Figure 0.1 Alexander Walker, Three Types of Beauty. *Beauty*. 1836. New York: Henry G. Langley, 1845.

system is highly developed in women with 'precise, striking, and brilliant' bodies, the nutritive or vital system is evident in the 'soft and voluptuous', while the thinking or mental system is conducive to a figure 'characterized by intellectuality and grace' (Walker 150). Though he describes 'distinguishing and judging of beauty in woman' as an 'art', his scientifically oriented method is less concerned with issues of aesthetics and personal adornment than later women writers such as Eliza Haweis (142). In this way, his work differs from most female-authored beauty manuals in that he adopts the male gaze in analysing and classifying the aesthetic merits and setbacks of particular features of women's bodies and is uninterested in the ways in which women might modify or 'improve' their appearance.

Walker's first type – the 'locomotive' beauty associated with the organs that enabled bodily movement – has an oblong face, broad shoulders, a moderate bosom and a proportional build that is 'precise, striking, and brilliant' (140). Walker does not fix women in one beauty type for life. While he indicates that the locomotive system is predominant in young women, he proposes that the vital system, which is more closely connected with fertility and reproduction and is definitive of his second beauty type, can develop as they mature (157). Out of the twenty-two illustrations included in most editions of the book, the first depiction of the locomotive type is the only one where the woman is standing rather than sitting or reclining. Her arms raised above her head, her hair hanging loose, and her gaze directed at the reader position her in sexual terms as in an erotic illustration, rather than a physiological, anthropological or artistic pose. Cooper suggests that there is a classed dimension to Walker's system in that women of the lower classes who perform physical labour are seen to have 'overdeveloped locomotive organs' (39). This class-based conception of 'overdevelopment' is no doubt linked with the highly sexualised pleasure inherent in the first illustration of the locomotive type. Walker's second type of beauty, the vital type, is strongly gendered, in that the vital organs are understood to be more developed in women because of their connection with reproductive capacity. For the vital type, good looks are imbricated with reproductive capacity – and women's rightful role as mothers – in terms of natural and sexual selection (Hartley, *Physiognomy* 112). Walker's description focuses on the roundness and fullness of the vital beauty; from her round face to a luxuriant bosom that 'seems to protrude on the space occupied by the arms', 'greatly expanded' haunches, 'ample trunk', and large thighs, the vital beauty has a figure that is 'soft and voluptuous in the extreme' (140).

In the mid-nineteenth century, as Hartley observes, '[t]he idea that superior physical beauty was the expression of higher mental development was quite commonplace' (*Physiognomy* 110). The pseudoscience of physiognomy suggested several mutual relationships between intelligence, character, morality and beauty; in the case of women, beauty was firmly connected with 'goodness' (Peiss 24). As a result, concealing the skin through cosmetics, in particular, could be viewed as 'hiding one's true character' (Lennox 11). Walker does not suggest that all three types of female beauty correspond with superior intellect given that he understands the mental organs to be more highly developed in men. However, the third type of female beauty, which he describes as 'nervous or thinking ... mental', accords with wider strands of Western thought that yoked beauty and intelligence together (144). Walker suggests that the oval-faced mental beauty has a 'high and pale forehead [that] announces the intellectuality of her character', with the inner characteristics of the woman discernible through a glance at her face (141). Unlike the descriptions of the first two types of beauty, Walker emphasises the inner qualities of the mental beauty, such as the sensibility evident in her 'intensely expressive eye' and the 'modesty and dignity' evident in her 'lower features' (141). As shown in the illustration, Walker's ideal intellectual beauty type has less pronounced breasts and curves in her form, corresponding with the reduced emphasis on her reproductive capacity in comparison with the second, vital type. The higher status afforded to this mental type is perhaps also evident in the way that the figure covers one breast and her pudenda with her hands, as does the frontispiece illustration of the statue of the Venus de Medici (first century BCE).[5]

As the century progressed, Walker's ideas about physiologically determined beauty types were superseded as the British society increasingly accepted that beauty practices and cosmetics could enable women to retain beauty into older age or remedy unappealing or 'deformed' features. Walker briefly refers to the role of diet and cultural factors in the promotion of beauty, such as education, 'good moral, social, and political conditions', and work that does not damage the body (167). Though he identifies 'defects' in each of the three bodily systems, unlike most beauty texts and advice manuals that would follow, and which I discuss in this monograph, he does not focus on the role of the individual woman in the production and maintenance of beauty. As Cooper points out, Walker's conception of female beauty emphasises its importance for human happiness and advancement as a species at the same time as labelling it inferior and maintaining 'masculine supremacy' (42). A woman's beauty exists to be evaluated by men, who use their superior intellect to select the right women to improve humanity. Walker locates beauty within the body, as produced by the predominance of one of three sets of organs, which are in turn influenced by external geographic and climatic factors. In some respects, this formulation of beauty absolves women of responsibility for their own appearance. By focusing on the relationship between various sets of human organs and female beauty, Walker ignores substantial engagement with ideas about thoughts and behaviours deleteriously influencing appearance and sidesteps debates about the merits and detriments of cosmetics, exercise and beauty regimens that would soon become central to advice manuals and intellectual accounts of beauty published in the second half of the century.

Conceptualising beauty in the nineteenth century: Contrasting perspectives, Part II, Eliza Haweis

Eliza Haweis's ideas about beauty are distinct from the treatises of male writers such as Walker because she acknowledges that beauty can be related to women's self-expression rather than being innate and, in turn, that beauty could be practically applied 'towards empowering women' (Ribeiro 266). Haweis was born in London and wrote about the decoration and adornment of the home and body in British periodicals and a series of books. *The Art of Beauty* (1878) was the first, followed by *The Art of Dress* (1879), *The Art of Decoration* (1881) and *The Art of Housekeeping* (1889). Talia Schaffer explains that many Victorian writers wrote on both interior design and bodily fashion and that '[m]any of the characteristic concerns of interior design manuals reappeared when writers discovered new ways of dressing women's bodies' (102). *The Art of Beauty* originated in a series of articles that Haweis wrote for *St. Paul's Magazine*, and Haweis also created the coloured frontispiece and numerous small line drawings throughout the book. The text is divided into three sections – 'Beauty and Dress', 'Beauty and Head-Dresses' and 'Beauty and Surroundings' – which by their very titles signal Haweis's aesthetic orientation, rather than the quasi-scientific approach typical of books about female beauty authored by men.

The manual[6] begins with the premise that personal beauty and adornment of the body is of 'the first interest and importance' to all people, with Haweis signalling that female beauty was especially significant (3). The language of biological imperatives underwrites the book's claims that 'the culture of beauty is the natural right of every woman', as by virtue of her sex she innately attracts male interest (3). Some beauty manuals, particularly earlier in the century, sternly warned against any significant attempts to alter the face or body beyond basic health and hygiene, with such practices seen as 'objectionable – as a hiding of inner truth' given the long-held association between appearance and character (Lennox 10; Marwick 36–7). Haweis, however, encourages young women to adorn themselves to heighten their beauty, and older women to continue to use methods that once enabled their beauty to be 'enhanced' but now 'conceal its fading away' (40). In this regard, Haweis was amongst a group of late nineteenth-century female beauty writers who 'integrated physiognomic rhetoric and ideas into their manuals both to pacify moralists and to defend the detailed beauty advice that they provided to readers' (Lennox 10). The methods that Haweis advocates reproduce prevalent ideas articulated in contemporary women's magazines and beauty manuals that discouraged any visible sign of artifice and that privileged the 'natural'. Lennox argues that such a practice constructed beautification as supplementing the science of physiognomy through nature and reinforced the idea that the face and body's ability to channel identity could not be subverted through artificial aids (10).

In *The Art of Beauty*, hygienic and cosmetic intervention are framed as fostering physical qualities as they ought to be seen or providing a delicate 'veil' for flaws, rather than attempts to entirely transform them. 'Nature must not be destroyed, but supported', Haweis argues, 'her beauties revealed, not stifled; her weaknesses veiled, not exposed; her defects tenderly remedied; and no fashion should be tolerated which simply tends to burlesque her' (40). Haweis's approach goes further than many pieces of beauty advice from the period – foreshadowing shifts in the 1880s as brand-name beauty products and services became more widely available and visible in magazine advertisements – in that it acknowledges that beauty regimens and fashion could aid in drawing out natural beauty and improving the appearance of, or curing entirely, aesthetic flaws.

The sense that intelligence or character influenced external appearance expressed in beauty manuals and women's magazines around mid-century suggested that mean-spirited and nasty individuals would see deleterious effects to their physical appearance as they aged. For example, in 'The Art of Preserving Beauty' from the British magazine *World of Fashion* in 1849, 'meanness of thought and selfishness' are implicated with 'Time' in 'unit[ing] age and ugliness together' (120). In contrast, Haweis's later *The Art of Beauty*, informed by the growing importance of women's physical appearance, entertains the reverse possibility of ugliness having a deleterious influence on character, 'surrounding and the chances of life' (6). She proposes that 'an immense number of ill-tempered ugly women are ill-tempered because they are ugly' (256). She acknowledges that ugliness is in fact an 'impediment' and a 'burden', which thereby supports her exhortation to all women to work to improve their appearance to overcome ugliness (6, 256). The unspoken assumption is that ugly people are treated differently and that this negatively influences the ugly woman's temperament. This logically supports Haweis's claims about the power of beauty and the necessity for women to cultivate it. She asserts that it is 'a kind of duty to make life beautiful to disguise deformity, to provide by care and forethought for others, a pleasure which costs so little and brings in so much even to the giver' and which 'tends to refine and elevate the mind, and increase the sum of human happiness' (9). This assertion synthesises ideas about women's purpose as providers of visual and other pleasures and the acceptability of beauty practices that can be medicalised as corrections to physical 'deformities' (rather than attempts to artificially pervert nature).

Haweis's ultimate argument is 'that no woman need be ugly' because every woman has 'points of attractiveness' (259). She acknowledges that increasing intellect is a respected practice, but argues that beauty and 'the study of "points"' still needs to be recognised as an 'honourable art' (257). Indeed 'art' is a term used in the title of many beauty articles and books in the period. According to Haweis, for the sake of women's advancement – even if they are the intellectual type – they must maintain a feminine external appearance, given that womanly 'graces' are a female requirement. Moreover, with a differing emphasis in comparison with professional male authors with quasi-medical and scientific motivations, she advocates for women to dedicate more time, money and research to adorning themselves provided the results ensure a proportional improvement in appearance. While young women would not want to fail to make the most of their beauty during their 'fresh youth', the apparently stale older woman ('whose first freshness is past') must similarly use 'the art which once enhanced beauty' to 'conceal its fading away' (4). Though Haweis promotes classical, historical styles of dress and critiques contemporary fashions for their distortion of the natural form, she is not opposed to beauty practices more broadly because of her deep appreciation of the centrality of beauty to 'visibility' as a woman. Haweis's embrace of the power of beauty as one of the few options for women to succeed in relationships or professions underwrites her lack of opposition to cosmetics and other methods for ensuring that women are able to capitalise on the attractive features that they do possess. In this way, Haweis prefigures the impending shift around which this monograph is based, in which, in the first two decades of the twentieth century, women would be 'pressure[d]' by a mass-produced and mass-marketed cosmetics industry 'to consume and change their bodies' (Nicholas 36).

Chapter structure

The following chapters are organised into three sections: 'Nature vs Artifice', 'Youth and Ageing' and 'Reshaping Female Beauty', which establish the overarching ideals and prohibitions that structured expectations of women's appearance, the specific advice that was reserved for girls and older women, and the eventual transformation of these norms with the increasing connection of beauty with consumer culture and the beauty regimen. The first section, 'Nature vs Artifice' considers the two opposing concepts that exerted the greatest influence on what was considered beautiful and what was regarded as unattractive or dangerous. Chapter 1, 'The Impossible Ideal: Beauty, Health and Character' interrogates the powerful mythology of the natural and healthy beauty that permeated advice in women's periodicals and advice manuals, as well as serving as the basis for punishment for fictional women who resorted to forbidden means, or who took excessive pleasure in their looks. I begin with this topic because the triumvirate of health, beauty and character were integral to idealised femininity throughout much of the century. Nevertheless, these qualities were not equally valued, with greater emphasis on healthful mindsets and practices as improving character for a lifetime, and repeated cautions that physical beauty was a fleeting attribute. This foundational principle about natural and healthy beauty as effectively producing a better person informed the association of cosmetics with personal harm and vanity. Medically influenced beauty texts, such as D. G. Brinton and George Napheys's *Personal Beauty* (1870), demonstrate how health was understood as a prerequisite for female beauty, particularly for male authors, while female authors of beauty manuals largely walked a fine line between catering to women's desire for measures to improve their appearance and ensuring their advice embodied the 'natural'. In fiction, Wilkie Collins's *The Law and the Lady* (1875) is a tragic demonstration of the fate that awaits the woman who is willing to risk everything to become beautiful, while George Eliot's *Adam Bede* (1859) is a cautionary tale for naturally beautiful women who take excessive pleasure in their looks.

Chapter 2, 'The Dark Side of Beauty: Cosmetics, Artifice and Danger', evaluates the flipside of the beauty equation, confronting the dangers associated with beauty and its pursuit. It spans a sixty-year period and all of the forms of print considered in this study in order to understand the predominant lines of thought about artifice that influenced a significant proportion of beauty discourse. Until the end of the century, beauty manuals (particularly those authored by men) and women's magazines often dissuaded readers from succumbing to the lure of cosmetic promises, which presents an intriguing conflict for the magazines that increasingly derived profits from cosmetic advertising. This chapter establishes how beauty and artifice were intellectualised in relatively consistent ways across time and for differing readerships, through the treatment of cosmetics in Mrs A. Walker's *Female Beauty* (1837) and minor celebrity, dancer and courtesan, Lola Montez's *The Arts of Beauty* (1858). It establishes how both an inexpensive magazine, *Woman*, and one with lavish production values, the *Queen*, similarly advocate for consistent methods of beautification that privilege the natural and warn against the use of any product or treatment that might be detectable, or which might cause the consumer to worsen their appearance. Fraudulent, criminal cosmeticians Anna Ruppert and Madame Rachel both make appearances in various guises in women's magazines, providing contemporary examples of the damage that sham cosmetics could cause to unsuspecting consumers. The danger posed by the likes of Madame Rachel to desperate women is captured in L. T. Meade's fictional rendering of her as 'Madame Sara' in *The Sorceress of the Strand* (1902), who is depicted as villainous for her conscious exploitation of women's vanity. However, even if women were assiduous in their avoidance of artificial enhancements, beauty, as a beacon of women's sexuality, was frequently portrayed as a danger in its own right. Young natural beauties, including Isabel Vane in Mrs Henry Wood's *East Lynne* (1861) and Sybil Vane in Oscar Wilde's *The Picture of Dorian Gray* (1890) exude sexual desirability and are at risk of embarrassment or a tragic fate as a result of their appearance.

Female beauty is most readily associated with youth, and its progressive decline with advancing years. Part II, 'Youth and Ageing', focuses on the requirements of beauty in the early and latter stages of a woman's life, in which both the pleasures and prohibitions surrounding appearance differed. Age was the greatest distinguishing function with respect to female beauty and determining what kinds of intervention and adornment were considered acceptable. Chapter 3, 'Beauty and Girlhood', considers how young women – who were at greatest risk of falling under the cloud of sexual impropriety through their toilette or dress – were advised to shape themselves with respect to beauty and the kinds of qualities that saw them depicted as beautiful or ugly. The most popular girls' magazine of the era, the *Girl's Own Paper* (1880–1914), and the related *Girl's Own Book of Health and Beauty* (1891?) are analysed for the way in which they fix beauty, health and character in a triangulated relationship for young women. Instructional advice to girl readers is subsequently traced to girls' fiction of the period, with Juliana Horatia Ewing's *Six to Sixteen* (1875) and Frances Hodgson Burnett's *The Secret Garden* (1911) embedding the widespread connection between health, beauty and a pleasant character in narratives intended for girl readers. Both novels emphasise the failings of unhealthy girls, whose flawed bodies and personalities render them unlikeable and of no meaningful benefit to others – a significant problem at a time in which girls' 'usefulness' ought to have been their supreme goal.

Many beauty products promised that they would enable users to retain or regain the markers of youth: a full head of luxurious hair with no bald spots, coloured rather than grey, a full set of teeth, a trim waist, and a clear and smooth complexion. As ageing was associated with qualities that were antithetical to female beauty, older women were situated somewhat differently with respect to the naturalised ideals I discuss in Chapter 1. In particular, older women could be viewed as grotesque for attempting to appear younger until cosmetic intervention was more widespread and acceptable. Beginning with women's magazines and beauty manuals, Chapter 4, 'Beauty and Ageing', compares a variety of advice and appraisals of older women that are united by consistent anxieties about how women might age disgracefully. It also evaluates instructions for staving off unappealing physical changes, registering movement from understanding ageing as something that must inevitably be accepted to a process to be fought 'by all reasonable means', as consumer products promised to extend the span of youthful beauty. It contrasts this discourse informed by consumer culture with expressions of distaste in fiction for the excessively made-up or fashionable older woman who attempted to display herself publicly in the same way as a young woman. Charles

Dickens's *Dombey and Son* (1848) and George Eliot's *Felix Holt, the Radical* (1866) both present somewhat pathetic and disturbing representations of older women who do not embrace the doctrine of successful prevention of the most unappealing physical changes associated with ageing.

The final section, 'Reshaping Female Beauty', turns from earlier debates about artifice to the gradual transformation of beauty ideals and practices at the turn of the twentieth century. These newly entrenched norms still retain cultural currency, including the emulation of the looks of celebrity women and the enactment of the daily beauty regimen. Chapter 5, 'The Celebrity as Beauty Icon', links the development of consumer culture surrounding beauty with the emergence of the female celebrity, who was created through the reproduction of glamorous photographs and illustrations and articles focused on celebrity style. Professional beauties and famous actresses, including Lillie Langtry and Sarah Bernhardt, helped to establish standards of beauty that could be replicated through consumption of the products that they endorsed or even lent their names to. This chapter reads the birth of the celebrity beauty ideal and the rise of the celebrity endorsement in cosmetic advertising through the illustrated periodicals the *Queen* (1861–1958), *Myra's Journal of Dress and Fashion* (1875–1912) and the *Sketch* (1893–1959). Famous actresses and singers became icons of good looks and taste not only through reproduction of their photographs and likenesses in editorial content and advertisements, but also through attention to the opulence of their private lives on stage and at home. In addition, purveyors of beauty products became celebrity brand names in their own right through their frequent advertisements, aiding in the establishment of trust for their products, as compared with earlier, unscrupulous figures within the cosmetics industry.

Chapter 6, 'Embracing the Beauty Regimen in British and American Women's Magazines', widens the monograph's largely British focus to show how the transatlantic reach of the cosmetics industry and celebrity culture in the 1890s and the early twentieth century displaced anti-cosmetic strictures and transformed ideals of both beauty and femininity. It traces the adoption of new beauty expectations in two very different British women's magazines, the *Queen* and *Woman*, and the American women's magazine, the *Delineator* (1873–1937), which was published by the Butterick Publishing Company in order to market paper clothing patterns.

Specifically, this chapter addresses the way in which an increasing number of advertisements for beauty products and techniques were rendered acceptable through conformity to the predominant editorial stance on naturalness and health within the beauty ideal. It also considers the simultaneous promotion and normalisation of the beauty regimen, which required women to perform a series of tasks on a daily basis to ensure the face and body remained in optimum condition.

These chapters provide an understanding of the ruptures and continuities that surrounded female beauty from the second half of the nineteenth century until the early twentieth century. While trends in women's corsetry, clothing and hairstyles were ever-changing, ideas about beauty – which were largely concentrated on the aesthetics of a woman's face – did not shift as quickly nor as readily. The pervasive construction of ideal beauty as something a woman was born with, and which she retained through moral and healthy behaviour and cleanliness, even by the end of the century, doggedly competed with new ideas borne out of the growth of the consumption of commercial beauty products. While beauty is often conceptualised as the straightforward by-product of prevailing aesthetic preferences, the growth of consumer culture in Victorian print disrupts the ways in which beauty norms were traditionally formed and transformed. Women readers consumed fiction, periodicals and advice manuals that not only shaped their views of how they desired to look but also provided them with the inspiration and information in order to buy the products and procedures that would help them to achieve it.

Notes

1. Paul Poiret was a leading French fashion designer associated with a modern look.
2. Aileen Ribeiro makes a related point that cosmetics serve to 'heighten the natural white and red of the complexion', and thus in visual art women often 'appear made up to a greater or lesser degree, but with a semblance of Nature' (34).
3. The two subsequent titles are *Intermarriage; or, The Mode in Which and the Causes Why, Beauty, Health and Intellect, Result from Certain Unions, and Deformity, Disease and Insanity from Others* (1838) and *Woman Physiologically Considered as to Mind, Morals, Matrimonial Slavery, Infidelity and Divorce* (1839).

4 The publication history of the book includes the following editions. UK: Effingham Wilson, London, 1836; Henry G. Bohn, 1845, 1846, 1849, 1852; Thomas D. Morison (Scotland), 1892. US: J. & H. G. Langley, 1841; William H. Colyer, 1844, 1845; Derby & Jackson, 1859.
5 By way of comparison, the frontispiece, a statue of the Venus De Medici, is the only other standing female figure illustrated. It depicts the classical statue of Aphrodite with the hands covering both the genitalia and one of the breasts, and the figure's gaze directed to the side.
6 I use the term 'beauty manual' for publications that provide some degree of instruction or advice for improving the appearance that readers may act upon, as opposed to purely intellectual accounts of beauty.

Part I: Nature vs Artifice

I

The Impossible Ideal: Beauty, Health and Character

> Be natural! A healthy life and mind
> The best cosmetics are, you'll surely find;
> The beauty of expression, *that* will last
> And charm, when all your other charms are past.
>
> Be natural! God made you as you are,
> And His creation you insult and mar
> By being other – keeping this in view,
> That Nature cannot be improved by you.
>
> M. Hedderwick Browne, 'To the Girls',
> *Girl's Own Paper* (1892)

Natural and healthful beauty was roundly encouraged in Victorian women's print culture. Browne's poem 'To the Girls', published in the *Girl's Own Paper*, distils the overwhelming tenor of beauty advice of the period. Through the hand of God, nature was the source of a girl's or woman's beauty, and her looks could be no more flawed than that of a flower, tree or animal. A forceful preference for the natural was informed by a reverence for God's creation in the magazine. The use of cosmetics, or slavish adherence to fashion, therefore, took on a transgressive function beyond that of simple aesthetic preference. Healthful practices and thoughts would improve the character, influencing the expression, or external representation of the internal self, and these qualities could last until old age, unlike physical beauty, which would inevitably degrade. These premises are important to account for when considering the representation of beautiful women in Victorian fiction and the beauty advice professed in women's periodicals and advice manuals.

This chapter considers how the unassailable logic about natural, healthful beauty created unmeetable expectations, fostered a culture of cosmetic secrecy and judged vanity harshly. The rhetoric of harm and danger associated with cosmetics situated them as the antithesis of health and in conflict with true, natural beauty. This generated a tension for the authors of beauty manuals who had to remain on the right side of God – as embodied by the natural – and yet somehow satisfy women readers with solutions for improving their appearance. The imagined relationship between the natural, the healthful and beauty prompted a number of men with medical backgrounds to produce advice about, or assessments of, female beauty, which carried with them the authority of their profession, and had very different motivations to female-authored beauty advice manuals. This chapter begins with an analysis of one such medically influenced beauty text, D. G. Brinton and George Napheys's *Personal Beauty* (1870), which provides a foundation for understanding how health was framed as a crucial measure for beauty, a yardstick by which to measure the acceptability of any method of improving the appearance, and a motivation for the increasing acceptability of women's exercise as the century advanced. I then consider how such stipulations about health, as well as the natural, were negotiated in Madame Bayard's manual *Toilet Hints* (1883), which explains to readers how they might add to 'nature's charms'. These informational texts expose the complexity of conforming to beauty discourses of the period, and the negative judgements applied to practices and attitudes that deviated from them. The most extreme consequences for such transgression are evident in depictions of women in fiction who seek to gain beauty by any means possible. This chapter concludes with a consideration of Sara Macallan in Wilkie Collins's *The Law and the Lady* who dies from her ingestion of arsenic in the quest for beauty, and Hetty Sorrel in George Eliot's *Adam Bede* who embodies the disgrace of the naturally beautiful woman who finds pleasure in her appearance.

Medical perspectives on health and beauty: D. G. Brinton and George Napheys's *Personal Beauty* (1870)

D. G. Brinton and George Napheys's *Personal Beauty: How to Cultivate and Preserve it in Accordance with the Laws of Health* is an illuminating example of a beauty manual that bridges the divide between the classificatory work of the likes of Alexander Walker and the manuals authored by women that focused on advice about how to improve the reader's appearance. Daniel Garrison Brinton was a union army surgeon in the American Civil War, who subsequently became a professor of ethnology and archaeology. Biographical notes in *Personal Beauty* establish his medical expertise as an editor of *The Medical and Surgical Reporter*, alongside his co-author George Henry Napheys, who is also noted for his medical work and publications, including his editorship of *The Half-Yearly Compendium of Medical Science*. While Brinton's knowledge seemed to be stretched in commenting on female beauty specifically, Napheys is noted as a member of the Gynaecological Society of Boston, and his assumed expertise relating to women was evident in his authorship of *The Physical Life of Woman: Advice to the Maiden, Wife, and Mother* (1869). Though this is an American publication, I include it as an example of the transatlantic presence of medicalised accounts of beauty, something to which I will return to in the final chapter as I consider the transatlantic circulation of the beauty regimen.

Brinton and Napheys explore personal beauty from the perspective of medical science and stipulate that they will not discuss dress or hair because they lie 'within the exclusive jurisdiction of the artist' (19). This exclusion seems like a coded reference to feminised aspects of adornment that were more typically discussed in books about beauty aimed at women readers as their explanation of the book's focus repeatedly connects beauty with art. In the introduction, Brinton and Napheys point to contemporary artists using Greek statues as models of beauty to exemplify 'the eternal laws of beauty', which are based in 'geometry' (13). The sole illustration in the book is a frontispiece that depicts a seated 'Grecian Female' in a loose gown, reflecting a universal, 'classic' idea of beauty that is commonly evoked in texts by male authors. Rather than focusing on the nature of beauty, the authors propose to investigate *'how it is to be got, and how it is to be kept'* (14). Brinton and Napheys set out to examine the human body as a whole and then in parts 'and show first what is the true artistic ideal of perfect form in each. Then we shall examine one by one the defects and imperfections to which each is subject, and how these may be remedied either by medical or by cosmetic art' (19). Their definition of personal beauty stipulates a 'combination of correct proportion and colour with perfect performance of function. Perfect performance of function requires health and grace; proportion and colour are under the control of fixed laws of taste' (Brinton and Napheys 19). In this way, the authors instruct readers on how to mobilise the alleged power of nineteenth-century medical expertise to forge an idealised 'beautiful' body so as best to conform with dominant ideas of feminine beauty. In doing so, they joined the ranks of other medical men of the period who contributed to circulating conceptions of women's bodies as beautiful, healthy and reproductive.

In the tradition of eighteenth-century aesthetic theorists who drew on classic traditions such as William Hogarth in *The Analysis of Beauty* (1753), *Personal Beauty* proposes ideal measurements for areas such as the forehead ('should be rather low and broad') and the most distinctive features of the female body, such as the breasts and the waist (Brinton and Napheys 70). Breasts are viewed as essential to beauty and the ideal they describe is youthful, with 'firm and elastic' tissue that forms 'true hemispheres in shape' (60). Very specific distances between nipples, the collarbone, and between the breasts themselves are specified, setting out perfect proportions. However, the authors claim that few European and American women meet these requirements owing to 'this artificial life of ours' (61), echoing a common criticism of modern life dating to the early modern period. They suggest such breasts do not exist in America, apart from in 'some vigorous young country girl, who has grown up in ignorance of the arts which thwart nature' (61). They criticise the use of breast 'forms' for harming the development of the bust, reflecting their general impetus to target means of beautification or cosmetic enhancement that hinder rather than enhance natural features. The first 'breast pad' was patented in the US in 1874, with a cotton cushion exterior and 'inflatable india-rubber breast pads' served as filling to make breasts appear larger (qtd in Gardner 103). While *Personal Beauty* describes breast forms as harmful to the body, it does promote a device for improving the shape of the breast through suction, which is similarly described to breast enlargement pumps that are sold today as an alternative to breast augmentation. Brinton and Napheys's reference to the potential of such a device to 'restore the organs in great measure to their proper shape, size, and function' suggests that they are referring to women's breasts that may have lost their fullness and symmetry after breastfeeding (62). It is unclear as to how such a device would not only improve the shapeliness of breasts, but also render them 'better adapted to fulfil their functions' (62). However, the notion that function, which is reliant on health, along with taste, is essential to beauty necessitates a medicalised understanding of the contraption. As femininity came to be understood as constructed through the purchase of an expanding range of consumer products, women were expected to continually defer to expert advice such as that of Brinton and Napheys so that they might make beauty choices aimed at improvement rather than harm (Beetham, *A Magazine* 8).

The crucial role of health in the conception of beauty is also evident in the discussion of corsetry and cosmetics. *Personal Beauty* posits that a woman of five feet in height should be at least twenty-five inches in waist circumference, increasing proportionally at half an inch in the waist for each additional inch in height. These measurements provide the basis for determining when corsets are laced too tightly, with compression beyond the desirable circumference being 'disastrous' in its impact on shoulder shape and the appearance of the breasts (Brinton and Napheys 65). If women do not obey their prescriptions in relation to health and corsetry, Brinton and Napheys warn that they will not be able to 'remain beautiful longer than they are young' (66). The emphasis on health reflects a wider tendency to focus on the ways that women destroy their own beauty through clothing, cosmetics or certain types of exercise, as I discuss in Chapter 2. Another target is the wearing of garters below the knee, which the authors claim is the reason why a 'handsome leg is a rarity, we had almost said an impossibility, among American women' (161). Unlike the wiser women of France and England who wear their garters above the knee, Brinton and Napheys explain that American women are ruining the shape of their calves through this practice and potentially causing the onset of varicose veins and ulcers.

The consideration of lip size and colour reveals conflicting ideas about what is considered healthful and therefore beautiful. For example, the authors suggest that thin lips can be increased in size through the application of silver plates, or increased by sucking them, thereby forcing blood into the area and 'consequently a greater amount of nutriment' (116). In contrast, girls who reportedly bite and suck their lips to induce redness, rather than an increase in size, are 'foolish' and liable to 'injure their shape' (119). This declaration is included in a discussion of attempts to make lips red, and sucking the lips is merged with prohibitions against 'colouring matter', such as lipsticks, which are a risk because they may be 'readily swallowed' (119). Unlike women's magazine articles and beauty manuals that repudiated coloured cosmetics on moral grounds, Brinton and Napheys's health-focused motivations concede that there is a less 'injurious' option in *rouge en feuilles*, which can impart a natural tint on the lips through the use of a moist cloth pressed onto the paper and then 'passed gently over the lips' (119). While most beauty advice of the period privileged the natural over what was seen to be artificial, these examples show the complexities arising when authors considered the added complication of 'health'. Nevertheless, the book does link the unnatural with the unhealthy in the case of brilliantly coloured cosmetics that contain 'unwholesome metals, lead and mercury' and methods for making the eyes sparkle (209).

While Brinton and Napheys rightly draw attention to the known harm of these metals in face products such as powders, which were intended to produce a flawless white complexion, their opposition to such products is not only grounded in the threat to life. Brilliant hues, they suggest, stand out to the observer as false, which defies what they term 'the perfection of art', achieved through 'an absolute resemblance to nature at her best, not to surpass her, nor fall behind her' (209). This opposition to cosmetics because of their contravention of 'natural' ideals of beauty and association with deceit was also commonly expressed in women's magazines and beauty manuals of the period. However, health concerns are more prominent in this manual, as reflected in the book's subtitle that specifies that its advice will accord with 'the laws of health'. If a woman's eyebrows required darkening, Brinton and Napheys caution against dyes because of the potential for harm to the skin or eyes, but instead recommend 'a pencil of dark pomatum' or smoking a needle over a candle flame as 'innocent' methods (82). However, surprisingly, they do not endorse the use of soap for women, even though it was the one product that was almost universally advertised, accepted and recommended in women's magazines. Their opposition to soap in the main does not stem from artistic concerns (although they argue that skin will be 'softer, whiter, and healthier' without soap), but on the grounds of health, given that they find most soaps are not 'perfectly "neutral"' and may contain a variety of harmful properties and ingredients, such as excess of alkali, 'rancid fat globules', colouring and 'irritating foreign substance[s]' (185).

Brinton and Napheys embrace the idea of beauty as an art that can be practised to advance single women's marriage prospects and ensure happiness within marriage. They situate the cultivation of beauty alongside other women's 'duties' relating to reproduction and as part of the 'infinite progress' of humanity itself, rather than positioning beauty practices and products as frivolous concerns (320, 321). They dismiss the idea that such 'arts encourage deceitfulness', pointing to the use of wigs, false hair and teeth, 'and a host of other devices to conceal deformities, which are now in universal use' (17). While tightly laced corsets, sucked-upon lips and white face powders are frowned upon for potential harm to health, as medical practitioners, they are not opposed to early manifestations of cosmetic surgery that can make a woman look her best for male suitors or her husband. For instance, in their discussion of nose skin that might extend to obscure the inner corner of the eye and produce a 'coarse look to the face', they advise that 'the knife of the surgeon is the only means that promises any relief' (84). In contrast, the authors oppose the cosmetic practice of enamelling, in which facial hair was removed and wrinkles filled with a white paste, followed by the application of powder and rouge, distinguishing between a medicalised 'defect' and vain practices that do not accord with ideals of health and a natural appearance (Rappaport 41). While both are cosmetic procedures, one of which is arguably of less medical risk in terms of the inherent risks of surgery, Brinton and Napheys distinguish enamelling as 'ridiculous and harmful' (255). While the dangers of surgery – especially in an era in which modern anaesthetic and antiseptic practices were still being developed – are glossed over, the authors point to the 'injury' possible through enamelling and equally to the fact that it is readily detectable 'by an eye at all practised in cosmetic arts' (255). A significant point in guiding the acceptability of cosmetic usage is whether such a practice appears natural, being undetectable from features that might naturally occur. Imitation itself is not described as distasteful if it can be transacted convincingly, but 'the failure in the attempt at imitation' does inspire revulsion, rather than physical harm (174). As such, a wig that accords with a women's age and appearance can be acceptable, but it is 'contrary to all good taste' to 'give to the top of the head an air of juvenility which is flatly contradicted by all other parts of the person' because the imitation is unsuccessful (309).

As a result, *Personal Beauty* often focuses on preventative measures for retaining beauty and delaying the onset of the markers of ageing, rather than ameliorating them once they have taken hold.

The conclusion of the book remarks that if all the measures recommended are undertaken that 'there will be little need for the purely venal cosmetic arts, such as paint, powder, patches, or rouge' (322). While the authors advocate for a strong mutual relationship between beauty and health, the emotions are frequently identified as a cause of the loss of beauty and as needing to be reined in to avoid deleterious consequences. This accords with Brinton and Napheys's declaration that facial expression – something that individuals can control – is what distinguishes people in terms of attractiveness given their assertion that most people are neither ugly nor beautiful (73). They suggest that half of the lines that form on a mature face are not the result of the passing of time, but 'of passion, of chagrin', and therefore can be prevented and diminished 'by a strong exertion of self-command', which represents a slightly differing manifestation of the idea that beauty and character were linked (255). The identification of movement, via facial expression, as a source of aged features is particularly intriguing given that facial exercises were a prescribed method for *avoiding* ageing later in the century, as I discuss in Chapter 6. In place of skin creams, women should aim to avoid facial expressions such as frowning and grimacing, squinting in bright light, and attempt to 'maintain as much command as possible over their facial muscles' (254). The authors suggest that the face is affected by 'violent emotions, especially of a dismal character'; the influence of emotion also extends to the hair, and indeed 'every part of our system' is discoloured and affected by our responses to life's trials (275). Quoting from Shakespeare's Sonnet 60, which touches on the loss of beauty with time, the authors contend that ageing may not necessarily cause decay in physical features, but that 'trouble', or an excess of negative emotions, are the true culprits.

Despite the logical focus on health in a book authored by two doctors, little attention is given to the benefits of exercise for women, according with expectations of feminine softness rather than muscularity and predating the physical culture movement for women. The book does support 'moderate exercise' for improving the symmetry of arm muscles, for example, but Brinton and Napheys assert that 'it is not in good taste for a woman to display a brawny, sinewy member' and maintain that women's bodies must be comprised of 'roundness' and 'gentle curve[s]' (148). These attitudes and subsequent physical interventions would transform by the end of the nineteenth century, with the growing onus in the West on the healthy body as a sign of inner and outer beauty, and the modern women's embrace of 'physical liberation along with familiar demands such as greater access to education, wider employment opportunities, and full citizenship' (Zweiniger-Bargielowska 107).

As Hilary Marland points out, even advice books – predominately those authored by women – that devoted significant attention to beauty advice and care of the body 'situated this within broader goals of producing healthy bodies and enjoyment of good health, and emphasised the importance of exercise' (65). To provide a counterpoint to Brinton and Napheys, *Beauty: How to Get it and How to Keep It*, which was published anonymously in 1885, encourages young women in particular to undertake a limited range of exercises, primarily types of physical culture and gymnastics. It formulates beauty as one of women's 'first duties' (7), implying that there was a form of work required for its cultivation and maintenance. However, this form of 'work' was distinctly different from the beauty regimen that I describe in Chapter 6. The manual proposes that 'perfect health' is the 'surest foundation' for beauty, giving the example of indigestion yellowing and muddying the skin (6).

Certain types of outdoor physical exercise became increasingly acceptable for girls and women in the latter decades of the nineteenth century, including horse riding, rowing, golf, lawn tennis, cricket and eventually cycling (Marland 91), and were linked with wider transformations in femininity brought about by changes in technology, dress and education. *Beauty: How to Get It and How to Keep It* summarises these changes by explaining that the invention of the sewing machine and change in fashion from long dresses provided girls and women with 'more leisure and greater freedom of movement' (8). Young women are encouraged to seize the possibilities of this new-found leisure time to 'reap the benefit in greater health and beauty' (8). This manual recommends the adoption of 'some simple system of gymnastics' and provided details of exemplary exercises (8). The language is medicalised with three 'physical defects' (rounds shoulders, stooping gait and a flat chest) named as capable of being 'cured' by daily practice of the exercises (8). As was frequently the case in discussions of cosmetics usage, the aim of exercise was not to enhance normal features, but to 'correct' flaws, deformities or the effects of illness. The significance of this distinction rests in the fact that it was acceptable for girls and women to harness the potential their features already had, but not to add something that was never there to begin with. A strange and specific example of this logic is evident in *Beauty: How to Get it and How to Keep It* with readers cautioned against utilising a 'nose-machine' to reduce the size of their nose. Such devices were regularly advertised in British periodicals for decades from the 1870s and promised to painlessly reshape the cartilage in the nose to improve its shape (Alex Ross Nose Machine 138). This beauty manual cautions that the unpleasant process of reshaping the nose through such a device 'should not be resorted to unless there is a positive deformity', particularly as 'the new-shaped nose may not suit the old place' (*Beauty: How to Get It* 18). Correcting 'defects' was, however, a very different prospect from improving features that were not beautiful, and concepts such as improving 'nature's charms', as I discuss in the following section, were mobilised in advice manuals authored by women in order to avoid transgressing prevailing ideals about healthy and natural beauty.

Madame Bayard's *Toilet Hints* (c. 1883): Adding to 'nature's charms'

The twin foundation of idealised beauty in the Victorian period were the natural and the healthy. Both were slippery categorisations that could be transgressed through almost any intervention in personal appearance. Many beauty manuals written by women attempted to delineate between the natural – and therefore acceptable – enhancement of the face, hair and body, and the artificial. While health also figures in beauty manuals that sought to provide advice about how a woman could appear her best, 'natural beauty' was a framing device in manuals such as Madame Bayard's *Toilet Hints* (c. 1883), providing a further complex set of instructions for how to negotiate prohibitions upon the unnatural and artificial. Marie Bayard was named as the editor of *Weldon's Ladies' Journal* (1875–1954), a British monthly dressmaking magazine. Her true identity remains unknown, but '"Marie Bayard" was a carefully crafted brand name epitomizing French expertise in fashion and needlework' (Van Remoortel 135). She also was named as the editor of *Toilet Hints; Or How to Preserve Beauty and How to Acquire It* (c. 1883), a guide to hair, skin and cosmetics, complete with recipes to combat 'personal defects'. The advice contained in this manual reflects a more general trend in earlier texts to distinguish acceptable 'natural' or 'healthful' attempts to remedy flaws from harmful or transgressive methods that were linked with the worsening of appearance or well-being.

In the preface, Bayard describes it as a woman's duty to spend time upon her appearance, but she cautions against excessive focus such that it might 'interfere with the higher duties of life' or 'occupy much time' (vii). These are clear signals for women to avoid anything that might compromise their moral responsibility for the care of others and which might plunge them into the territory of vanity. The book promises 'ample and simple means to remedy any personal defects, or further add to those charms which nature has already bestowed upon them' (viii). The language here is important in that it signals correction of physical flaws that deviate from the norm, which imparts an almost medicalised justification for 'remedy' or treatment; it also tellingly refers to the enhancement of favourable qualities already imparted by 'nature', legitimising making the most of beauty that is already inherent in each woman.

The book promises to provide recipes for skin blemishes, advice for the prevention and cure of wrinkles, and recommendations for pre-made products. On the surface this might appear counter-intuitive with respect to the overwhelming rhetoric surrounding natural beauty and healthful practices. However, the advice itself stops much shorter than the wholesale recommendation of artificial practices, and largely prescribes methods that do not involve the use of cosmetics. For instance, the first recommendation for a bad complexion is treatment of 'impure blood' through mineral waters, and consumption of moderate amounts of the right foods (15). As a French woman, or at least a woman assuming a French persona, Bayard suggests that Parisian women do not use soap on their faces, instead applying 'soaked bread' (15). The list of food products to treat the skin also extends to 'real cream', 'rice-starch powder' (18) and cucumber (20), ensuring connections with the nutritive properties of food and avoiding the negative connotations of artifice or harmful ingredients.

Bayard advocates the prevention of ageing when young, maintaining that skin care would ensure 'fewer faded and wrinkled skins when old, and there would be no need for cosmetics' (19). Visible ageing is framed as the result of neglect among girls and women, with everyone having the potential to retain skin 'ever soft and fair' rather than 'requiring extraordinary cosmetics, when the skin beings to show signs of decay' (19). The language of 'preservation'

(18) is combined with a preference for 'more natural' options to avoid being 'offensive to the eyes of others' (20). Bayard dismisses any talk of using rouge, which would fall foul of her stipulation and which she declares unfashionable in any event. She provides an undetectable substitute: readers with white complexions are advised to rub their cheeks with a gold coin.

Her preference for treatments to remain undetectable and to cause no harm to the user motivates Bayard's provision of home-made recipe substitutes for commercially available products. She warns the reader to '*Never* buy liquid white' because it contains lead and ruins 'skin, and health, and clothes' (21). In contrast, Bayard's recipe is purportedly impossible to detect, as long as the user does not apply a thick 'unnatural' coating to the skin (21). The factors that potentially lead to offence are the act of consumption itself and the noticeability of an unnatural attempt to improve the appearance. Somewhat incongruously, given the repeated advice to avoid cosmetics, and liquid white in particular, the advertisements at the beginning of the book include a full-page devoted to Rimmel's Toilet Requisites. The products listed include *blanc marimon*, an 'innocuous white' that was promoted as equally suitable for the stage and drawing room, eyebrow pencils, Velvetine toilet powder, and kohl (xiv). The presence of the advertisement – as in many women's magazines – alongside repeated admonishments *not* to use such products suggests a widespread culture of secrecy surrounding the use of cosmetics.

An additional prohibition is advice regarding anything that Bayard does not deem beautiful, which is evident in her discussion of blue tattooing to falsely create the appearance of veins on pale skin. She refuses to explain how the technique is performed regardless of any reader demand because it does not improve the appearance and therefore 'cannot be too severely condemned' (21). Bayard similarly condemns false hair, which she cautions is the most ruinous to real hair. She warns her readers to not even contemplate a false fringe (bangs), and dramatically states that she would rather wear her hair 'as short as a French soldier's than wear a single false curl' (32). The only way to preserve the health and colour of the hair is through the mundane method of keeping it clean, while those with dark hair may retain its youthful colour through washing it with red wine and iron. Home-made beauty concoctions and natural remedies such as these had an ancient history that Victorian manuals referred to, even citing specific recipes. Bayard acknowledges that some ancient recipes may have been 'nasty, but they were never dangerous', constituting a lament of the contemporary cosmetic landscape with the risks of lead, caustics and arsenic potentially hidden at every turn (40). Like liquid white, hair dyes are also flagged as containing lead and causing 'fearful illnesses of *body and brain*, and even death' (40). Dyes for auburn and yellow hair are singled out for utilising 'caustics' which burn the hair, causing it to break and become shorter and thinner (40). The twin anxieties of loss of health and worsening of the appearance are a familiar combination for dissuading the use of artificial beautification methods.

Bayard's longest and most emphatic denunciation is reserved for stays (corsets), which were the subject of long-running debates about health in Victorian print culture and in works such as Brinton and Napheys's *Personal Beauty*. Such was the commonality of medical condemnation of corsets that corset-maker Roxey A. Caplin's 1856 publication *Health and Beauty, or, Corsets and Clothing Constructed in Accordance with the Physiological Laws of the Human Body* comments upon 'medical men' who target corsets as a source of injury to internal organs and restriction of the motion of the spine (viii). Caplin is eager to draw the distinction between the opinions of medical men who do not understand the practicalities of dress and those of female consumers, who have intimate knowledge of their bodies in ways that male doctors do not and who regard corsetry as essential.[1]

Nevertheless, while Bayard is interested in women making the best of their appearance by natural means, she draws the line at 'cheap stays' that cause bodily harm (37). Sculptors of the period, she declares, were unable to sculpt women who were as beautiful as those in the past. The figures of the contemporary models have been destroyed by cheap corsets that work by

> squeezing in one part [of the body], and thus caus[e] the others to bulge out in exaggerated proportions. Stays ruin the figure, and there can be no truly perfect figure after having worn tight stays for any length of time. If once you begin to wear stays you cannot do without them, for they weaken the back, which can no longer keep straight without stays. (37)

Bayard's primary concern is long-term health damage, restricted breathing and pain, suggesting those who design fashions that require stays 'commit next to murder' (Bayard 57). This is coupled with the ongoing dependency created by their use and the ruination of a woman's figure, the precise opposite of their intended effect. However, it is important to recognise that the concerns expressed by Bayard and 'medical men' in beauty texts were not the prevailing view, and that corsets were worn by most women. Condemnation was usually reserved for the tight lacing of corsets, which was not only understood as harmful to health, but deleterious to a woman's appearance, in contrast with regular corset wear (*Beauty: How to Get It* 7). As Valerie Steele suggests, corsets 'allowed women to articulate sexuality in a socially acceptable way. The corset was also supposed to make women look more "beautiful" by concealing physical features that were less than "ideal"' (*Corset* 35). The amelioration of flawed features, as I have suggested, was generally acceptable in a way that attempting to 'improve' or enhance average features was not.

The common accusation surrounding the use of artificial methods of temporarily altering the body's appearance is that they worsen the appearance by causing long-term damage to health. Noticeable change to the appearance of the face or the body was therefore frequently linked with bodily harm, deformity, disease and even death. The only healthful kind of beauty was therefore one that was natural, and women who did not measure up to the aesthetic standards outlined by the likes of Alexander Walker or the illustrations of women found in fashion plates and advertisements were thoroughly warned about the harm that might come to them if they sought too radical a change beyond that which could be achieved by conservative measures.

Cosmetics and dangers to health in *The Law and the Lady*

While the rhetoric of naturalness was pervasive in beauty manuals and women's magazines, some women were using products and methods that were frowned upon, or which were unknowingly – and knowingly – dangerous. The culture of secrecy surrounding more transgressive methods of beautification is integral to the death of Mrs Sara Macallan, and subsequent trial of her husband, Eustace, for her murder, in Wilkie Collins's *The Law and the Lady* (1875). The protagonist, Valeria, resolves to clear her husband's name and sets out to prove his innocence and uncover the true cause of his first wife's demise. One of her first discoveries is a photograph of Mrs Macallan, who is 'not young', 'hard-featured and ugly, with the marking lines of strong passions and resolute self-will plainly written on it' (Collins 83). The multiple mentions of Mrs Macallan's 'self-willed hard-featured face' yoke together emotion and character with physical appearance (83). Mrs Macallan's ugliness is due in part to her character and the inscription of her strong feelings on her face, something that many beauty manuals warned against, as I discuss in Chapter 2.

Nevertheless, Mrs Macallan has arguably followed all of the other directives of the period to cultivate her demeanour, dress and voice. In the trial testimony, which Valeria consults as part of her investigation, the nurse who attended Mrs Macallan, Christina Ormsay, speaks to her refinement in all of these respects:

> She spoke and acted like a well-bred lady. Then again, as to her personal appearance. Plain as she was in face, she had a good figure; her hands and feet, I was told, had been modelled by a sculptor. She had a very pleasant voice and she was reported when in health to sing beautifully. She was also (if her maid's account was to be trusted) a pattern, in the matter of dressing, for the other ladies in the neighbourhood. (133)

While the rhetoric of health and self-improvement was pervasive in beauty advice throughout the second half of the nineteenth century, Mrs Macallan's ugliness runs contrary to it – she has been unable to remedy her plain face by any of the approved strategies available to her, despite 'the great anxiety of her life' being to make herself as attractive to her husband as she could (158). Valeria's inquiries uncover Mrs Macallan's jealousy of her husband's attractive cousin, Mrs Beauly. Mrs Macallan works herself 'into one of her furious rages' one morning after Mrs Beauly has spent the night, asking bitterly 'Is she more beautiful than ever this morning?' (125). While she may have resented Mrs Beauly's looks, Mrs Macallan did not neglect the opportunity to attempt to improve her own appearance, asking Mrs Beauly 'what artificial means she used to keep it [her complexion] in good order' (159). Mrs Beauly upholds expectations of the period, purportedly 'knowing nothing whatever of cosmetics' and resenting the question (159). Aviva Briefel's reading of the novel suggests that Mrs Macallan's death constitutes a 'cosmetic tragedy' but that it also warns of 'the dire consequences of not being able to achieve physical enhancement' (465). Mrs Macallan does not embrace all options for beautification (she eschews paint, for instance), which means she does not transgress beauty norms. Most importantly, however – given her yearning to do so – she also fails to be beautiful for her husband.[2]

Collins makes it clear that strategic beautification is necessary for women in their interactions with men. Valeria, though not 'ugly' like Mrs Macallan, begins her quest for information with her husband's friend Major Fitz-David. However, Fitz-David likes to surround himself with young, beautiful women, such as his unnamed 'over-dressed', opera-singing protégée. When Valeria arrives at his home, his chambermaid assists in rearranging her hair so that Valeria looks her best. However, the chambermaid also finds her complexion to be in need of artificial assistance, something to which she guiltily acquiesces in order to obtain the Major's confidence:

> 'Where do you keep it?' she asked.
> 'What do you mean?'
> 'Look at your complexion, ma'am. You will frighten him if he sees you like that. A touch of colour you *must* have. Where do you keep it? What! You haven't got it? you never use it? Dear, dear, dear me!'
> [...]
> She came back with a box of paints and powders; and I said nothing to check her. I saw, in the glass, my skin take a false fairness, my cheeks a false colour, my eyes a false brightness – and I never shrank from it. No! I let the odious deceit go on; I even admired the extraordinary delicacy and dexterity with which it was all done. (55)

Valeria's discomfort with the process is evident in her description of the chambermaid's 'wicked forefinger' directing her attention towards the mirror (55). The chambermaid, however, knows the power of skilfully applied cosmetics, telling Valeria that she is now one of the prettiest women in London and talking up the effectiveness of pearl powder (which provided an iridescent glow to the skin). This power is especially important for women who lack power and need to cultivate their influence upon men for their own advancement. The Major is a prime example of a man who lets down his guard and commits 'many a rash action' when encountering a pretty woman (72). Valeria's transformation is proof of this fact, in that the Major allows her to look through his belongings to seek a clue about her husband's trial, despite his sense of loyalty to Mr Macallan. It is not coincidental that the Major's blue velvet book of 'love-tokens from various ladies' (82) contains locks of hair from each woman, indicating the Victorian fetishisation of locks of hair in lockets and rings as well as symbolising sexual availability as each woman has given part of herself to the Major (Heaton 104). While beauty is a power over men that women ought to seize, according to Collins's narrative, there is a distinction between measured application of cosmetics in the right circumstances, and the courting of danger in order to enact a wholesale transformation.

While the narrative intrigue relies upon uncertainty about whether Mrs Macallan was poisoned and testimony from various witnesses that they had never known her to use arsenic to improve her appearance, her mother knows better. She testifies that her daughter had repeatedly said 'there was no risk she would not run, and no pain she would not suffer, to improve it [her complexion]. "Men" (she had said) "are all caught by outward appearances: my husband might love me better, if I had a better colour"' (158). Valeria's experience with Fitz-David establishes this fact: men are easily influenced by beautiful women. Beauty manuals and magazine advice columns sounded warnings – and applied moral judgements – about the use of an array of products, creating a strong impetus toward concealment and denial of their use. Indeed, in her history of the Victorian beauty industry, Jessica Clark explains that 'consumers went to great lengths to conceal their beautifying practices' and that these processes were confined by 'parameters of secrecy' (7). Mr Macallan's lawyer asks if women typically mention 'the secret artifices and applications by which they improve their personal appearance' or if a woman who wishes to be attractive to a man would tell him 'that the charm by which she hoped to win his heart – say the charm of a pretty complexion – had been artificially acquired by the perilous use of a deadly poison?' (Collins 170). The assumption, and the reality of Sara's ill-fated path, is that secrecy and deception are inherent in the consumption of beautifying products whether arsenic, false hair or false teeth (170). Moreover, when she fails to improve her appearance by these means, she commits suicide, expressing her regrets to her husband in her final letter: 'Farewell, my dear. I wish I had been a prettier woman. A more loving woman (towards you) I could not be. Even now', and signs off 'your poor, ugly, SARA MACALLAN' (366).

While Sara is an example of a failed user of artificial beauty aids, the 'plump, round-eyed, over-dressed girl, with a florid complexion and straw-coloured hair' who had attracted Fitz-David's attention has become his wife by novel's end (62). Significantly older than his wife, Fitz-David is submissive to his attractive mate, '[s]itting behind the chair on which his imperious wife sat enthroned' and almost waiting 'for her permission to open his lips and speak' (379). He remarks 'Isn't she beautiful?', praising her figure and voice in a manner that indicates the elevation he feels as a man paired with a younger, attractive woman (379). Fitz-David's wife has successfully enhanced her appearance and is therefore, Briefel proposes, 'able to perform her social functions' as a woman (465). The novel nevertheless also suggests that there is something awry with the relationship in which a beautiful younger woman holds power over a man. Fitz-David's wife is not even named and disturbs patriarchal power structures through her control. Moreover, her flushed skin, plumpness and overdressing imply not only excess with regard to her appearance, consumption and sexuality, but also a tendency towards vanity. *The Law and the Lady*, then, articulates the delicate balance that must be achieved by women between cultivating their appearance so as to hold the attention of men, and an excessive vanity that can undermine the gendered hierarchy and lead to fatal harm.

Punishing the natural beauty in *Adam Bede*

A significant portion of this monograph discusses the way Victorian print culture frames a 'right' way and innumerable 'wrong' ways of maintaining, retaining and enhancing beauty. However, natural beauties could be condemned for exhibiting serious flaws in character, such as vanity or overt sexuality, meaning that ideal beauty was rarely 'ideal' or without consequence. The very notion of cosmetics needing to be undetectable to be acceptable, not only adhered to rhetoric about nature versus artifice, but signalled that women should not be discernibly focused on their appearance. Women who dressed themselves with excessive ornamentation or visible cosmetics on their faces – those who could be seen to be consciously cultivating their sexuality – were inevitably derided in both fiction and advice literature. Naturally beautiful, but vain, women who were conscious of their influence upon men, such as Hetty Sorrel in George Eliot's *Adam Bede*, may not die by novel's end, but suffer significant punishment and humiliation. Eliot's fiction is particularly revelatory for consideration of beauty, as she includes what Richard Altick dubs 'Identikit inventories of a woman's features' in her novels and utilises a fictional convention in place since the beginning of the century by which the influence of physiognomy linked physical features with character traits (330).

The novel establishes an initial contrast between the plain and austere appearance of the Methodist lay preacher, Dinah Morris, and the prettiness and fussy ornamentation of the blacksmith's daughter, Bessy Cranage (known as 'Chad's Bess'). 'Chad's Bess' exhibits pride in her features, such as her plump, red cheeks and her 'pair of large round ear-rings with false garnets in them', and the Hayslope villagers pity her as a result (19). In contrast, Dinah is a modest woman, with a slim figure and 'total absence of self-consciousness in her demeanour' (20). Dinah wears a Quaker cap that covers her hair, and has a pretty 'small oval face, of a uniform transparent whiteness, with an egg-like line of cheek and chin, a full but firm mouth, a delicate nostril, and a low perpendicular brow, surmounted by a rising arch of parting between smooth locks of pale reddish hair' (21). Unsurprisingly, Bessy's gemstones are artificial, while language associated with nature and purity ('whiteness', 'egg-like') describes Dinah. When Bessy watches Dinah preaching, she puzzles over whether a woman who would wear such an unflattering cap experiences pleasure and satisfaction, unable to fathom femininity and a woman's happiness divorced from visual display. Dinah recognises the dangers of vanity and directly confronts Bess for her preoccupation with jewellery and clothing:

> 'Ah, tear off those follies! cast them away from you, as if they were stinging adders. They *are* stinging you – they are poisoning your soul – they are dragging you down into a dark bottomless pit, where you will sink for ever, and for ever, and for ever, further away from light and God.' (28)

She brings Bess to tears with her dramatic language and cruel reminder that her cheeks will eventually shrivel, her hair will grey, and her body will degrade.

This exchange about Betty's earrings prefigures the opposition between the titular protagonist's two romantic interests – Dinah, and her cousin Hetty Sorrel, which Bonnie Zimmerman describes as one of many instances in which Eliot contrasts 'artificial, "made" things and those of nature' (213). Significantly, both women are orphaned, which leaves them without maternal guidance regarding their appearance and romance. Each takes a differing path, with Dinah eschewing any conscious attempts at beautification or ornamentation while Hetty is preoccupied with catching glimpses of her appearance in polished surfaces and gaining the attention of her suitors. Zimmerman points out that Eliot's 'principal symbol for Hetty Sorrel, the unnatural woman, is jewelry' (213). As with Bessy's false garnets, earrings are a recurring symbol of artifice throughout the novel, in part, because 'they require nature itself be mutilated by piercing the ear' (Zimmerman 213). Indeed, as Hetty prepares for a dance for which she will be accompanied by Adam, she spends a long time in her bedchamber attending to her toilette and looking at herself in the 'old specked glass' (226). Hetty has been cautioned by Adam about being modest in her dress and has resolved to wear no ornamentation apart from a lace tucker. She even removes her usual small round earrings, which prompts her to lovingly gaze upon a pair of gold, pearl and garnet earrings that had been bought for her by Captain Arthur Donnithorne, the young squire to whom she is attracted, and who will eventually seduce her:

> O the delight of taking out that little box and looking at the ear-rings! Do not reason about it, my philosophical reader, and say that Hetty, being very pretty, must have known that it did not signify whether she had on any ornaments or not; and that moreover, to look at ear-rings which she could not possibly wear out of her bedroom could hardly be a satisfaction, the essence of vanity being a reference to the impressions produced on others; you will never understand women's natures if you are so excessively rational. Try rather to divest yourself of all your rational prejudices, as much as if you were studying the psychology of a canary-bird, and only watch the movements of this pretty round creature as she turns her head on one side with an unconscious smile at the ear-rings nestled in the little box. (226)

The language of nature that conventionally corresponds with idealised beauty is repurposed to speak to Hetty's status as a 'pretty' being that exists for the pleasure of others, and whose behaviours, like that of the canary, are quaint and inexplicable to more intelligent beings. While Adam seeks a woman to love who does not focus upon her appearance and decorative trinkets, Hetty spends significant time rehearsing for the dance by looking into the mirror, thinking about her neck and arms, and the dress she had adjusted the day prior. Her fixation on the earrings must be read in light of the pair of earrings she initially places in her ears to impress Arthur, which are large and made of coloured glass and gilding but 'looked just as well as what the ladies wore' (137). The mere sight of the earrings given to her by Arthur brings pleasure to Hetty because they have real monetary value and, as such, signify male esteem and desire that confirm her beauty. Moreover, they signal her inappropriate class aspirations, as a milkmaid who fantasises about living in luxury as an upper-class lady.

The overarching narrative about beauty that develops in print culture of the period is that natural beauty corresponds with goodness and ideal femininity, while artifice is connected with undesirable traits and tragic fates. The instance above where Hetty is likened to a canary is but one of many in which Hetty – and her beauty – evoke comparisons with infants and baby animals:

> It is a beauty like that of kittens, or very small downy ducks making gentle rippling noises with their soft bills, or babies just beginning to toddle and to engage in conscious mischief – a beauty with which you can never be angry, but that you feel ready to crush for inability to comprehend the state of mind into which it throws you. Hetty Sorrel's was that kind of beauty. (76)

The connection with animals and small children (both understood in scientific discourse as savage in various respects) links Hetty as a woman with two Othered categories (Shuttleworth 4). Her depiction also does not adhere to the more general principle about natural beauty being associated with innocence and vulnerability. Nancy Ann Marck suggests that Eliot's narrator aligns beauty with deception rather than virtue: 'Since the reader may take beauty as a sign of goodness and construct a conflicting interpretation of Hetty's motives, the act of reading character must be guided by the wise narrator, who in fact links Hetty's beauty to her narcissism' (455). The greatest condemnation of Hetty's vanity derives not only from her decision to have sex out of wedlock with Arthur Donnithorne and subsequent pregnancy, but her eventual conviction for infanticide. As the middle-class woman's primary role and function was to serve as a wife and mother, Hetty's catastrophic failure in both endeavours must be read as related to her excessive preoccupation with her beauty, and its association with sexuality.

Hetty welcomes attention from both Arthur and Adam, signalling her lack of virtue. The telling aspect of her pleasure in being adored is her blush. The first instance occurs when Arthur visits her when she is churning butter in the dairy, and she is conscious of his gaze, giving off a 'coquettish air' (76). Her blush when he enters is not 'distressed' but 'inwreathed with smiles and dimples, and with sparkles from under long curled dark eye-lashes' (76). Ruth Bernard Yeazell notes that nineteenth-century science did consider the 'physiological resemblance of a blush to other forms of sexual flushing and excitement', yet even prior to this 'lovers of the modest woman read an erotic promise in her blushes – all the more so, no doubt, because so little other than her cheek was conventionally available for contemplation' (74). Hetty's initial blush evokes youthful innocence with her dimples and sparkling eyes, but her awareness of being looked at and desire to retain Arthur's gaze might be read as 'erotic promise' by Arthur, certainly when factoring in that he later takes her virginity and her social respectability. The next instance occurs with Adam when she is picking cherries and is startled to the degree that she drops the basin of fruit, and once she sees Adam 'she turned from pale to deep red' (198). With respect to John Everett Millais's famous portrait of a young girl entitled *Cherry Ripe*, Pamela Tamarkin Reis observes that 'the word "cherry" meant young girl and referred also to the hymen and virginity, Millais's title announces, none too subtly, that the little girl, like the cherries, is ripe and ready to be plucked' (203). Hetty's failure to keep hold of the basin of fruit prefigures her premarital seduction, and her movement from enticing to repellent. In her examination of eighteenth-century literature and fruit imagery, Liz Bellamy notes that women and the pineapple are alike in that both 'should be consumed when they reach ripeness, suggesting their objectification as comestibles and luxury goods that are inherently transitory and subject to rapid deterioration. Both women and pineapples are liable to rot' (Bellamy 7). Though Adam has a positive, visceral response to Hetty's blush, his heart beating 'with a new happiness' (198), he cannot possibly desire her once she has become 'rotten'. The equation of female beauty with sexuality opens up both to the possibility of spoilation and decay, which sends many beautiful young heroines like Hetty to tragic fates in Victorian literature.

The pious and practical Dinah proves to be a faithful advocate for her disgraced counterpart, remaining with Hetty in prison while she awaits her execution (which is commuted to transportation after Arthur's intervention). For her exemplary conduct and unadorned natural prettiness, Dinah is rewarded with a mutually satisfying marriage with Adam and a safe and happy home with his family. The stark contrast between the outcomes for each character have a connection with appropriate female morality. Nevertheless, Hetty and Dinah also represent two models of beauty, one which seeks out male attention through artificial adornment and one which almost refuses it through modest dress. *Adam Bede* is an example of how the cautions about artifice and female display found in advice literature and the periodical press were also evident in Victorian fiction.

Conclusion

The beauty manuals I have examined in this chapter demonstrate that the Victorian beauty ideal was tied to expectations of the natural and healthful, which placed unrelenting and frequently contradictory conditions upon how a woman cultivated her appearance. These expectations were almost impossible to conform to, in that almost any intervention beyond the realm of the hygienic, such as cleansing the face, was contested. Moreover, differing kinds of beauty texts, whether written from a medical perspective or intended to provide advice to women for making the best of their appearance offered distinct stipulations as to what was an acceptable practice and which methods improved beauty. Even exercise, which had clear health implications and benefits for the wellness and appearance of the body, was difficult terrain to negotiate, with particular exercises considered harmful or unfeminine at various stages throughout the century. As Madame Bayard's advice manual suggests, exceptions were made for 'arts' that might be seen to 'assist' nature, such as the corset, so long as it was not tightly laced (Steele, *Corset* 54). This exception links with the tendency in beauty advice literature to accept methods of beautification that enhanced features that were already present or corrected deformities: for these purposes the natural was not being perverted.

For those women who were not blessed with the features that were regarded as beautiful, attempts to improve their appearance were largely troublesome if there was any way they might be conceived of as unnatural, artificial or harmful to health. In the most sobering examples, both real and fictional women, such as Mrs Macallan in *The Law and the Lady*, died from their use of unknowingly dangerous cosmetics or direct ingestion of harmful substances, showing that cautious attitudes to commercial beauty products were not entirely baseless and moralistic. In my discussion of *The Law and the Lady* and *Adam Bede*, I have sought to demonstrate how the ultimate impossibility of models of female beauty in advice texts is made manifest in the punishments meted out to beautiful women in fiction who exhibit excessive vanity or who succumb to demands upon their sexuality. For the women who actively cultivated sexual allure or visibly called upon cosmetics, dyes and other products deemed artificial, there was a higher level of condemnation connected with their perceived danger to themselves and others. The following chapter turns to the dangerous attractive woman and the menace of the quest for beauty, particularly in relation to cosmetic artifice.

Notes

1 Caplin's book includes an example of the emphatic criticism that corsets received from male physicians. She cites 'Dr Copeland's *Medical Dictionary*' published by Scottish physician James Copland as the *Dictionary of Practical Medicine*: 'These noxious and unnecessary articles of clothing – these mischievous appliances to the female form, useful only to conceal defects and make up deficiencies in appearance – are rendered still more injurious by the number of unyielding, or only partially yielding, supports with which they are constructed on every side' (qtd in Caplin ix). Copland maintains motion of trunk and spine is restrained, 'the nutrition of the compressed parts impaired', and the metal busk at the front 'has an injurious effect which has been universally overlooked' (qtd in Caplin ix).

2 This idea of failing to be beautiful is usefully read considering Eliza Haweis's contemporary ideas about the significance of female attraction and her definition of two different classes of girls, 'the Visible and the Invisible' (Haweis 259). A girl becomes Invisible when she 'fails to attract' (259). Indeed, the woman who does not attract might very well lose her status as 'a woman', which Haweis illustrates through an

obvious metaphor: 'just as a magnet that has lost its magnetism might be called a good stone, a weight, a stopper, or what not, but hardly a magnet' (259). The Visible, magnetic girls, including 'the handsome, the talented, the brilliant, the learned, and the indispensable in any way' will inevitably marry if they wish to do so, or 'blossom on the margins of the learned professions' (259). The second class of girls she describes, who need to become Visible and allow their beauty to 'be seen', include the 'The Nonentity', 'The Ill-educated', 'The Stupid', 'The Ordinary or Plain', 'The Discouraged' (260).

2

The Dark Side of Beauty: Cosmetics, Artifice and Danger

While beauty is a desirable quality in women, it is also often understood as signalling a threat. The term *femme fatale*, for example, refers to 'dangerously attractive' women (Braun 2). Much of this danger resides in a woman's sexual allure. In her influential study of fashion and eroticism, Valerie Steele argues that the very 'concept of beauty is sexual in origin, and the changing ideal of beauty apparently reflects shifting attitudes toward sexual expression' (*Fashion and Eroticism* 5). Aileen Ribeiro similarly suggests 'beauty in a woman often cannot be divorced from desire and specifically from sex' (15) and, relatedly, notes that cosmetics have 'sexual implications' (16). This chapter builds upon the foundation of Chapter 1, which distinguished between artifice and acceptable measures for enhancing the appearance and maintaining hygiene in beauty manuals. It examines the ways in which beauty was connected with danger in the Victorian period in three diverse kinds of print: the beauty manual, the periodical press and the novel. Cosmetics, dyes and other commercial products were situated within wider debates 'about the legitimacy of artifice and appropriateness of styles of dress and adornment that were overtly erotic' (Steele 126). While magazine advertising increasingly featured beauty products, the harmfulness of dangerous cosmetics to health and the potential damage to natural features from cosmetic usage were routinely emphasised in non-fiction, leaving the woman reader torn between competing ideals. Fictional depictions of cosmeticians extrapolated the dangers associated with cosmetics to harm and crimes that far exceeded deceptive products and treatments, as in L. T. Meade's *The Sorceress of the Strand* (1902). More frequently, however, Victorian fiction depicted natural beauty itself as a danger for young women, with its sexual implications being sufficient to lead to a tragic downfall and death in numerous novels, including Mrs Henry Wood's *East Lynne* (1862) and Oscar Wilde's *The Picture of Dorian Gray* (1890). These novels are representative of the enduring and pervasive association of beauty with sexuality and thereby the potential of a girl or woman's downfall.

Eliza Lynn Linton's 'The Girl of the Period', an unsigned article that appeared in *The Saturday Review* in 1868, hit a raw nerve about the changing behaviour and appearance of young British women in the mid-nineteenth century. As Kristine Moruzi suggests in her study of girls' periodicals, 'Linton's critique of the Girl of the Period ... suggests a deep anxiety about the control that girls are assuming over their own lives', which departed from 'the virtuous womanly ideal of the past' (1). Given the sexual resonances of cosmetics, the first line of Linton's article unsurprisingly attempts to define the Girl of the Period, describing her as 'a creature who dyes her hair and paints her face, as the first articles of her personal religion' (2). The Girl of the Period through her use of cosmetics and focus on extravagant fashion resembles women of questionable morality and potentially courtesans and sex workers who were breaking middle-class social codes surrounding sex. Linton's explicit comparison is to the 'demi-monde', a term which refers to women who had abandoned adherence to respectable norms of appearance and behaviour (3). She finds with dismay that their 'frantic efforts to excite attention' through extravagant dress is being imitated by the Girl of the Period, who 'cannot understand why she should be condemned for an imitation of form which does not include imitation of fact' (3). Even the very perception that fashion was being used by young women 'deliberately trying to attract men' to highlight their 'sexual beauty' was scandalous (Steele 132). By Linton's reckoning, however, the Girl of the Period 'does not please men', who are willing to flirt with such a girl, but not to marry one, given that respectable men 'prefer the simple and genuine girl of the past' (8). While the Girl of the Period is troubling because she is selfish and fails to modify her behaviour when chastised, she also reveals the ways that cosmetics and fashions were often understood as impractical, as facilitating artifice and as dangerous. Linton observes that her tastes are exaggerated, such that a trend for gowns that sit above mud in the street will be modified by the Girl to raise 'hers midway to her knee', or if bonnets are worn in a way that 'shall protect the wearer's face without putting out the eyes of her companion, she cuts hers down to four straws and a rosebud' (3).

Linton's essay sensationalises the topic of girls' appearance and the ways in which these troubling girls respond to current directives surrounding trends in hair, clothing and cosmetics. Whether considering skirts, hats or hair, Linton finds that the Girl of the Period gravitates toward what is most unreasonable in terms of utility and what is most shocking in relation to gender, class, sexuality and even race. Most alarming is the association of exaggerated reactions to beauty trends with racial otherness and mental illness:

> If there is a reaction against an excess of Rowland's Macassar, and hair shiny and sticky with grease is thought less nice than if left clean and healthily crisp, she dries and frizzes and sticks hers out on end like certain savages in Africa, or lets it wander down her back like Madge Wildfire's, and thinks herself all the more beautiful the nearer she approaches in look to a negress or a maniac. (3–4)

Linton refers to the popular men's hair oil and signals the Girl of the Period's excessive take on cosmetic trends that suggest her uncontrollable nature and the way in which her whims distance her from white, middle-class femininity. She also references a beautiful character, Margaret Mudochson, in Sir Walter Scott's *The Heart of Midlothian* (1818), who descends into mental illness after she is seduced and her infant murdered. This reference indicates how nineteenth-century fiction frequently connected beautiful, sexual female characters with negative outcomes including disgrace, poverty, madness and death, as I will discuss later in this chapter in relation to Ellen Wood's *East Lynne* and Oscar Wilde's *The Picture of Dorian Gray*. In the following section, I consider two beauty manuals that offer negative assessments about the use of cosmetics and highlight the potential outcomes of their use – from embarrassment through to death.

Beauty manuals and cosmetics

While attitudes towards cosmetics shifted by the end of the century, leading into a fuller embrace of commercial products, as I examine in Chapter 6, scepticism and discouragement of their use was frequent until late in the century across treatises on beauty, beauty manuals and the women's magazines I examine in the following section. An 1879 article from *Myra's Journal of Dress and Fashion* entitled 'Health and Personal Attention' is relatively representative in the primary points and concerns it raises about cosmetic use. First, it acknowledges that cosmetic usage has been common among women since ancient times: 'The arts of the toilet are as old as Thebes' ('Health' 187). Second, it singles out women who use coloured cosmetics or 'paint and powder' liberally as engaged in 'deception' (187). In place of such deception, echoing the privileging of natural and healthful beauty I outlined in Chapter 1, the author prefers the enhancements provided by fresh air, exercise and water, which are, in fact, more effective at imparting 'a ruddier glow and more pearly tint to the face than all the rouge and lily-white in Christendom' (187). Third, if any 'artificial' product must be used then it must be applied 'artistic[ally]' and used 'well' (187), particularly for cosmetics that must be applied with discretion, such as rouge. Fourth, most commercially available cosmetics are nevertheless labelled as dangerous, with harmful ingredients in common products listed, including red-lead, bismuth and arsenic, and may make a woman's appearance worse. The author's case in point is 'public singers' whose 'hideously coarse complexion ... is partly due to their use of bismuth powder' (187). Finally, if a woman must try to actively change her appearance, then she ought to try making her own harmless preparations. This article provides recipes for 'Almond Bloom' and 'Devoux French rouge', and advises correspondents such as Henriette, who asks about a preparation for wrinkles and loose skin, to consult a particular chemist to obtain 'Glycerole of Tannin' (187). By the last decades of the century, beauty norms were cemented and prohibitions on cosmetics were replaced by advice on which cosmetics should be used and how they should be used.

But how did these commonly held ideas about beauty and artifice come to be so widely held and embedded in the advice of the very women's magazines that would eventually come to rely on cosmetic advertising? Here I consider two beauty manuals, one published early in the century purportedly by Mrs A. Walker (Alexander Walker's wife), and the other by a minor celebrity, Lola Montez, published mid-century, in order to show the prehistory of these precepts. Some of the ideas these books present are closely tied to enduring beliefs about women that long underwrote patriarchy, such as the disproportionate emphasis on women's beauty and decreased value of women as they aged. Nevertheless, they also denied the hope that the span of the idealised youthful appearance could be extended by beauty products and practices. These authors are representative of the beauty manual genre that helped to propagate and circulate dominant Western ideologies of beauty, such as the privileging of the impossible 'natural' ideal, the remnant threads of which continue to influence contemporary culture, often in deleterious ways for girls and women.

Mrs A. Walker's *Female Beauty, as Preserved and Improved by Regimen, Cleanliness and Dress* (1837) provides a clear sense of how beauty regimens and cosmetics were regarded in print at mid-century as potentially harmful and with the capacity to degrade a woman's appearance, and likely the way discourses about beauty at this stage was heavily influenced by physiological and scientific publications.[1] Indeed, the full title of the book clarifies that the advice contained within aims to influence 'the forms, complexion, and expression of each individual ... rendering cosmetic impositions unnecessary' (Walker n.p.). For Walker, the definition of a cosmetic included both products that might be used for 'cleansing and purifying the skin' and those for 'artificially embellishing and giving a factitious colour' (32). While Walker seemingly gives credence to the possibility of efficacious cosmetics, she chooses to apply the term in *Female Beauty* 'as signalling only the artificial, complex, costly, and inefficient means' (32). Like many manuals, Walker acknowledges that women have adopted cosmetic practices since ancient times, such as milk baths. However, while she concedes that such methods derived are less harmful, she similarly finds them to be 'dirty' and to 'clog the skin, and injure it in the end' (33).

Cosmetics of the present day often rely on referencing natural products such as fruits, plant extracts and beeswax to signal their harmlessness and efficacy, but Walker is not engaging in a similar opposition between the 'artificial' and the 'natural', given that she finds that both can be injurious and claims that nature 'never meant that people should plaster food over the outside of their bodies' (33). Rather than calling on nature for products that might enhance or preserve female appearance, beauty is framed as natural and at risk of loss or damage from cosmetics, particularly those of dubious origin. For example, Walker refers to 'the pretended cosmetics sold by general perfumers, and by a great number of ignorant persons who call themselves chemists' that are comprised only of 'vinegar or spirits of wine scented' (37). While she acknowledges the potential of such products to clean the skin, she suggests that acids and spirits destroy 'the imperceptible unctuous moisture that nature exhales' and that '[t]he delicate tissue of the cuticle requires' (37). Similarly, when 'pretended remedies' are applied to conditions where the skin is disturbed by 'a disordered state of the system', they can have a dangerous effect because the skin afflictions are themselves 'an effort of nature to re-establish or preserve the health' (39).

Other types of cosmetics more properly signal harm to health through the inclusion of substances such as lead, which Walker notes causes paralysis, convulsions and colic. The notion that such harm might be worth risking for beauty are squashed by the assertion that cosmetics destroy the complexion, impelling a vicious cycle of detrimental consumption: 'As soon as the deluded dupe removes the paint from her face, she sees in her glass a skin so wrinkled, and a countenance so ghastly, that she redoubles the application of cosmetics, till she has finally ruined her complexion and destroyed her health' (40). The language of beauty as natural and subject to destruction by 'pretended cosmetics' is again inherent in the description of 'the natural brilliancy of the tint' being destroyed and the 'wither[ing]' of 'the most blooming and the softest skin' (46). At one end of the cosmetic spectrum are those with false claims that prove to be harmful, and at the other 'are mere decoctions, pastes, pomades, &c. which have no claim to the pompous titles with which ignorance and quackery decked them out' (32). The extended figuration of cosmetics as either harmful or ineffective in this manual leaves little scope for improving the appearance beyond washing the face.

The emphasis on cleanliness as one of the few acceptable methods of improving the appearance is readily evident in the preponderance of advertisements for soap in women's magazines in the second half of the nineteenth century, and the household-name status of soap brands such as Pears. Walker declares in a section of the book devoted to 'Artificial Paints' that remarkably beautiful women – and most especially women who have managed to retain their beauty into older age – have 'rejected with disdain all cosmetics, and have been indebted for the whiteness of their skin, and the dazzling brilliancy of their complexion, to the most simple but regular attention to cleanliness' (59). Walker frames women's addiction to cosmetics as have a traceable lineage from the Roman

Empire (as documented in the works of Juvenal) to the nineteenth century. She places herself in the tradition of men such as Celsus who understood the quackery of the cosmetics of the period, but points to the women of the past to demonstrate 'the antiquity of such delusions' relating to overcoming ageing (47). The 'charlatans and perfumers' of the early to mid-nineteenth century offer 'dazzling promises' to women 'troubled with an oily or scaly skin, red spots, pimples, or extreme paleness', situating cosmeticians in a long line of swindlers who exploit women's vanity for profit (39).

Lola Montez's *The Arts of Beauty* (1858) similarly shows that manufactured cosmetics and the artifice with which they were connected were roundly condemned at mid-century, with a few very specific qualifications. Montez was an Irish-born woman who led a colourful life as a courtesan, dancer and mistress of King Ludwig I of Bavaria, before she died at the age of 39 from the complications of syphilis. Her manual reproduced existing recipes for home-made cosmetics, washes, pastes, creams and powders that she claims were originally used by celebrated European beauties, and she entreats her lady reader that if she must use 'helps to beauty' then she must 'become *her own manufacturer*' (xii). One of the primary reasons given for self-manufacture is because of cases of harm, as also mentioned by Walker. Alison Matthews David's *Fashion Victims: The Dangers of Dress Past and Present* (2015) documents numerous types of toxic clothing in the nineteenth century, as well as identifying branded cosmetic powders that contained lead and caused a form of palsy (22). Montez was aware of these dangerous products and asserted that patent cosmetics 'have ruined the finest complexions, and induced diseases of the skin and of the nervous system, which have embittered the life, and prematurely ended the days of their victims' (xii). Montez lists the ingredients of a cosmetic sold at a profit of 1,700 per cent that, even more alarmingly, included a generous proportion of 'corrosive sublimate', or mercury chloride (xiii). Similar warnings about cosmetics would persist in beauty manuals until much later in the century. *Beauty: How to Get It and How to Keep It* (1885), published by *Tit-Bits* magazine, for example, continued to describe cosmetics as 'injurious', giving only a 'passing beauty' that prompts a vicious cycle in which 'the cosmetic must be used more frequently, and in larger quantities, till even that is useless, the skin is utterly ruined, and first paint and then enamel have to be resorted to' (10). There were notable examples of harmful products throughout the century, yet the ongoing hyperbole about manufactured cosmetics contained in advice manuals, such as *Beauty*'s admonition that cosmetics worked almost like a drug addiction with diminishing effects over time, far exceeded the likelihood of women experiencing harm, especially as brand name products established their reputations over time.

Montez describes beauty practices as 'arts', a commonly applied term in beauty advice literature that alludes to the careful judgement required to ensure a woman's appearance remained appealing (xii). She focuses on '*modern arts*' that she has seen in practice that do not conform to expectations of healthful beauty, such as the women of Bohemia drinking the waters of 'arsenic springs' to impart a whiteness to their skin (41). Montez suggests that once 'habituated to the practice' that women must maintain the habit of consuming the arsenic water 'or death would speedily follow' (41). Young girls are similarly successful in obtaining pale skin through the consumption of chalk, slate and tea grounds, but these practices are likewise described as destructive to well-being and beauty itself: 'it destroys the health, and surely drives out of the face the natural roses of beauty, and, instead of a bright complexion, produces a wan and sickly one. Every young girl ought to be impressed that whatever destroys health spoils her beauty' (41). Nevertheless, Montez is far from suggesting that natural and healthy equates with inaction. She argues that it is, in fact, 'a woman's *duty* to use all the means in her power to beautify and preserve her complexion' (39). These may be 'rational' and 'natural' methods, but in addition 'there are many artificial devices by which a lady may keep up and show off her attractions to great advantage, and for a long period' (32). Because a woman's face 'is such a public thing' and there is 'no hiding-place for an ugly face', it is unsurprising that women attempt all methods possible (40).

Montez condones the use of natural methods for improving the appearance in a way that Walker's publication from two decades earlier does not, showing the gradual process by which beauty interventions became acceptable. She even reproduces recipes for various preparations, including the Vestris's Paste purportedly used by the recently deceased actress Madame Vestris to prevent wrinkles each night while she slept. Nevertheless, like Walker, she also devotes substantial attention to detailing the kinds of cosmetics that must be avoided and to habits that are seen to destroy the skin, indicative of the ongoing policing of coloured cosmetics and other methods equated with artifice. Coloured cosmetics violated accepted rules about beauty practices needing to be in accord with nature, rather than eclipsing it. For this reason, Montez does not caution against the use of rouge, particularly if a woman has been unwell and 'loses her roses', given that it leaves most of the face in its natural state and does not conceal 'the language of the heart', which she suggests the complexion expresses (48). This sentiment accords with the idea that cosmetics served as a mask or disguise of women's true character, and fuelled their association with deceptive women in fiction. The rule for usage is that the tint provided by the rouge 'should always be *fainter than* what nature's pallet [sic] would have painted' (48). A woman who transgresses these instructions and applies colour such that she is 'violently rouged', ensures that her features appear coarse, her countenance fierce, and transforms her 'into a vulgar harridan' (49).

As a consequence of the emphasis on the natural, cosmetics such as lipstick and eyeliner fall into the category of 'paint' within the pejorative term 'powder and paint'. This accords with earlier French cosmetic categorisations, in which products that 'embellished beauty through improvement, such as creams and lotions', were distinguished from 'fard', including face powder and rouge, that 'masked imperfections and created the illusion of color' (Martin 13). Montez describes a fair woman who draws on black eyeliner or uses dark hair dye as having a 'frightfully ... mutilated nature' (55). The language applied to women who transgress the line of what is natural relates to revulsion, particularly from men. For instance, in her discussion of the use of 'artificial red' paint on the lips, Montez suggests that men instantly detect its use and will 'shrink back with disgust from the idea of kissing a pair of painted lips' (58).[2] While powder was often described as acceptable if it was used sparingly, excessive use was similarly understood as a 'vulgar trick', aligning with perceptions of cosmetic use as a form of deceit designed to mislead men (49). The woman who does not use powder artfully, but applies it hurriedly and excessively, with her face appearing as if she 'just came out of a meal-bag', appears 'ridiculous' and 'disgusting to gentlemen' (49). Most disgusting of all is the older woman who would no longer naturally have a blush in her cheeks who uses rouge, rendering herself 'a horrible sight – a distortion of nature's harmony' (49), a common sentiment throughout the century that Chapter 4 examines in detail.

Moreover, for Montez, artificial means cannot actually replicate the imagined effects produced by nature, such as the 'delicate charm associated with the idea of "nature's dewy lip"', seeing as '[t]here can be no *dew* on a painted lip' (58).

The recourse to extreme examples of degraded beauty, the provocation of disgust, and severe illness and death caused by the unacceptable – more artificial – end of the cosmetics spectrum were commonplace in both intellectual treatises on beauty and beauty manuals. In addition to repeated cautions about the repulsive effects of paints upon men, Montez also warns about the potential for artificial aids to ruin beauty (India-rubber bosoms destroy 'the beauty of the part') and health (52). Montez claims to personally know of 'paralytic affections and premature death' linked to the use of paints but acknowledges that 'there never was a time' when fashionable women did not use 'this disgusting trick' (48).

These more sensational attempts to discourage the use of 'artificial' cosmetics could be taken further into the realm of fantasy in fiction, with women who were preoccupied with appearance and artifice depicted as villains. Unlike beauty manuals published in book form, however, women's magazines had to mediate between these prevalent discourses and the growing number of cosmetic products that could seek to place paid advertisements within their pages.

The place of cosmetics in women's magazines: the cases of *Woman* and the *Queen*

In the second half of the nineteenth century, periodicals with vastly different price points and intended readerships in class terms, were relatively consistent in their editorial stance on cosmetics, and their cosmetic and beauty advertising, while often for different products, made similar claims in relation to naturalness, harmlessness and discretion. In both editorial and advertisements, magazines such as the *Queen* and *Woman* inevitably critiqued or avoided reference to cosmetics, instead advocating the maintenance of youthful beauty through health and a hygienic daily regimen. The *Queen* was an illustrated publication founded by Isabella and Samuel Beeton in 1861, and was sold to publisher Edward William Cox and merged with *The Lady's Newspaper* in 1863 (Beetham, *A Magazine* 89). It had lavish production values, including its broadsheet format and hand-coloured fashion plates.

The paper was sold in weekly issues for 6d, signalling, along with its print aesthetics and editorial assumptions about reader income, that it was intended for wealthy readers. However, it was likely also consumed by aspirant women who would not have the means to purchase many of the products advertised within it or the status to move within the social circles often discussed. Fashion and luxurious living were significant preoccupations, but the magazine also included domestic advice such as gardening tips and recipes. The *Queen* mentioned that it was overseen by an 'editress', but Helen Lowe (editor from 1862 to 1894) remained anonymous. In contrast, *Woman* (1890–1912), was a 'cheerful but conservative' penny weekly that was dependent on advertising, and had lesser aesthetic qualities in comparison with more expensive magazines (Beetham and Boardman 87). During the 1890s, the magazine was edited by novelist Arnold Bennett who adopted several female pseudonyms (including 'Sal Volatile' and 'Lady Betty') to maintain the expected 'feminine persona' of women's magazines (Beetham, 'Periodical Writing' 227). *Woman* combined short fiction with informational articles, fashion and beauty notes, dress patterns, domestic tips and advice columns.

In this section, I examine the tensions evident in these women's periodicals between adhering to prevailing natural ideals in editorial content and the necessity of advertisements for beauty products. Margaret Beetham explains that '[t]he relationship between advertising and editorial copy was ... potentially even more fractured than between other elements of the magazine" (*A Magazine* 140). While the physical separation of advertisements on, or inside, magazine covers helped to create distance from the content over which editors had full control, the 'invisible role played by advertising revenue in financing the press' was visible in the predominance of advertisements (*A Magazine* 143). The potential effect of advertised products on a magazine's reputation is alluded to by *Woman*'s claim that it only accepted advertising for products that it had tested, even if, as Beetham suggests, this was likely untrue given the copious advertising it included in each issue (*A Magazine* 180).

Advertisements published in *Woman* for products that were associated with artifice attempted to conform with the predominant ideal of natural, healthy beauty. Coloured cosmetics, such as blush, were the most policed of all beauty products within these – and indeed most, if not all – women's magazines. Given the erotic associations of coloured cosmetics, they had the potential to endanger a woman's moral character. As such, advertisements continually seek to deny or obfuscate that the products they promote are indeed cosmetics. A spurious ad for 'Narubine (Regd.) (Natural Blush)' in *Woman* describes the way the 'clear and colourless liquid ... *gradually and imperceptibly* produces a lovely peach-like blush, perfectly natural in tint, bloom and appearance' when applied to the cheek (21, original emphasis). The copywriter ties herself in knots to describe a product that imparts colour but which is devoid of colour. The blush produced is 'lovely' but it is also 'imperceptible', helped no doubt because of the 'natural' quality of the result, which is accentuated through comparison with the downy softness of a fruit (21).

The distinction between acceptable methods for improving the appearance and potentially morally or physically harmful products is especially evident in advertisements that pertain to hair loss or greying hair. False hair was often condemned in beauty manuals, with Madame Bayard suggesting that in 1883 that in cases of hair loss and disease 'false hair only increases evil' (42). In magazines, hairpieces and toupees were often advertised with illustrations of the various types included, but these advertisements were not always accompanied by the same claims about undetectability made by many cosmetic ads. One advertisement for C. Bond and Son's wigs and hairpieces in *Woman* in 1892 describes the products, which are designed for concealing baldness or grey hair, as 'the most perfect imitations of nature' (C. Bond and Son's xx). Colouring of the hair was, however, regarded as problematic, and advertisements were more likely to refer to 'hair restorers' than dyes. An advertisement for Jean Stehr's hair colouring in *Woman* in 1896 does use the word 'colouring', but tempers this with the qualification that the product is 'natural' and free from harmful chemicals (Jean Stehr's 7). In addition, the smaller print describes the 'consultations' that Stehr himself conducts in which he 'treat[s]' 'Greyness and Faded Hair' drawing on his 'long experience' and 'thorough knowledge of Chemistry' (7). The idea of medicalised 'treatment' sidesteps the association of dyes with unacceptable artificiality, detectability and even harm to health.

Very few editorials, therefore, discuss the cosmetics that fall outside of the acceptable realm of self-improvement occupied by healthful activities and maintaining cleanliness. One rare example from *Woman* in 1894 adopts the pretence of a visit to a 'Parisian

Beautifier' to deliver several cautions about cosmetic use. In 'The Art of "Making-Up"', *Woman* interviews 'Madame M-----' who, with her daughters, beautifies wealthy French women. Madame M makes several pronouncements that deflect common anxieties about cosmetic usage. First, she denies the transformative potential of cosmetics, emphasising that they do not pretend to turn 'ugly women into beautiful ones' ('The Art of "Making-Up"' 9). Instead, the focus is on instructing women about taking 'care of their beauty', in accordance with accepted rhetoric about preserving youthful features, as well as improving features 'where the features are good' and adding to existing beauty (9).

The emphasis on the inability to create beauty where it did not naturally exist was crucial in response to male anxieties about cosmetics that had appeared in the periodical press for decades. For instance, in 1862, during coverage of fraudulent beautician Madame Rachel's legal proceedings against one of her clients for unpaid debts, newspaper articles expressed anxiety about the deceit being perpetuated on men when nature was usurped through processes such as her enamelling technique. Enamelling involved the removal of facial hair, cleansing of the skin with alkaline washes, then filling of any wrinkles or uneven facial features with a thick white paste, sometimes containing lead, followed by the application of powder and rouge. The *Glasgow Herald* remarked:

> We feel alarmed when a beauty looks as if she were going to be betrayed into a smile lest her cheek should suddenly become fractured. We shall watch with tremendous apprehension when some beauty applies a pocket handkerchief to her nose, lest four or five guineas worth of its exquisite proportions should come away with it. (Qtd in Rappaport 66)

Madame M, therefore, emphasises that cosmetics cannot create beauty where it does not already exist. She also promotes the artistic nature of cosmetic use and critiques women who are artificially made up. She describes her encounter with a young society lady who looks 'horrible!' because of her excessive use of powder and coloured cosmetics: 'Two vivid spots of rouge, hard, and as accurately defined as if put on with a stencil, glowed upon her cheeks ... Her lips were too red ... and spoilt by careless outlining. Her eyes were blackened far too much; her eyebrows heavy and badly shaped' ('The Art of "Making-Up"' 9). Although this article purportedly provides an insight into the practices of a make-up artist who works with society ladies, Madame M's opinions on 'cosmetiques' discourage their use and favour natural methods that were generally accepted in women's magazines. She advises that beautiful women do not need cosmetics and also generates alarm about the permanent burden of cosmetic use by suggesting that once a woman begins to apply cosmetics, she must continue to use them. Madame M instead recommends several practices that are 'natural' and which may be taken up simply for 'temporary occasions', such as holding a saucer over a flame to gather lamp black to lightly darken the eyebrows and eyelashes. She also recommends beetroot juice as 'an innocuous substitute for rouge' applied with a camel-hair brush and then toned down with chamois leather ('The Art of "Making-Up"' 9).

Though attitudes towards cosmetics were shifting by the end of the century, the harmfulness of particular solutions was still commonly outlined, sparked by the reality of numerous spurious cosmetic products and practices throughout the century, ranging from deceptive to fraudulent and dangerous. Moreover, there continued to be incidences of fraudulent cosmeticians and dangerous beauty products even as they were gradually embraced. Throughout 1891 and 1892, advertisements for London lectures by the self-styled 'celebrated American skin specialist' Anna Ruppert (Anna Shelton) appeared in the *Queen* and other British publications (The Celebrated American Specialist n.p.) (Fig. 2.1). The advertisements also mention her 1892 book on 'natural beauty', as well as various products, including a skin tonic. While originally marketed as 'Face Bleach' in the United States, the tonic is described in one advertisement as harmless and invisible: 'It is not a cosmetic as it does not show on the face after application' (Mrs Anna Ruppert xxxii). Another of Madame Ruppert's advertisements reproduced the accepted rhetoric surrounding beauty typical of women's magazines, encouraging women to 'Be beautiful not with artificial means, but naturally so' (Madame Ruppert xl). The reality, however, was that Ruppert's product was dangerous; after a chemical analysis, the skin tonic was found to include the dangerous ingredient 'corrosive sublimate (bichloride of mercury)' ('Editor of "Health News"' 67). Prior to this revelation and her subsequent discrediting, Ruppert had nevertheless appreciated the importance of marketing her products as natural and non-cosmetic in accordance with the predominant

68 Consuming Female Beauty

Figure 2.1 The Celebrated American Specialist advertisement. *Queen* 3 December 1892, n.p. Bodleian Library.

editorial stance of most women's magazines, regardless of their true composition.

Cosmetics and crime in L. T. Meade's *The Sorceress of the Strand* (1902)

Before the case of Anna Ruppert, however, the multiple fraud trials of criminal cosmetician Madame Rachel in the 1860s and 1870s informed the most culturally significant discussions of scandalous cosmetic practices in Britain. Even decades after her notorious dealings, she inspired a fictional character, 'Madame Sara', who amply demonstrates the ways in which cosmetics, artifice and the deceptive appearances they could produce were hyperbolically associated with moral ills and potential danger to both unsuspecting men and women. Sarah Rachel Leveson (Madame Rachel) notoriously defrauded and blackmailed clients that visited her London salon, and was well known for her practice of 'enamelling'. In her beauty manual, Montez proposes that if Satan had ever exerted 'any direct agency in inducing woman to spoil or deform her beauty, it must have been in tempting her to use *paints* and *enamelling*' (47). The practice was widely ridiculed and criticised for its disguise of a woman's facial expressions, in accord with ideas that the concealment of the true appearance or emotion was linked with deceptive conduct. The 'face bedaubed with white paint and enamelled' cannot show pleasure, hope or love 'through the incrusted mould' (Montez 47). A fictional exaggeration of Madame Rachel's life was serialised as *The Sorceress of the Strand* by L. T. Meade and Robert Eustace in *Strand Magazine* in 1902, joining *The Picture of Dorian Gray* and *The Strange Case of Dr. Jekyll and Mr Hyde* in debating 'the capacity for external beauty to hide internal deviance' (Halloran 178).[3] The novel is set in London in 1899, which is over thirty years after Madame Rachel's two fraud trials in 1868, signalling the intrigue that continued to be associated with cosmetics and cosmeticians, even as they inched towards more widespread acceptance. The mythology and sensation surrounding dangerous beauty remained current in fiction at the turn of the century, perhaps owing to capacity to exaggerate and extend the severity of its consequences.

While the historical Madame Rachel was not known for her beauty or youthful appearance, the figure of Madame Sara in Meade and Eustace's detective story is strikingly beautiful and looks remarkably young. Sara is 'very fair, with blue eyes, an innocent childlike manner, and quantities of rippling gold hair' (Meade 120). Two factors render this description unnatural: first, 'that by birth she is a mixture of Indian and Italian' parentage; and second that her actual age is likely more than 50, despite multiple assessments of her age as no more than 25 (120).[4] Sara's mastery of cosmetics means that she misleads those she encounters regarding both her race and her age, intensifying the concerns I described earlier about their potential to enable deception. Elizabeth Carolyn Miller suggests that her appearance is 'undoubtedly artificial and calculated' (323) serving to highlight 'makeup's role in the text as a signifier of the breakdown of social hierarchies', regardless of their greater visibility and usage by the turn of the century (324).

The early ways in which this more calculated and artificial kind of beauty were framed as unnatural and dangerous are sensationally demonstrated by Madame Sara in *The Sorceress of the Strand*. Madame Sara appears in simple dress on most occasions ('almost like what a girl would wear'), but she makes a notable appearance in 'rich Oriental stuffs made of many colours, and absolutely glittering with gems', including diamonds in her hair and around her neck (129). While an excess of adornment, particularly on an older woman, would ordinarily be critiqued for the twin crimes of vanity and ridiculousness, as I discuss in Chapter 4, Sara manages to not only evade them, but to outshine the younger women present. The explanation is not merely beauty, but 'charm – charm which carries all before it' (129). The choice of the word 'charm', the description of her shop as 'a magician's cave' (125), and the later fearful reference to her 'cast[ing] a spell' with her appearance allude to the way that female beauty came to be linked with almost supernatural (and thereby threatening) powers over men (129). As Carol Dyhouse observes in her book on the subject of glamour (2010), the word, which would come to indicate a sophisticated type of sexual allure, 'meant something akin to sorcery, or magical charm' in the nineteenth century (1). Her deceptively white and youthful beauty enables her to take in almost everyone she meets, providing a lure and a screen for dubious business practices and outright criminal conduct. However, what is most disturbing is that Madame Sara's artifice is undetectable, and she has the look of an 'innocent' and 'natural girl' (121). Cosmetics provide the means to 'mask her criminal tendencies ... behind a facade that is not only accepted but admired by society' (Halloran 178). There is little suspicion of Madame Sara and her reputation among most of her clients is above reproach. Edith Dallas, an unmarried woman approaching the age of 30, for example, calls her 'the most marvellous woman in the whole of London' and her adoration of the beautician is framed as 'amount[ing] to idolatory' (120).

Madame Sara is involved in numerous crimes and deceptions throughout *The Sorceress of the Strand*, and her business is 'all sorts of curious secrets, but principally in cosmetics' (120). The novel begins with Dixon Druce, manager of Werner's Agency 'the Solvency Inquiry Agency of all British trade' (117), on a ship bound for Southampton from Madeira. He encounters his old school friend Jack Selby, who shares with him his knowledge about Madame Sara, who has recently been mysteriously occupied in Brazil. When Druce meets Sara, she describes her business as a 'perfumery shop', signalling associations with the more reputable end of the beauty industry. However, her reference to 'some perfectly innocent secrets' obtained 'partly from the Indians and partly from the natives of Brazil', including her recent visit to the state of Pará, home to the Amazon river and rainforest (122), indicates practices that hold a dubious mysticism and connote a threatening exoticism in a period in which whiteness was central to constructions of beauty. In Pará she inquired 'into certain methods by which my trade can be improved' (122), mirroring Madame Rachel's marketing practices of claiming to source particular products from Africa (Magnetic Rock Dew Water of Sahara), Asia (Chinese leaves for the cheeks and lips), and the Middle East (Arab Bloom Powder, Royal Arabian Cream) (*The Extraordinary Life and Trial* vi–vii). While beauty was firmly linked with whiteness in Victorian Britain as I detailed in the introduction, beauty products connected with exotic locations carried with them the belief in potentially magical properties.[5]

There is speculation that Madame Rachel may also have been involved in the practice of backroom abortions,[6] which is also replicated in the insinuations made about the character she inspired in Wilkie Collins's *Armadale* (1864), Mother Oldershaw. Madame Sara 'does what is necessary for her clients', including 'small surgical operations' and dentistry (120). As with her reputation among her clients, men associated with intellect, such as Professor Piozzi, are also convinced that Madame Sara is 'as good as she is beautiful' (189). While the Professor believes her to be 'the cleverest woman in London', Dr Eric Vandeleur, the police surgeon who acts a detective in the novel, is sceptical of her venturing into the domain of science: 'that scientific knowledge which Madame possesses, and which is not a smattering, but a real thing, makes a woman at times – dangerous' (189). Implicit in Vandeleur's comment is the idea that a woman's ability to work within the masculine domain of science and medicine already implies a threat to the safety of others, especially in light of the speculation about Madame Rachel's sideline in abortifacients. Druce's description of her rooms is heavy with medicalised language, with implements and tools reminiscent of a laboratory:

> There stood polished oak square table, on which lay an array of extraordinary-looking articles and implements – stoppered bottles full

of strange medicaments, mirrors, plane and concave brushes, sprays, sponges, delicate needle-pointed instruments of bright steel, tiny lancets, and forceps. Facing this table was a chair, like those used by dentists. Above the chair hung electric lights in powerful reflectors, and lenses like bull's-eye lanterns. Another chair, supported on a glass pedestal, was kept there, Madame Sara informed me, for administering static electricity. There were dry-cell batteries for the continuous currents and induction coils for Faradic currents. There were also platinum needles for burning out the roots of hairs. (127)

Other rooms have a wooden operating table and apparatus for administrating chloroform and ether. This interior is in no way suggested by the shop's exterior, which displays innocuous 'pyramids of perfume bottles, with scintillating facet stoppers tied with coloured ribbons', nor by the engraved nameplate on her private house which reads 'Madame Sara, Parfumeuse' (125). Madame Sara uses her beauty practice to extort money from vain women, however she more clearly transgresses gender norms than Madame Rachel through her expansion into the masculine realms of surgery and science, which she then perverts through an attempt to blackmail a client.

One of the major crimes of the novel involves an elaborate scam that begins when a young woman, Antonia Ripley, seeks to have a wart or mole removed from her neck. Though Miss Ripley had been advised by Italian doctors that the placement on the neck meant that removal without scarring would not be possible, Madame Sara promises success and counsels Miss Ripley not to remove the bandage from her neck until she returns to the clinic. The reason for this caution is revealed to be a complicated attempt at extortion, as Sara has used nitrate of silver to write damning words on her patient's neck while she was unconscious. The operation was performed under red light, and as soon as the skin is exposed to ordinary light, the flesh would be eaten and would permanently tattoo the following words on Miss Ripley's neck: 'I AM THE DAUGHTER OF PAOLO GIOLETTI, WHO WAS EXECUTED FOR THE MURDER OF MY MOTHER, JUNE 20th, 18— ' (157). The scheme was designed as blackmail to obtain a pearl necklace, but is foiled when a nurse bathes Miss Ripley's neck with cyanide of potassium to neutralise the effects of the nitrate of silver. This aspect of the narrative links the artifice of the cosmetic and beauty industry with immoral crimes in a

The Dark Side of Beauty 73

way that taints the very idea of commercialised beautification and reproduces broader beauty ideals that equated 'simplicity with naturalness and virtue, and artifice with deceit' (Steele, *Fashion* 120). It also echoes the small number of well-publicised cosmeticians whose products were dangerous, such as Madame Ruppert, or associated with puffery like the products and salon treatments offered by Madame Rachel, as well as the swell of advice provided in beauty manuals to exercise extreme caution or entirely avoid commercial preparations.

Moreover, *The Sorceress of the Strand* judges young women like Miss Ripley, who are dissatisfied with their natural appearance and risk not only scarring and but also further disfigurement through cosmetics and cosmetic surgery. By dabbling with them, these women place themselves in positions of harm and danger. Selby understands the 'temptation' for 'plain women' to improve their appearance with 'cosmetics and complexion pills', but like the pronouncements made in much beauty advice, he is bemused as to why a young and beautiful woman like his own wife, Beatrice, would be visiting Madame Sara (130). Younger women have more to lose through compromising the fleeting years in which their 'bloom' will be natural and hair untouched by grey, and because the sexual connotations of coloured cosmetics could tarnish their perceived innocence and purity in ways that would be less troublesome for older women. Beatrice has been visiting Madame Sara for a toothache given her claims towards dentistry, but despite the legitimate medical motivations for her visit, Selby describes her as 'infected' by the same 'strange state' that has taken hold of Edith Dallas, one of her repeat clients (130). Edith is 'nervous and depressed', her young face 'haggard', and becomes sensitive to the mere mention of Madame Sara's name (125). While the change in her character may be attributable to Sara's devious dealings, the ageing of Edith's face while purportedly undergoing beauty treatments accords with the repeated advice of many beauty manuals and magazines that claimed that cosmetic usage would harm looks and induce ageing.

The specific vanity of women is also signalled by the way that women fall victim to Madame Sara and are 'unanimous about her charms and her genius', while men such as Druce are either sceptical of her practices or ethics, or know enough to exploit her abilities (149). One of the male criminals revealed in the narrative, Petro de Castro, confesses on his deathbed that he was aided in his schemes to obtain gold by Madame Sara, who made him a wig and painted a face on his bald skull; he calls her 'one of the greatest criminals of her day' (185). While men work with her in the world of business, Druce alludes to the potential trail of male victims given Madame Sara's 'wit and brilliancy': 'I hated her for that beauty, which effected such havoc in the world' (218). Sara's beauty is falsely constructed by undetectable make-up that makes her look in her early twenties, with the novel yoking 'deceptive' beauty with deceptive criminal conduct. Madame Sara profits by her conscious use of artificial beauty and is framed as a villain for her deliberate manipulations, according closely with consistent condemnation of artificial beauty throughout broader print culture including women's magazines and beauty manuals.

Beauty and tragic fictional fates

Many Victorian novels depict naturally beautiful young women who are subject to cruel fates because of their beauty, seemingly contradicting the non-fictional valorisation of natural beauty. The youthful beautiful woman, through the lure and potential of her sexuality, is often subject to a sorry outcome in Victorian fiction. Characters associated with artifice might be villainous and calculating, as in the example of the beautiful Madame Sara, or framed as the object of pity like Collins's Mrs Macallan, especially if they are older women, yet young natural beauties are repeatedly endangered or set on a tragic course by their appearance. While the rhetoric of beauty manuals identified women's complicity in harming their health through seeking beauty, being sexually desirable was itself a risk for numerous young female protagonists. Two very different novels, from the mid- and late nineteenth century, Mrs Henry Wood's *East Lynne* (1862) and Oscar Wilde's *The Picture of Dorian Gray* (1890), exemplify the trope of youthful – and presumably acceptable – beauty as a danger that might lead to a woman's embarrassment and demise.

Wood's doomed heroine, Lady Isabel Vane, begins the novel 'with her bright colour, her beauty, her dark flowing curls, and her agile figure' and before her miserable death at its conclusion – while still comparatively young – she has been reduced to a 'grey, broken-down woman' with 'disfiguring marks' (389). When thinking of the predominant tone in beauty manuals that made significant judgement on vain women, such an outcome might be expected as a punishment for excess and self-involvement. However, despite her name, Isabel Vane is naturally beautiful and unaware of protocols and perceptions surrounding clothing and adornment. In part this is because the motherless girl has been raised primarily at her father, Lord Mount Severn's, property in Wales, ensuring that she 'had hitherto been secluded from the great world' and 'was little like a fashionable young lady as it was well possible to be' (12–13). When attending her first party at a duke's residence, she does not choose to wear her diamonds and responds when questioned as to her lack of adornment: 'I did not like to be too fine', answered Isabel, with a laugh and a blush. 'They glittered so! I feared it might be thought I had to put them on *to look* fine' (16). Isabel is conscious of how a choice to '*look* fine' through wearing striking jewels might be interpreted as vanity by the party guests. Nevertheless, on another occasion, she also demonstrates an ignorance of how finery might be perceived, or at least a greater concern for emotion and love than protocols surrounding dress. When her father takes ill, precipitating her loss of home and wealth, she is dressed elaborately after an evening out, this time in her diamonds. Her attendant, Marvel, asks her to change her 'rich dress', but she refuses in case the protracted process of undressing and dressing might prevent her rushing to her father if she was called to him urgently (86). When she refuses, she questions what is unsuitable about her clothing: 'What does it signify? Who thinks of my dress?' (86). This question is symptomatic of Isabel's broader failure to understand how her beauty impacts upon how she is treated by several women and many men, and it plays an important role in her disgrace and loss of her children. After the loss of Isabel's father, who had sold the family property and left her penniless, her only option is to stay with her uncle and aunt, Lord and Lady Emma Mount Severn. Lady Mount Severn is highly envious of beautiful young women, and 'would as soon have invited a leper' as Isabel with her youthful 'unusual beauty' (112). Though her character and behaviour are never slighted at this point, Lady Mount Severn informs Isabel that she 'was a hated intruder, her presence only suffered because there was no help for it' (112).

Lady Mount Severn's jealousy serves as a significant motivation for Isabel to marry. Though she does not yet love Mr Carlyle, who is struck by her beauty on first glance, his proposal provides an opportunity for Isabel to escape her hostile living situation and return to her familial home, which he had earlier purchased from Isabel's father. Nevertheless, another woman with heightened sensitivities regarding women's dress and appearance will soon make Isabel's married life similarly unbearable. His sister, Miss Cornelia Carlyle, insists upon remaining to aid in the management of the household, and while not overtly jealous has a hatred for particular kinds of dress, including 'long dresses' and 'corded petticoats', and opinions at odds with Isabel's in the spending of money on clothing for the couple's eventual children (45). In contrast with Isabel, several other women in the novel are associated with markers of vanity and exhibitionism. Isabel's perceived rival for Mr Carlyle's affections, Barbara Hare, for example, buys excessive finery (her 'head is stuffed up with it' (189)). Afy Hallijohn is similarly preoccupied with beautiful outfits and exhibits herself publicly in elaborate clothing; she stands in a crinoline and fancy bonnet 'bold as a sunflower, exhibiting herself and her splendour' (529). Annarose Fitzgerald suggests that Isabel's shortcoming is the fact that she is unable 'to see True Womanhood as a fashioned rather than a natural trait' (304). Where Afy and heiress Emma Vane understand that their actions, comments and dress are integral to appropriate class and feminine performance, Isabel is perceived as having a 'natural' status, something she cannot regain after her imminent fall (Fitzgerald 304). Her fraught relationships with Cornelia and suspicion of her husband's secretive relationship with Barbara nevertheless make her easy prey for Francis Levison, who is charmed by her beauty, and encourages her to elope to France, where he deserts her soon after she has borne his child.

To worsen the situation, Isabel is disfigured in a train accident, which also kills her illegitimate child. She had already observed a decline in her appearance, such as a worn face and sunken eyes, due to protracted illness and – she imagines – her 'wretched mind and heart' (284) for abandoning her husband and children. The rail accident, however, transforms Isabel with a facial scar, knocks out some of her teeth, turns her hair grey, and leaves her with a limp and a stoop. The changes to her height, speech and lower face provide the impetus for Isabel to alter her appearance further through green spectacles and loose clothing so that she may assume a new identity as governess Madame Vine, and allow 'Isabel Carlyle' to be understood as dead. Eventually her strange and 'almost ugly' appearance allows her to return to the

Carlyle family home and to spend precious time with her children under her assumed governess identity (620). It is telling that, for a woman who is repeatedly mistreated or used because of her beauty, her embrace of ugliness allows her the rare opportunity to reclaim some control of her destiny and to fulfil her desires, in that case to be with her children again briefly before she dies.

Wilde's Sibyl Vane, who shares the same surname as Isabel, arguably takes charge of her destiny, but her tragic suicide as a 17-year-old is a similar deathly fate for a beautiful young woman. While *The Picture of Dorian Gray* is most obviously a novel about ageing and beauty of character in comparison with a beautiful physical exterior, the specific cruelty and sadness associated with beautiful women is tragically played out through the actress Sibyl's brief life. The eponymous Dorian falls in love with Sibyl after seeing her perform at a low-rent theatre, becoming enamoured with the idea of an actress, who contains more mystery than '[o]rdinary women', whom '[n]o glamour ever transfigures' (75). Here the dual connotations of glamour in terms of beauty and a magical illusion are fused in the figure of the actress. Lord Henry Wotton, friend of Basil Hallward (the artist who paints Dorian's portrait) remarks that he has loved many an actress, while Dorian retorts that he must mean 'horrid people with dyed hair and painted faces' (75), to which he replies: 'Don't run down dyed hair and painted faces. There is an extraordinary charm in them, sometimes' (76). This distinction between girls such as Sibyl and 'horrid', 'painted' women is further nuanced by Henry's earlier reduction of women to two kinds, 'plain and coloured' (70). Henry is not troubled by paint as a way to 'try and talk brilliantly', in the manner of '[o]ur grandmothers' for whom '[r]ouge and *esprit* used to go together' (70). Contemporary women are charged with using paint to fulfil a vain and unnatural desire to look ten years younger than their own daughters, rather than to enhance their character.

Like Isabel, Sibyl is squarely associated with a natural, innate beauty and is distanced from women who are more conscious of cultivating their appearance or who seek to deceive. Dorian's smitten descriptions of her to Harry of her emotional effect are laced with floral metaphors: her face, small and 'flower-like', her eyes 'violet wells', her lips 'like the petals of a rose' (74). Elsewhere her lips are 'petals', her hair like 'dark leaves round a pale rose' (113), the curves of her throat those of a 'white lily', and in animal comparisons her voice is that of a 'caged bird' (89), 'something of the fawn' evident in her 'startled eyes' (121). The overwhelming picture of Sibyl is one of innocent naturalness, in contrast with the typical falsity associated with the actress or her own mother's unpleasant artifice, such as her 'crooked, false-jewelled fingers' that, when waved, imbue her words with 'grotesqueness' (89).

However, when Sibyl falls for Dorian to the degree that her acting ability becomes severely impaired, 'stagey', and her gestures 'absurdly artificial', he rejects her as 'nothing' without her art, just a mere 'third-rate actress with a pretty face' (123, 129). The artificiality of Sibyl's acting (rather than her appearance) taints her artistic power, leaving her with mere prettiness, rather than the 'beauty' that Dorian had always ascribed to her. She commits suicide in her dressing room with what her mother describes as 'something dreadful they use at theatres ... it had either prussic acid or white lead in it' (145). Prussic acid is better known today as cyanide and was an ingredient in products such as face washes, while lead was added to some washes, face powders and hair products (Rappaport 31, 234). Though Sibyl is evidently a young, natural beauty, her death comes at the hands of a presumable cosmetic, as with the death of Mrs Macallan in *The Law and the Lady*. Like Wood's Isabel, Sibyl's beauty sets in motion the course of events that lead to her death, and the link between her fate and appearance is only sharpened by the source of the poison.

Sibyl joins Dorian's 'beautiful' mother, Lady Margaret Devereux: she dies young as a result of 'a mad passion' for a man (52). Like Dorian, both young women evade the 'hideousness of age', never knowing crow's feet, grey hair, and crêpey necks (182). However, they join many other beautiful, and relatively blameless, young women protagonists in Victorian fiction whose natural beauty is implicated in their demise or disgrace. In contrast with the advice manuals of the period that caution against the dangers of cosmetics and artificial aids, the sexual threat of youthful beauty is enough to bring about the demise of some Victorian heroines. Female beauty is itself a danger to women.

Conclusion

A traversal of sixty years of British print culture, including beauty manuals, women's magazines and fiction, shows enduring ideas about the dangers of female beauty. While the cultural emphasis on female beauty as a lure for men that brings with it inherent dangers is long-standing, the variety of texts discussed in this chapter exemplify two related strands of thinking about the dangers posed by beauty – and the quest for beauty – for women propagated throughout much of the nineteenth century. Most common are stipulations surrounding artifice and the need to avoid products and practices that are embarrassingly detectible or which, counter-productively, only hasten the loss of markers of youthful beauty such as smooth skin or lush manes of hair. Documented instances of harmful cosmetics and unscrupulous cosmeticians, such as Anna Ruppert and Madame Rachel, enabled the punctuation of the warnings contained in beauty manuals and women's magazines with examples that were based in real-world harm. Masses of advice about the appropriate way to negotiate feminine appearance cumulatively suggest a right and a wrong way to deal with grooming and personal appearance, with 'nature' inevitably being the preferable, and safe, course. This rhetoric nevertheless ignores the way that beauty in itself – even when free from artifice or calculation – imperilled young women, and how this danger was commonly represented in Victorian fiction. Women's sexuality, and its manifestation through their physical attraction, was a danger whether youthful and 'natural', or aged and 'artificial'.

Notes

1 Robyn Cooper speculates that *Female Beauty* is the production of Alexander Walker, whose work I discussed in the introduction, rather than his wife (Mrs A Walker), to whom the book is attributed (35). There is minimal biographical information about Walker and the publication history of *Female Beauty*, which makes it impossible to confirm whether Walker simply utilised his wife's name for a book that was more explicitly concerned with instructions to women readers about their appearance and dress. Another possibility is that the publication was jointly authored.
2 The association of cosmetics with poisoning and death is extrapolated to the effect that the painted woman might have upon men. Montez describes the visceral reaction of men to painted lips and other facial features: 'Many a time have I seen a gentleman shrink from saluting a brilliant lady, as though it was a death's head he were compelled to kiss' (47).
3 Mother Oldershaw in Wilkie Collins's sensation novel *Armadale*

(1866) is a beautician and an agent for back-room abortions; the character was modelled on Madame Rachel (E. C. Miller 75).

4   Dixon Druce estimates her age at no 'more than five-and-twenty', in answer to which Mrs Selby tells him that Sara was a bridesmaid thirty years prior at her mother's wedding: 'She declares that she never changes, and has no fear of old age' (122).

5   This would evolve into a greater emphasis on the scientific in the twentieth-century marketing of cosmetics, as seen in the continued practice of retail sales staff for some cosmetic brands dressing in white, laboratory-style coats. Madame Sara's dubious international 'importations' and practices are nevertheless paired with recourse to science and medicine.

6   Elizabeth Carolyn Miller clarifies that there is no explicit proof that Madame Rachel's crimes extended beyond 'extreme puffery and an occasional attempt at extortion' (314). However, she suggests that her advertising brochure *Beautiful For Ever!* 'does echo advertising copy for late-Victorian abortion-inducing patent medicines' (314).

Part II: Youth and Ageing

3

Beauty and Girlhood

Beauty is but a flower
Which wrinkles do devour.
                  Nanette Mason, 'Plain Looks and Good Looks',
                                  the *Girl's Own Paper* (1891)

An illustration by Sydney Cowell in the *Girl's Own Paper* (1880–1954) in July 1896 captioned 'They Had the Beauty of Youth and Health' (632) (Fig. 3.1) shows two young women posing by a riverbank, nestled among wild flowers. The title points to the two central pillars of beauty in this period. Moreover, the possessive use of 'had' references the reality that beauty will inevitably be lost over time, or prematurely, if illness or recklessness destroys health. Girls were poised on the cusp of adult sexuality, marriage and motherhood, and their beauty was especially prized. Yet as the automatic possessors of youth and thereby, quite often, beauty, girls are subject to specific forms of advice about maintaining their appearance in comparison with those found in broader Victorian print culture for women. Instructions about beauty for girls were often embedded within other expectations about good behaviour, virtuous character and morality. Like the illustrated girls with roses adorning their hats, girl readers would be expected to follow pronouncements about appropriate dress and grooming while negotiating idealised visions of natural beauty. For girls this balancing act was framed as crucially important given that the actions of their youth could either ensure their beauty in the present and in the long term, or prematurely usher in a displeasing or prematurely aged appearance.

84   Consuming Female Beauty

Figure 3.1 Sydney Cowell, 'They Had the Beauty of Youth and Health'. *Girl's Own Paper* July 1896: 632.

Beauty ideals for girls were intimately connected with the concept of health in late nineteenth-century print culture. The healthy girl would necessarily have a cheerful character and a pleasing appearance. In contrast, in the *Girl's Own Book of Health and Beauty* (1891?), Gordon Stables, a former Royal Navy surgeon who wrote the medical advice column for the popular British girls' magazine, explains that unhealthy girls could be neither beautiful nor happy:

> Brightness of eyes, clearness of complexion, and happiness of expression, belong only to the possessor of health. A girl who is but indifferently well, is self-conscious, ill-at-ease in society, not clear in eyes, and very often sallow as to skin. She is not happy, she may powder and paint herself, she may 'make up' as to eyes and eyebrows, and hair but still I say she is not happy; she cannot smile the smile that wells up from the heart, and goes curling round the eyes, lighting up the face like a summer's sunrise. No, she cannot smile, she can only make faces with her mouth ... (n.p.)

The guidebook is typical of representations of girls in fiction and advice of the period in its correlation of health with beauty and happiness. Health – and consequently beauty – were not only linked with a girl's emotions and character, but also with the responses of those who encountered her. Negative emotional responses to 'fast' and fashionable girls, such as those expressed in Linton's 'The Girl of the Period', were intimately related to norms of chaste girlhood and underscored the value placed upon 'natural', unthreatening forms of beauty. Girls were cautioned about artificial cosmetic aids, with inner qualities and disciplined behaviour promoted as the true means to a pleasing appearance. Cosmetics could be seen, as Valerie Steele notes, as deceptive, potentially concealing 'the evidence of true inner emotions that would normally be expressed by blushing or growing pale' (*Fashion* 125). As a result, there is no advice to be found in publications for girls about measured or 'artful' cosmetic usage. 'Authentic' beauty was not only understood as 'natural', but as intimately related to desirable internal traits that would manifest on the face.

The *Girl's Own Book of Health and Beauty* implicitly argues against any form of external cosmetics by glorifying the relationship between inner health and pleasing external features. Stables recounts a story of a Scottish girl bathing in a stream, describing the way her simple toilet produces a beautiful complexion: 'Ah!

but she had health also. And that is the secret. That alone can secure a beautiful complexion' (99). Wistful examples such as this are balanced with quasi-scientific explanations for Stables' advice. He argues, for example, that a good complexion is impossible

> if there be anything the matter with the blood. The skin will be dry and harsh if the blood is not sweet, it may be muddy almost, and the eye that ought to sparkle with health will be dull, even fishy – pardon the adjective, it is expressive, – the pupils will not be dark, nor the whites clear. (21)

Crucially, the healthy, and therefore beautiful, girl 'is reasonably happy':

> And the mind should feel as light and buoyant as the body, a healthy girl should feel a pleasure in merely living, she should be capable of taking an interest in everything that goes on around her, in all she sees, in all she hears, in all she reads, and in all that concerns the well-being of her fellow creatures, and honest toil itself should be an enjoyment to her, and not a worry, not a penance. (54)

Moreover, the healthy girl enjoys life, is inquisitive, well-read and hard-working, which were all qualities that were seen as essential for the woman that the girl would become. As Kristine Moruzi and I show elsewhere, modern girls were 'expected to be useful' (431) through work within or beyond the home. It was not acceptable for this new girl 'to think only of herself' (431), but to derive pleasure, as Stables suggests, from helping others through her labour. The healthy girl is physically and psychologically capable of enjoying her leisure time and the work of caring for others, and, in turn, these qualities bring happiness and comfort to those around her.

Hilary Marland shows that health advice for girls became especially prominent in Britain from the 1880s. The new healthy girlhood discussed in these texts was understood as 'vigorous' and 'bright-eyed' in comparison with the 'wan, drooping, nervous' mid-Victorian girl (Marland 42). Girlhood was a crucial period for the cultivation of health, in part because it involved a girl's reproductive maturation through the onset of menstruation. Stables makes an oblique reference to this fact when he calls 'the last five years of a girl's teens ... the most critical part of her whole life, for soon after, or about fifteen ... she is no longer a child' (195). As Deborah Gorham points out, the onset of puberty was seen to alter girls' physical health needs, but also heralded the requirement that she dress and 'adopt physical deportment' compatible with her future role as a wife and mother (97). This expectation encoded ideals of usefulness and strength that would be essential in homemaking and child-rearing. Girls' magazines were the most common site in which these views were promulgated, and this chapter will consider how the highest-selling girls' magazine of the late nineteenth century, the *Girl's Own Paper*, linked together beauty, health and character. In turning attention to girls' fiction, I will argue that the unhealthy girl cannot be productive or useful to others and thereby inspires feelings of distaste and pity in others that issue from perceptions of flaws in both her character and appearance. In contrast, the healthy girl who can aid others is understood to be beautiful inside and out. Two novels published more than three decades apart, Juliana Horatia Ewing's *Six to Sixteen* (1875) and Frances Hodgson Burnett's *The Secret Garden* (1911) signal the enduring views about the interconnection between health, beauty and a pleasing character in girls across the late Victorian and Edwardian periods.

Pleasing others and being physically attractive were not qualities associated with boys' health, as is evident in the gendered differences in Stables's 'health library' series. *The Girl's Own Book of Health and Beauty* focuses on the relationship between diet, hygiene and exercise habits and girls' outward appearance. The manual has chapters on food, water, air, baths, exercise, the toilet, sleep, indigestion, colds and obesity, and includes a cautionary story about the tight lacing of corsets. In the *Boys' Book of Health and Strength* (1892?), which includes portraits of Stables and 'several celebrated Athletes' along with a letter from a 'Champion Scottish Athlete', health is valued for what it can contribute to well-being and athleticism, rather than looks (n.p.). In contrast, the 'Athletics for Girls' chapter in the girls' book begins with the aphorism, 'The beauty of a man is his strength, the beauty of a woman is her hair' (66). In the girls' guide, Stables cautions foolish girls who will approach the book 'in search of nostrums and recipes to ensure them an artificial beauty', clarifying that the book shows how 'health – bounding saucy health – is the fountain from which all true beauty springs' (n. p.). Steele comments on Stables's use of this phrase, acknowledging that it has some basis in truth, but 'as an argument it also served to devalue the erotic aspects of physical beauty' (*Fashion* 126). She suggests that Stables's argument about health was distinct from more common exhortations directed at women about moral self-improvement. However, with respect to girls, the correlation between health and beauty was almost always emphasised in order to steer them away from excessive emphasis on vanity, the harms of which I discussed in the previous chapter, which would tarnish a girl's character. As Marland observes, even guides that were explicitly focused on beauty 'emphasised the importance of exercise as well as the fostering of good behaviour and character', a tendency which is only magnified in girls' magazines that had long-term reputations as acceptable reading material to maintain (65).

Beauty and character in the *Girl's Own Paper*

Religiously oriented magazines such as the *Girl's Own Paper* sought to downplay the value of girls' physical beauty as a transitory quality, privileging the long-term potential of other types of beauty, such as those relating to character, intelligence and piety. The temptations of beauty culture and its potential to 'spoil' a young, implied readership ensured that it was a frequent topic within non-fiction articles. In this section, I discuss a representative selection of articles from Medicus's regular column and other contributors to the magazine, as well as some of the advertisements for products relating to cleanliness that were deemed acceptable for publication, demonstrating how the beauty ideals I have detailed in previous chapters were communicated to the next generation of women.

In the brief article 'The Face of an Angel' from 1885, Darley Dale identifies youthful beauty as being enjoyable 'for a season' (28). In contrast, beauty of intellect can counteract 'rugged features and redeems them from the charge of plainness', yet its prevalence is even rarer than that of youthful beauty (28). The one type of beauty open to all and which 'never fades, but daily increases' is that of 'holiness' (28). Unlike most beauty publications aimed at women, the *GOP* regularly provided advice by men regarding beauty, and even from members of the clergy. The firm association of girlhood beauty with morality opened it up to religious commentary. 'Beauty Lore' by Reverend T. F. Thiselton Dyer focuses on the mythology surrounding beauty in literature throughout the ages, drawing attention to poetry and fiction in which 'beauty is unfortunate', including the Cinderella tale in which she is 'persecuted on account of her charms' (521). Like Dale, Dyer highlights 'beauty's transitory character', an aspect on which he finds 'poetry has largely dwelt' (521). However, his discussion of beauty's connection with misfortune goes further than Dale's emphasis on the possibility of other types of beauty only being heightened with time. Dyer concurs with ancient Greek physician and philosopher Galen in suggesting that beauty is connected with negative outcomes because 'Many who have been distinguished for their loveliness have neglected the education of their mind' (522). The reason for this oversight of other types of potential, and for the magazine's repeated exhortations for girls to cultivate their intellect or spirituality, is because the beauty of young women is linked with power. Medicus refers to an old maxim, for example, that suggests 'Beauty draws more than five yoke of oxen' ('Beauty in Woman' 247).[1] However, this power is most often connected with danger (as a 'fatal gift'), when a beautiful girl does not also possess a refined mind and soul through being well read, appreciative of God and nature, and able to contribute to a lively conversation ('Beauty in Woman' 247).

In her study of Victorian girls' periodicals, Kristine Moruzi demonstrates that the *Girl's Own Paper* helped to create 'a new aesthetic of beauty ... entwined with moral qualities, robust health, and physical capability instead of an abstract idea of beauty' (87). 'Invalid' girls, for example, needed to transform to become not only healthy and beautiful, but also productive and useful (Moruzi 88), linking aesthetic appeal with the capacity to serve others. An emphasis on beauty and intellect, as with the focus on health, foregrounded personal qualities that could be worked on and improved, avoiding the idle and unproductive time that the *GOP* found troubling for girls (Moruzi and Smith 431). Moreover, an explicit physiognomic connection was often made between a pleasing character and a pleasing appearance, meaning that the unattractive girl effectively only has herself to blame for her looks and for how she would age. In Nanette Mason's 'Plain Looks and Good Looks', she goes further than Dyer in suggesting that 'beauties are often stupid', and that '[i]n many cases it is a natural defect, for which they are not to be blamed' (374). While in other cases, Mason highlights that beautiful girls and women:

hope by the aid of their faces to get successfully through life, and so take no pains to sharpen their wits. The plain-looking, despairing of their faces, take up polishing their minds. This is how we see many lovely features utterly expressionless, as if the girls who owned them were waiting for their souls; and plain features full of brightness and animation, as if their owners had received souls long ago. (374)

Beauty is repeatedly framed as a trap for girls who may neglect aspects of their character and intellect through complacent reliance on their looks, which are nonetheless temporary (beauty's 'empire lasts but for a day'), and are at constant risk of being spoiled through cosmetics or through failings in personality (Mason 374). Mason warns that both 'mean feelings', including anger, vanity and pride, and 'degrading passions' destroy beauty and leave a permanent taint on otherwise attractive features. As she describes, 'A waspish disposition soon gives a turn to the mouth that is unmistakeable, and you can read a sneering mind in the nose just as plainly as if "sneer-well" were printed across the forehead in big letters' (374). The connection between the mind and external appearance was presumed to work in both ameliorative and deleterious ways, such that being 'sweet and cheerful' was essential to the 'art of being beautiful for ever, and of rendering natural charms irresistible' (Mason 374). The girl has a unique responsibility to preserve and improve her looks while she is young, as she is charged with the power to avoid 'occupying a place in the dismal catalogue of ugly old women' (Mason 375). While this implies that girls occupied a critical life stage within which to make or break their appearances for their complete lifespan, it simultaneously reinforces that the promises of cosmetics for older women were emphatically hollow. Moreover, the girl who is beautiful must also manage 'her dangerous gift' intelligently or she will risk joining the ranks of beautiful women who are 'neither happy nor fortunate' (Mason 374).

With a readership of girls aged from approximately 12 until their early twenties and a strident editorial stance against such products, coloured cosmetics or artificial beauty aids are unsurprisingly absent from the *GOP*'s advertisements. Ads for corsets and clothing do appear regularly, along with those for soap and products closely associated with the cleanliness or health of the skin. Rowlands' Kalydor face wash was frequently included in the advertising supplements, promising in an 1886 advertisement to

Beauty and Girlhood 91

ROWLANDS' KALYDOR

is a most cooling, healing, and refreshing wash for the face, hands, and arms of ladies playing tennis, yachting, boating, driving, and all exposed to the scorching rays of the sun and heated particles of dust. It eradicates most effectually all freckles, tan, sunburn, stings of insects, prickly heat, eczema, &c., and produces a

BEAUTIFUL AND DELICATE COMPLEXION.
It is warranted to be perfectly free from all lead, mineral, or poisonous ingredients, or oxide of zinc, of which most cosmetics are composed, and which ruin the skin, and, to prevent fraud, has on the stopper a 6d. Government stamp. Beware of cheap noxious imitations, as Rowlands' Kalydor is the only genuine article. It can now be had in bottles of half the usual size at 2/3, including Government stamp.

Figure 3.2 Rowlands' Kalydor advertisement, *Girl's Own Paper*, 'Lily Leaves'. Extra Summer Number 1886, n.p.

'cool', 'heal' and 'refresh' skin damaged by sun and dust exposure ('Lily Leaves' n.p.) (Fig. 3.2). This language is typical of the brand-name beauty products featured in *GOP* advertisements that focus on counteracting or prevention of 'damage' rather than promising any improvement to the base level of a girl or woman's attractiveness. 'Lovely skin' is also understood as entailing the entire body that might be visible to others, including the neck, hands and arms, enhancing the connection with healthful maintenance of the skin and treatment of temporary, medicalised blemishes and discolouration, such as pimples, eczema and burns (Rowlands' Kalydor, 'Feathery Flakes' n.p.). At the same time, while ads for Rowlands' Kalydor acknowledge this preparation as a 'cosmetic', they seek to distance it from harmful kinds of product that contain 'lead, mineral, or poisonous ingredients, or oxide of zinc' and 'which ruin the skin' (n.p.). Beetham's Glycerine and Cucumber, an emollient for softening the skin, likewise highlights its effectiveness for damage caused by weather (such as frost and cold winds) or heated homes, and cautions against 'Injurious Imitations' in an 1887 advertisement (n.p.).

As the magazine's long-term health columnist, 'Medicus', Gordon Stables made frequent comments on beauty matters and was outspoken in his opposition to cosmetics. In 'Is Beauty Evanescent?', he offers a cautionary story about a girl who has lived 'too well', neglected her health, and caused her complexion to decline (631).

His hypothetical girl resorts to cosmetics (he cannot bring himself to use the word 'Paint') as she has seen tempting advertisements in women's magazines. The girl wonders if she can use them without being detected, but resolves that it cannot hurt:

> It is only a little harmless powder, and it is more to protect the skin than anything else; and has not one as good a right to wear powder for this purpose, as to carry a parasol on a sunny-shiny day in summer? Certainly one has. So she crosses the Rubicon. A neat little parcel comes for her by post one day; it is flowers, perhaps, or a book, or it is nobody's business what. (Medicus, 'Is Beauty Evanescent?' 631)

The girl's secretive order of powder brings with it 'deleterious' and 'injurious' substances (631–2). Medicus then shifts his discussion to address girl readers about 'baneful beauty washes', which are 'ten times more dangerous' and which hold the prospect of making a girl's face resemble a 'duck's foot' ('very rough and yellowish-red') or 'Malaga raisin' ('very much wrinkled') (632). Worst of all, the slippery slope of cosmetic usage means that the girl who uses a face wash will soon find that she must powder her face and 'make up' or she 'would not be in a fit condition to enter society' (632). It is here that the connotation of the term 'make up' as ameliorating some kind of deficiency becomes evident.

Nevertheless, there is hope for the girl who was tempted by the cosmetic advertisement, as she might take up Medicus's advice and restore her looks. The address then shifts to a thinly veiled address to readers who may have been transgressing his advice in the guise of a question: '"Suppose, Mr. Medicus," someone may say, "suppose a girl who has been using cosmetics for some little time were to abandon this habit, is there hope for her?"' (632). He advises the young girl that there is hope to remedy damage she may have caused, whereas the older woman must remember the she 'cannot defy the ravages of time' (632). The transitory nature of beauty is emphasised to encourage the cultivation of 'the beauty of mind' (632), which is a superior form of beauty that can humble that of aesthetics alone. Medicus cites the example of unattractive women he knows 'whose presence and conversation simply fascinate and captivate men, and in whose society mere beauty looks like a painted doll or hairdresser's dummy' (632). The use of the inanimate forms of the doll and dummy dehumanise the kind of beauty that girl readers may idolise, supporting the repeated prioritisation of spiritual and intellectual kinds of beauty that in effect relate to particular traits of character.

Medicus links beauty and character in ways that regard beauty as 'noble' so long as it is disconnected from vanity, pride and superficiality ('Beauty in Woman' 247). The balance must be struck between a girl looking her best and thinking too much of her appearance,[2] between making reasonable calls 'in the aid of science and arts' and unappealing artificiality ('Beauty in Woman' 247). Society is the home of too many a 'painted doll' who is 'just as frivolous and heartless as she is artificial – a painted fraud, in fact, and I pity the poor fellow who is snared into marrying her' ('Beauty in Woman' 247). Stables combines three prevalent views about beauty: that cosmetic usage entails knowing deception; that cosmetic usage or a focus on appearance coalesced with a vacant or cruel personality; and that the lure of artificial beauty could entrap unsuspecting men. At their core, girls or women who makes recourse to artificial methods must be unhappy, and therefore they cannot make their husbands happy either: 'One cannot bestow upon those around them that which they do not possess themselves' ('Beauty in Woman' 247). The primary acceptable method for seeking beauty is health, which can bring both an attractive complexion and the 'power to please others' ('Beauty in Woman' 247).

Apart from her unhappiness, one of the key character flaws associated with the girl who uses cosmetics is that she is deceptive. In 'Beauty' in 1888, the girls who ignore advice about cosmetics and are 'rouged, powdered, and pencilled' trouble Medicus to the extent that he wonders 'if the world is getting worse' (717). He describes the use of cosmetics as a form of openly conducted deceit that 'can have no good effects on the moral character':

> Many girls moving in what is called good society, a sadly mixed compound, nowadays, are little better than walking frauds, perambulating fibs. I will not put it any stronger, but I can let my imagination whisper to me what some of these 'angelic beings' look like in the morning before they are ready to emerge from their rooms. ('Beauty' 717)

Recourse to paint is equated to lying, and similarly the insinuation that these girls must appear hideous prior to the application of make-up chalks up another point of sympathy for unsuspecting men who may be have no true sense of their beloved's appearance prior to marriage. Conversely, the deception entailed in cosmetic use is also framed by Medicus as *failing* in attempts to trick the spectator. The girl who applies carmine to her lips and pencil to her eyebrows is 'transformed ... but very transparently so' ('Beauty' 717), with detectability understood to being caught in the act of deception. In this catch-22 scenario, the clumsy beautifier who relies on artifice will be judged harshly by all who look upon her, while the more careful girl who crosses the cosmetic line jeopardises her character and invites trouble into her relationships through concealing her 'true' appearance.

This is not say that the *GOP* wholly discouraged girls from looking after their appearance. Mason's article, for example, suggests it is only the 'queer girl' who does not devote effort to looking her best (374). She affirms Aristotle's view 'that beauty was superior to all the letters of recommendation in the world', equating good looks with 'real power' and highlighting the difficulty of overcoming 'prejudice' against plainness (Mason 374). In the unattributed article 'The Service of Beauty. Personal Beauty', there is a rare moment of critique for girls who eschew vanity, 'wear anything that comes in their way' and 'are entirely indifferent to their appearance from the aesthetic point of view' (299). To be 'careless about the impression we leave on the eye' is declared to be a fault, rather than a feature of merit ('The Service of Beauty' 299). Less time devoted to appearance is not the measure of a girl's virtue, but she must look 'pleasant and harmonious' through taking her cues 'from Nature and the artists' (299). The author refers to the rational dress movement[3] of the 1880s that 'worked to reform women's dress for reasons of physical and intellectual health' (Kortsch 77) in order to explain that contemporary girls will find it much easier than in the past to find dresses that will be 'appropriate and beautiful, without being unpleasantly conspicuous' (299).

Medicus/Gordon Stables likewise encouraged girls to ensure they looked their best, distinguishing vanity and cosmetic usage from the aesthetic benefits of health and cleanliness. In 'Beauty: A Duty', Stables (publishing under his own name) suggests beauty is 'a duty you owe to everyone around you' and that he never thinks 'anything less of a girl who tries to make the most of her good looks' (222). In 'A Bundle of Hints on Beauty', where he also describes beauty as a 'duty', he provides reliable recipes through which girls can prepare their own products from ingredients found at a chemist (Medicus 612). The products for which he provides recipes are largely related to hygiene (such as tooth powder and paste), scent (toilet vinegars and potpourri), and the most innocuous of powders used on the body (violet powder and powdered starch), rather than any cosmetic purpose. However, the extent of Medicus's advice consistently warns about the dangers and detectability of artificial aids, and encourages girls to improve other aspects of the self. In 'Beauty: A Duty', he provides cautionary stories of the real-world 'Madame R--- ' who 'used positively to enamel the faces of ancient dames' with 'a coat of some stuff so thick that the unhappy woman could not even smile without cracking it', and the hypothetical 'Miss Blondeau' who submits herself to a fraudulent cosmetician (Stables 222). Miss Blondeau crosses the point of no return with her cosmetic usage. She endures suffering, runs up a staggering bill for procedures and products including 'crow's feet excisions', removal of 'buccal wrinkles', electrolysis, enamel, and rouge, and ages herself further in the process: 'The crow's feet have given place to scars, there are the cicatrices of what appears to be burns here and there as if she had fallen on the bars of a grate, and the corner of one eye is drawn up which gives poor Miss Blondeau a sort of Chinese squint, not at all prepossessing' (222). Such excessive language of graphic disfigurement warns girls of the risks of engaging with cosmetics and provides inherent criticism of the decision to beautify artificially in the first place.

According to Medicus and the broader editorial stance of the *Girl's Own Paper*, the only acceptable path of action for the girl who wishes to be beautiful is the pursuit of health. The wise girl who notices flaws in her skin does not make immediate resort to 'the puff-box' but thinks of the medical causes for dull complexion, such as 'an inactive liver', which can induce dark circles under the eyes or 'a slight dim or yellow tinge near the nose' (Medicus, 'Beauty' 718). She appreciates that she will need to alter her diet to include more vegetables and exclude rich foods, maintain habits such as rising early and pursuing 'wholesome, happy exercise', in addition to taking what Medicus claims 'is now pretty well-known as "The Girl's Own" bath' (a quick wash in hot water, followed by 'the delightful and invigorating cold sponge tub') each morning ('Beauty' 718). These spartan methods will not only clarify a girl's complexion and brighten her eyes within one week, but will positively affect her emotions, along with making her calm and good-tempered in her interactions, linking the triumvirate of beauty, health and character.

In the advice presented to girls, beauty is commonly discussed as something that girls can lose. Contravention of the natural beauty ideals I outlined in Chapter 1 is the primary route to beauty's loss for the individual, and for the classes of girl who are foolishly fashionable. The girl who takes up the powder puff will not be beautiful, according to Medicus, after she has turned 21, leaving younger girls who eschew cosmetics to snipe about her being '"an old thing" when she is not within hearing' ('Beauty' 718). This loss can also be extrapolated from examples of individual girls to entire classes of girls and women. An article by 'The New Doctor' in 1898, for example, makes a class-based contrast between 'dirty little ragamuffins' in the Whitechapel slums who have 'far finer complexions' then the 'leaders of fashion' in Mayfair (6). This provides evidence that cleansing the skin is not the cause of 'a fine cheek', but 'the outdoor life, the not too liberal diet, the absence of stimulants, the early hours, and the loose clothing of the urchin that give her her good complexion' (6). In fact, bad complexions are understood as more common among the upper classes because of their cosmetic usage.

As beauty was – and indeed continues to be – tied to youth, girls attracted a particular focus for being vulnerable to the dangers that beauty, and thereby sexuality, brought with them. The pervasiveness of beauty advice in the *Girl's Own Paper* is testament to the unique anxieties that surrounded girls' appearance and behaviour. The magazine sought to redirect girls' attention from external methods of beautification towards internal improvements through the development of health or character. From an adult, editorial perspective, this strategy sought to encourage girls to develop qualities in other aspects of life that were tied to idealised femininity, and for the girl reader, attention to the cultivation of her intellect and morality would have the further inducement of improving her looks.

Girlhood health, beauty and character in fiction

The class implications of an excessive focus on beauty and fashion I have just discussed are also evident in girls' fiction. The two highly popular children's novels I consider in the following section express negative judgements of women who are excessively focused on their own appearance, especially mothers. Moreover, they encourage the progress of their girl protagonists toward an idealised healthy femininity that is closely entangled with appropriate maternal and wifely qualities that produce positive affective responses in those who encounter them. In this section, I focus on the reactions that girls' appearances provoke because of the ways in which girls' transgression of norms of beauty, health and virtue were viewed as especially detestable and shocking, as evident in the extreme reaction to painted girls in Linton's 'The Girl of the Period'.

Scholars including Beverly Lyon Clark, Nina Auerbach, U. C. Knoepflmacher and Michael Newton observe the initial plot similarities between Ewing's *Six to Sixteen* and Hodgson Burnett's *The Secret Garden* and the likely influence of Ewing on Hodgson Burnett. Both works begin with girls who are resident with their families in India and who, on being orphaned, return to England to live with relatives. Both girls had beautiful mothers and were usually cared for by ayahs. Both novels first appeared in serial form: *Six to Sixteen* in *Aunt Judy's Magazine* (an English children's periodical, from January to October 1872) and *The Secret Garden* in *The American Magazine* (an American periodical for adults, from October 1910 to 1911). In addition to differences in the initial target readership for these stories, there are also differences in the ways in which the girls develop into healthy young women. *The Secret Garden* explicitly blames the Indian climate for Mary Lennox's sour personality and looks at the beginning of the novel and imbues the Yorkshire moors – where she lives with her largely distant uncle Archibald Craven and invalid cousin Colin – with the power to enervate her mind and body. In *Six to Sixteen*, the death of her father affects Margery (Margaret) Vandaleur's health and she must choose between the different models of femininity she encounters in England, specifically that of vanity as enacted by her relative Matilda, or health as embodied by her friend Eleanor, for whom her 'biography' is written. Nevertheless, despite their plot variances, both novels critique fashionable femininity, upholding the view that artifice and disconnection from nature could bring about illness and distract from the maternal aspects of idealised femininity.

In *Six to Sixteen*, Margery's late mother is described to her by several people as 'the prettiest woman they ever saw' (Ewing 12). Mrs Vandaleur dies when Margery is 6, and the most readily available memory that she has of her mother is of her beauty and dress, rather than moments of play or love: 'I can remember her brief appearances in the room where I played in much dirt and contentment, at my ayah's feet – rustling in silks and satins, glittering with costly ornaments, beautiful and scented, like a fair dream' (Ewing 13). There are no grotesque or alarming aspects to Mrs Vandaleur as with the sexualised 'girl of the period' and her use of artificial cosmetics. However, the lack of naturalness – and thereby maternal instinct – in her beauty is evident in Margery's description of her mother's cheeks as 'like the petals of a china rose' (Ewing 13), ornamental and cold to the touch. This maternal distance is reflected in Margery's narration of her mother's death, which is brief and devoid of emotion (Ewing 20). In comparison, her father's death provokes long nights of crying and impacts negatively upon her health, transforming her into a 'very thin, weak child' (Ewing 28).

While living in India, Margery is socialised by both her mother and her ayah to understand the affective potential of her appearance and to take pleasure in being looked at. She is 'shown off' in the drawing room when guests visit. Margery is conscious of her own pride and that of her ayah when wearing her pink silk dress, hair styled in ringlets and matching pink shoes 'and was wont rather to strut than walk into the room upon my best kid shoes [. . .] and I was not a little vain of them' (Ewing 14). At this point in the novel, Margery is being socialised into a type of femininity preoccupied with external appearance, and is learning to take pleasure in attracting the favourable attention of other people. After her father dies, Margery stays with her mother's cousin, Aunt Theresa, and Major Buller. One of their daughters, Matilda, becomes the next female figure who inducts Margery into expectations of dress and makes her aware of scrutiny – not just admiration – from girls and women. It is Matilda who introduces the negative affective potential of dress, and who ultimately demonstrates that excessive vanity could provoke ill health. The daughters display their best dresses for Margery and also provide her with an inventory of the items they are anticipating in the mail from England. Matilda, who is fashionable with her stiff 'lawyer's wig' curls, subjects Margery to a barrage of questions about her hair, clothing material and dressing procedure (Ewing 14). Dress is so entwined with Margery's emotional response to her father's death and life as an orphan as to become indistinguishable. Matilda delivers a cruel blow by reminding Margery that she will no longer be allowed to wear her pink silk dress, but will be required to wear black for a year after the loss of her father (Ewing 18). Margery is, of course, distressed at the loss of her beloved father, but as is depicted in the accompanying illustration, she is also miserable because she can no longer derive pleasure from admiring reactions inspired by the pink dress. Aunt Theresa, however, orders a fashionable black mourning dress, which deprived Margery's 'deep mourning of much of its gloom' (Ewing 28).

Dress is imbricated with Margery's affective potential as an orphan, as is evident when she plays out imagined scenarios in her mind:

> Sometimes it was agony to me to hear the oft-repeated tale of my parents' death, and then again I enjoyed a sort of gloomy importance which gave me satisfaction. I even rehearsed such scenes in my mind when I was in bed, shedding real tears as (in the person of Aunt Theresa) I related the sad circumstances of my own grief to an imaginary acquaintance; and then, with dry eyes, prolonging the 'fancy' with compliments and consolations of the most flattering nature. I always took care to fancy some circumstances that led to my being in my best dress on the occasion. (Ewing 29)

Here Margery senses the importance, and experiences the fulfilment, of being looked at, even when these feelings issue from the painful experience of her parents' death. Her fantasy of wearing her most impressive clothing while being pitied as an orphan further demonstrates her awareness of the social influence of dress and her own pleasure in the act of making an emotional impact. These visualisations of her affective potential are enacted in a role play that Margery conducts in front of her aunt's full-length mirror. Wanting to see whether she shares her mother's 'expressive eyes' (Ewing 28), Margery is displeased by her reflected expressions and then rehearses the act of meeting someone: 'I threw all the grace and graciousness of which I was conscious into my manner, and holding out my hand, said, in a "company voice," "*charmed* to see you, I'm sure"' (Ewing 30). Margery is highly embarrassed when her aunt and great-grandmother walk in during her performance (Fig. 3.3). While Margery blushes and perceives shame and indignity, her grandmother smiles and then becomes tearful. The scene is poignant because Margery's knowledge of womanly

Figure 3.3 Illus. Mrs W. Allingham, *Six to Sixteen*. London: George Bell and Sons, 1886.

public conduct is limited to memories of the admiration that surrounded her mother and because she will always lack a mother to induct her into appropriate femininity as she matures. The remainder of the novel shows Margery confronted with a range of models of feminine conduct and appearance, primarily those of her peers, Matilda and Eleanor Arkwright, whose father is a friend of Margery's uncle.

Fashionable Matilda is an example of the way in which a preoccupation with producing favourable affective responses based on beauty and fashion alone is debilitating to a girl's character and health. At the age of 12, she suffers from 'very severe headaches' which cause her to faint (Ewing 47). The novel makes it explicit that Aunt Theresa's focus on her daughters' appearance has contributed to Matilda's poor health because she suffers mental anguish at the thought of failing to measure up to external scrutiny. Matilda becomes 'irritable, moody, and perverse' (Ewing 57) and reluctant to appear in company because of her sensitivity to judgements about her plain appearance; she has always heard her mother and her friends 'discuss, approve, and condemn their friends by the standard of appearances alone' (Ewing 53). Jackie Horne argues that the narrative rejects Aunt Theresa 'as a model for a good mother' because she cares more about fashion than raising a 'healthy girl, particularly a girl prepared for the rigors of colonial wifehood' (256). Matilda suffers a swollen face, squinting eyes and choking throat when anyone looks upon her, reactions that are attributed to her 'ill-health' (Ewing 59) and serve as a cautionary tale of excessive emphasis on beauty and dress among girls on the cusp of maturation.

Healthy and practical Eleanor, who lives with her family on the Yorkshire moors and eventually attends Bush House school with Matilda and Margery, functions as the antithesis of Matilda. She is unfussy about her appearance, does not bother to style her hair in front of a mirror, wears 'thick boots' and eschews crinoline (Ewing 49). Her rejection of ostentatious adornment is firmly yoked with her robust mental and physical health that make her the ideal candidate to be Margery's life-long best friend and, eventually, a marriageable woman. The first meeting of the three girls encapsulates Eleanor and Matilda's differing perspectives on the extent to which aesthetics should interfere with personal comfort. When a piece of hat trimming blows into Eleanor's eyes, she stuffs it unceremoniously into the band, while Matilda is horrified that it is being crushed because it 'looks so pretty' (Ewing 50). Margery's initial acceptance of the healthy model of girlhood is signalled by her realisation that the kind of elaborately dressed women she has been admiring are not the most desirable model to emulate, in part because of the way their faces reflect their lack of character and their inability to impart a lasting emotional response on the viewer:

> The faces of the fine ladies I had envied were a little apt to be insipid in expression, and to pass from the memory; but my great-grandmother's quick, bright, earnest face was not easily to be forgotten. I made up my mind that when I grew up I would not wear a large *chignon* after all, nor a bonnet full of flowers, nor a dress full of flounces, but a rather short skirt and buckled shoes and grey curls, and a big hat with many bows, and a green satin driving-cloak lined with fur. (Ewing 39)

Through her brief encounters with her great-grandmother, who is practical enough to ride in a run-down carriage and take the reins herself, Margery recognises the importance of the face as a carrier of pleasing emotions above that of the kind of elaborate clothing that her mother would have worn and which Matilda aspired to wear. The fashionable woman is largely separated from the healthy body, particularly through the depiction of Matilda as emotionally and physically frail.

The Arkwrights' home on the Yorkshire moors, where Margery eventually lives with Eleanor, produces a different kind of girlhood. As Claudia Mills points out, at the Arkwrights' farmhouse Margery 'comes to relish bracing mountain air, vigorous outdoor exercise, hearty food, the company of boys and dogs, and most of all, the pursuit of intellectual hobbies' (73). In this healthy home, industriousness, usefulness and well-being are emphasised over appearance. Near the conclusion of the novel, when Eleanor and Margery visit the Bullers after a long period of absence, 17-year-old Matilda attends her coming-out dance. The last description of her in the novel observes her looking 'pale' and 'somewhat dishevelled' (Ewing 110) at the dance, combined with a spell in which she almost faints and is struck down with a headache. The unhealthy girl has developed into an unhealthy woman, and within the context of the dance, Matilda is unable to fulfil the basic aspects of the ritual that builds toward romance and marriage. In contrast, Margery informs the reader that Eleanor is married, an effective demonstration of the way in which healthy girlhood gives way to idealised, marriageable womanhood, while unchecked unhealthy girlhood (preoccupied with aesthetics and deprived of exercise, fresh air and industriousness) is incompatible with the qualities required of a wife and mother. Ironically, *Six to Sixteen* suggests that the harder a girl works to gain pleasing affective responses to her appearance through external measures, the less successful she will be.

In its similarities with *Six to Sixteen*, *The Secret Garden* is an example of the pervasiveness and longevity of views about the interconnection between health, beauty and character in British girls' fiction. At the beginning of the novel, 6-year-old Mary Lennox lacks each of the three aspects of the imagined triangular relationship between health, beauty and the production of a character that evokes positive affective responses. Like Margery, Mary is raised by her ayah and likes to look at her pretty mother 'from a distance': 'Her hair was like curly silk and she had a delicate little nose which seemed to be disdaining things, and she had large laughing eyes. All her clothes were thin and floating, and Mary said they were "full of lace"' (Burnett 4). Mary's mother is almost ethereal in her finery, and her emotions, both positive and negative, are inscribed on her face. In contrast, Mary is consistently ill, her face and hair are an unattractive shade of 'yellow' (Burnett 1), her body is scrawny, and her character is extremely disagreeable with her pig-like selfishness.

Mary's unappealing physical and personality traits are not depicted as innate, but as the product of the environment of India, emotional neglect by her mother and indulgence at the hands of her ayah and other native servants. Mrs Lennox's inadequate maternal instinct is evident in her instructions to the ayah to 'keep the child out of sight as much as possible' (Burnett 1). Mrs Lennox's failure to fulfil her expected duty as a woman – particularly in the colonial context of British India – is firmly connected with her misuse of her beauty, which she channels into fine clothing, parties and entertaining. This flawed aspect of her character does not taint her external appearance in the same way as Mary's abrasive personality is mirrored in her 'sour expression' (Burnett 1) and 'ugliness', which sees her described as a 'young plucked crow' (114). While Mrs Lennox is already a mature woman, Mary still has the potential to transform from ugly to pretty, both externally and internally.

Moreover, Mrs Lennox is punished for her hedonistic lifestyle – encouraged by her beauty – through her own death, her husband's death and the abandonment of her daughter. When Mrs Lennox is informed that the cholera outbreak has reached an alarming point and that she should have evacuated several weeks prior, she regrets that she 'only stayed to go to that silly dinner party' (Burnett 4). Her focus on entertaining at the expensive of maternal caring also leaves Mary without the expected empathetic responses to others, most notably in the face of her parents' death. As Mrs Crawford (who cares for Mary briefly before she returns to England) remarks, explicitly linking aesthetics with the transmission of desirable personality traits: 'Perhaps if her mother had carried her pretty face and her pretty manners oftener into the nursery Mary might have learned some pretty ways too' (Burnett 13). In this way, the novel constructs a relationship between physical appearance and emotion in which one influences, and might even transform, the other. Ben Weatherstaff, the gardener at the estate of her relatives at Misselthwaite Manor, is the first to make

Mary aware of the correlation between her unattractive appearance and her character: 'We're neither of us good lookin' an' we're both of us as sour as we look. We've got the same nasty tempers, both of us, I'll warrant' (Burnett 51). While elderly Ben's curmudgeonly nature is entrenched, *The Secret Garden* shows that in young people transformations in health can in turn improve character and physical appearance.

In keeping with expectations of healthy girlhood beauty, exercise in the countryside is the catalyst for the transformation of Mary's well-being both externally and internally, much as fresh air is one of the only balms for Matilda's pains and irritability in *Six to Sixteen*. When Mary arrives at Misselthwaite, her 'yellow' complexion, limp hair, thinness and lack of appetite signal her poor health. Walking and running on the moors has the effect of 'stirring her [Mary's] slow blood and making herself stronger by fighting with the wind' (55), replacing the 'sour buttermilk' (93) in her veins and filling her lungs with 'fresh air blown over the heather' that 'was good for her whole thin body and whipped some red color into her cheeks and brightened her dull eyes' (56). This mirrors the process described in the *Girl's Own Book of Health and Beauty* in which Stables explains that athleticism induces 'perfect action of the skin', making it 'clear and transparent, and the pure, healthy blood that circulates beneath it is seen in the soft-delicate bloom on the cheeks and in the carmine of the lips', as well as making the hair and teeth beautiful (67). The gift of a skipping rope from servant Martha further directs Mary's outdoor exercise and promises to strengthen Mary's limbs, and transform her appearance to be attractively feminine. Outdoor exercise increases Mary's appetite to the point where she can take pleasure in the taste of porridge, something which Martha, with her folk wisdom, recognises. She tells Mary to keep playing outside 'an' you'll get some flesh on your bones an' you won't be so yeller' (56). Crucially, outdoor exercise also makes Mary a happier girl who can enjoy her experiences of the world and other people and can be useful and bring happiness to others.

Beauty ads of the period were as often concerned with girls and women gaining weight as with losing it. As Mary fills out, growing stronger and fatter to the point where she needs new dresses, other aspects of her appearance improve, including her hair, which has grown thicker. In Stables's guide book, he describes the hair as the prime indicator of a girl's overall health noting the 'the hair cannot be in health if the body be not so' (103–4). Nature, and an appreciation of the beauty of the world outside, impart healthful beauty onto Mary herself. This is particularly important within *The Secret Garden*'s narrative as her transformation into a pleasant and healthy girl enables Mary to bring health to her invalid cousin Colin. As she enthusiastically runs to Colin to announce the arrival of spring, she carries its smell and markers of health on her body:

> The next minute she was in the room and had run across to his bed, bringing with her a waft of fresh air full of the scent of the morning.
> 'You've been out! You've been out! There's that nice smell of leaves!' he cried.
> She had been running and her hair was loose and blown and she was bright with the air and pink-cheeked, though he could not see it.
> 'It's so beautiful!' she said, a little breathless with her speed. 'You never saw anything so beautiful! It has *come*! I thought it had come that other morning, but it was only coming. It is here now! It has come, the Spring!' (246)

The sour girl who first arrived at Misselthwaite Manor could not have derived happiness from the beauty of nature, nor could she have transferred this excitement and zest for life to another person. Mary now has the ability to be affected profoundly by the outdoors and this capacity not only transforms her own appearance into one that is marked by signs of natural health (flushed cheeks and loose, billowing hair) but her desire to share these pleasures. Colin's father, Dr Craven, eventually notices that his invalid son has been transformed by his outdoor rambles and play. Mrs Medlock claims the same for Mary, but there are some clear differences in their respective transformations, and how they are perceived by adults as a result. Where Colin becomes lively and strong, Mary is, in Mrs Medlock's estimation 'downright pretty since she's filled out and lost her ugly little sour look' (Burnett 327). While there are healthful aspects to the change in Mary, her movement from ugly to pretty is equally important. The degree to which her appearance evokes first negative and then positive reactions and emotions in various viewers is unique to Mary's development. When Mrs Medlock describes the new situation in which Mary and Colin laugh together gleefully, she reflects on Mary's former expression and character: 'The glummest, ill-natured little thing she used to be' (Burnett 327). Mary herself, who had never displayed any self-consciousness about her appearance, recognises that her image in a mirror 'looked quite a different creature from the child she had seen when she arrived from India. This child looked nicer' (Burnett 191). The change that Mary registers is one that acknowledges that she is both more aesthetically pleasing and that she now appears to be nicer because of her happiness, which stems from her new-found health and beauty.

In the novel's conclusion, the explicit connection between positive thoughts and health is described as a new discovery of the 'last century' (353). Bad thoughts are equated with a 'scarlet fever germ' (Burnett 353) that may infiltrate the body and contribute to a lifelong debility. It is only Mary, however, who is explicitly discussed in this context, even though Colin's hypochondria and negative outlook contributed to his own miserable confinement in his bedroom. In addition, her 'disagreeable thoughts' don't merely make her feel ill when she is not, like Colin, but 'affected her liver and her digestion and made her yellow and tired' (Burnett 354). Burnett's theories about the relationship between a disagreeable character, blood purity and an unhealthy appearance closely accord with those of Stables in his discussion of the liver in *The Girl's Own Book of Health and Beauty*. He explains that 'you will never get the skin to look healthy if the liver is out of order, or if indigestion be present' (245). Mary's health suffers for her thoughts, and so too does her ability to be regarded as pleasant-looking according to feminine expectations for girls. Beauty expectations were therefore not only explicitly concerned with controlling girls' external appearance based on notions of acceptable sexuality, usefulness and reproductive health, but also with moulding the characters and emotions of health. Stables claimed that 'there can be no beauty without health', but the ideals of the period meant that there could also be no beauty without pleasing and selfless femininity.

Conclusion

In Ewing's opening dedication of *Six to Sixteen* to her friend Eleanor Lloyd, she diminishes the achievement of her novel and proposes that 'it contains no attempt to paint a model girl or a model education, and was originally written as a sketch of domestic life, and not as a vehicle for theories' (v). Regardless of Ewing's conscious intentions, her novel influenced ideologies about girls' health, beauty and character that remained pervasive in Britain into the Edwardian period. Heroine Margery is presented with two opposing types of girlhood – one based in vanity and the other in health and usefulness – and it is abundantly clear as to which model produces happiness in the girl and those whom she encounters. Burnett's novel similarly makes the connection between physical appearance and its interdependent relationship with felt emotion and affect upon others. In both novels, nature is one crucial factor in the development of a healthy body and a healthy outlook, appropriately grounded in a feminine desire to care for and please other people. The endurance of this girlhood ideal across four decades is apparent not only through the comparison of these two novels, but also through placing them alongside the unchanging beauty advice contained in the *Girl's Own Paper* throughout the last decades of the nineteenth century. Consistent direction provided by Medicus and other less frequent contributors warned that 'abominations' such as cosmetics would never be necessary if girls focused on maintaining their health ('Beauty' 717).

Moreover, beauty articles in the magazine promoted a two-way relationship between character and appearance that echoed the rhetoric embedded in the novels I have considered. There could be 'no true beauty of face if the mind be neglected', and even the girl with attractive features possessed no more 'real beauty' that a fashion-plate illustration or clothing dummy on display (Medicus, 'Beauty' 717). This rhetoric meant that girls were encouraged to understand their physical appeal to be dependent on development of their personalities, such as the cultivation of intellect through reading and nurturing of empathy through appreciation of nature ('Beauty' 717). It was no doubt convenient to link girls' desire to be beautiful with conservative feminine ideals of behaviour and self-improvement, however this type of advice correlated with broader beliefs in the period about relationships between character, physical features and dress, as well as immorality and artifice. For the woman who had left behind the girlhood period to which beauty rightly belonged, there was far more opportunity to transgress these norms given that there was less at stake to lose, as I examine in the following chapter.

Notes

1 In Dyer's book *Folk-Lore of Women as Illustrated by Legendary and Traditional Tales, Folk-Rhymes, Proverbial Sayings, Superstitions* (Chicago: McClurg, 1906), his source for this saying is cited as *New Help to Discourse* from 1721.
2 In 1899 Medicus similarly warns about 'over-doing it' in relation to a girl's concern about her appearance; she must not think about her looks too much or allow herself 'to become a piece of human vanity' ('Beauty in Woman' 236).
3 Kortsch notes that beauty in dress was yoked with health and rationality by those who worked to reform women's dress in the period, such as the Rational Dress Society, the Rational Dress Association and the Healthy and Artistic Dress Union (77, 79).

4

Beauty and Ageing

Both young and older women were cautioned against using cosmetics, but the rationales for each stage of life differed. By the early twentieth century, it was more common for women's periodicals and beauty manuals to promote the idea that older women must combat fading looks by almost any means necessary so long as they did not attempt to foolishly – and futilely – recreate the charms of their youthful selves. Women's magazines and advertising that featured older women celebrities offered up a virtually impossible ideal of youthful appearance maintained into older age purely through a daily regimen of undetectable and hygienic body care. Discussions of beautification for older women shift from the sensation and pitying attitudes associated with Madame Rachel's salon and her mature clients around the 1860s. In this chapter, I examine the differing beauty strategies for older women described in beauty manuals, women's magazines and advertisements by the final decades of the century, which both offered hope for lifelong beauty and, at the same time, blamed women's character, thoughts and mental health, in addition to their hygiene and grooming methods, for any degradation in their appearance as they aged. Finally, I consider two novels published at mid-century, Charles Dickens's *Dombey and Son* (1848) and George Eliot's *Felix Holt, the Radical* (1866), focusing on the revulsion associated with women's ageing and loss of beauty in order to exemplify the minimal scope afforded for women to age well until much later in the century.

But at what age might a Victorian or Edwardian woman be regarded as 'old'? Life expectancy at birth rose to the upper forties by the end of the nineteenth century, though this figure is skewed substantially by infant mortality rates (Heath 9). Most people who survived infancy could expect to live into their fifties, and it was not uncommon for people to survive into their eighties and nineties. Kay Heath explains that conceptions of what constituted middle age, however, did not strictly accord with life expectancies and varied for men and women. She suggests that literary evidence often puts women as nearing middle age at 30, particularly as this marked the point at which women's value on the marriage market would rapidly dwindle; this contrasts with men, who could still be regarded as eligible bachelors and as not yet having reached middle age at 40 (Heath 10–11). Teresa Mangum suggests that most popular advice texts saw women's ageing tied to their reproductive capacity and, as such, menopause, occurring approximately between the ages of 45 and 55, was seen to trigger the onset of old age (99, 106). The association between female beauty, fertility and being in 'bloom', as detailed by Amy M. King in *Bloom: The Botanical Vernacular in the English Novel* (2003), therefore also brought with it metaphors of withered or faded flowers as women moved beyond their reproductive years. In contrast, old age for men was tied to the point at which they could no longer work, which could extend beyond their forties and fifties. Ageing for women was therefore intimately connected with perceptions of a woman's sexuality, and therefore her beauty, given its association with youth and fertility. Many advertisements for beauty products in Victorian women's magazines promised that they would enable consumers to retain the markers of youth: a full head of luxurious hair with no bald spots, coloured rather than grey hair, a full set of teeth, a trim waist, and a clear and smooth complexion. As ageing was associated with qualities that were antithetical to female beauty, older women were situated differently with respect to the naturalised ideals that were predominant in discourses aimed at girls and younger women. Specifically, older women could be viewed as grotesque for attempting to dress like young women, wear or colour their hair like girls, or mask their aged skin with the heavy application of 'powder and paint' to replicate youthful features like a rosy blush to the cheek.

The ages mentioned in beauty advertisements correspond with the view that the thirties marked the threshold for women entering middle age and no longer being considered youthful and at the peak of attractiveness. A pamphlet for Mr Kirkham's Patent

Medicine that included an advertisement for Madame Dupree's Berlin Toilet Soap from 1890 promises 'a return to youthful beauty' and specifies that the soap can make 'a lady of thirty-five appear but twenty-five' ('Mr Kirkham's'). A 1904 beauty manual by Lady Jean, *Beauty as a Fine Art*, confirms that it is 'Not many years since a woman of thirty-five was considered of middle age', noting a change in which 'the woman of forty, with her combined charm of the mental, the spiritual and the physical, is just entering upon a long summer of useful and enjoyable existence' though 'anything that threatens to rob her of the outward sign of youth is combated and defied by all reasonable means' (5). The process by which women moved from understanding ageing as something that must inevitably be accepted to a process to be fought 'by all reasonable means' within her disposal is what I am interested in examining here, in addition to identifying the methods that were regarded as crossing the line into 'unreasonable' means.

For older women in the nineteenth century, being visibly made up became tolerable as the century advanced, though the degree to which the cosmetics might be acceptably detectable was still a point of contention. Valerie Steele asserts that mature women were of less concern in their use of cosmetics because they would likely be in more need of their assistance and, given the sexual association of cosmetics, would suffer less damage to their moral character than girls who had their 'innocence' to preserve (*Fashion* 127). Nevertheless, there is a wealth of space in advertisements, beauty manuals and novels of the period devoted to discussing the potential ageing effects of cosmetics on already aged skin and – a significant focus for this chapter – on the disgust that the overly made-up older woman might provoke. Both factors encouraged evasive language in the advertising of cosmetics that continually sought to market them as health or hygiene products, distancing them from the negative connotations of cosmetic products. A brochure for Plantol soap that was likely produced in the 1890s or early twentieth century (Fig. 4.1) cautions that 'powders, lotions, rouges, &c' spell '*Ruin to Skin* and Complexion' and 'draw attention to what they are intended to conceal'. Not only are these kinds of cosmetics described as failing in their mission to camouflage or repair dry, wrinkled or red skin, but the ad warns that they *cause* 'premature ageing'. This is one in a long line of attempts to frame damaged and wrinkled skin as induced by women's own ill-advised behaviour as they aged.

LADY THOUGHTFUL.

Lady Thoughtful always keeps some tablets of *Plantol Soap* (Floral) in the house, she spreads it about in the linen-cupboards and wardrobes. It helps the soap (which like good wine improves with age) to mature, and diffuses an agreeable perfume through the clothes. Thus she secures a double service at a single cost.

Figure 4.1 Undated advertising brochure for Plantol soap. John Johnston Collection of Printed Ephemera, Bodleian Library.

As I suggested in Chapter 2, manufactured anxieties about cosmetic usage ensured that most beauty products attempted to describe themselves as something other than a cosmetic. Hair restorers, for example, promised to renew grey hair – one of the most telling signs of ageing – to its original colour. Advertisements for hair products commonly emphasised that they were not dyes, though these claims were surely fabricated given that, even today, no such product exists that can reverse the process of greying hair. In addition to returning colour, an ad for Rossetter's hair restorer from around 1880 also claims to prevent hair falling out and to give the hair 'the lustre and health of youth'. Blackham's hair restorer promises to restore 'youthful colour and lustrous beauty' within a few days (Fig. 4.2). Dyes transgress ideas about what kinds of artificial aids to beauty are acceptable, and the principle of preserving beautiful features, rather than masking or concealing signs of ageing. Nevertheless, in small print at the bottom of the

Beauty and Ageing   113

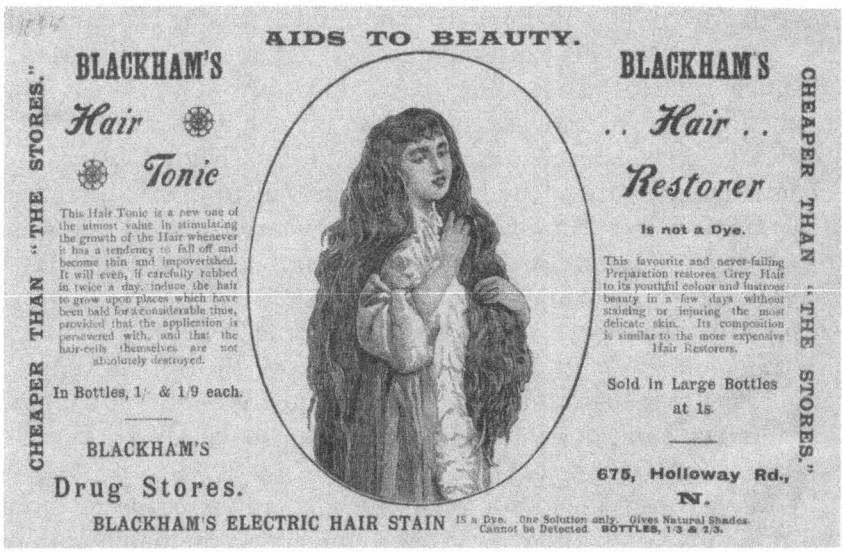

Figure 4.2 Blackham's hair products, pamphlet. John Johnson Collection of Printed Ephemera, 1895. Bodleian Library.

Blackham's ad is mention of the company's Electric Hair Stain, which is declared to be a dye, but which reassures the potential purchaser that it 'cannot be detected'. Though there was substantial movement toward greater acceptance of cosmetics such as powder and rouge in the late nineteenth century, lingering views about natural or God-given beauty, as well as the unpleasantness of an older woman attempting to present herself as youthful, ensured that cosmetic advertisements repeatedly denied the artifice involved in their products and highlighted the prevention of skin ageing in place of concealment.

Methods (acceptable and taboo) for regaining a youthful appearance

Soap was the most acceptable of commercial products for preserving youthful skin, and it developed an association both as a cause and treatment for aged skin. As Lori Anne Loeb points out in her study of Victorian advertising, the amount of physical work required to keep a household clean 'might render women prematurely decrepit' (117). Anxieties about work-related physical decay were deployed in Sunlight Soap's famous advertising caption from the 1880s – 'Why does a Woman Look Old Sooner than a Man?' – which transformed laundry work into one of the areas that women needed to monitor to maintain their appearance. More common, however, as I discuss in detail in Chapter 5, was the deployment of actresses and famous figures in advertising, as in an 1887 advertisement for Pears' Soap published in *Myra's Journal of Dress and Fashion* including praise from actresses and singers Lillie Langtry, Adelina Patti and M. Fortescue (165). Another Pears advertisement, from the same magazine in 1888, promises a radical suppression of ageing, with a 50-year-old woman supposedly resembling a girl (Fig. 4.3). It features Mrs Georgina Weldon, an amateur soprano, campaigner against lunacy laws and well-known litigant (Pears 325).

While advertisements for beauty products focused on methods for retaining youth and were usually embellished with illustrations of young women, celebrity women provided exceptional examples of older women as icons for emulation. The fame associated with celebrity women such as actress Sarah Bernhardt could disrupt the usual visual emphasis on young faces. Moreover, the artistic skills of actresses like her could relate to the artistry of retaining youthfulness into middle age. An advertisement in *Woman* for 'Camelline for the Complexion' (Fig. 4.4) headed 'Women who never grow old' pictures three actresses in middle age (iii). It carries testimonials from 'Miss Ellen Terry', 'Mrs Kendal', 'Mdme Adelina Patti', 'Mdme Jane Hading' and 'Mrs Bancroft', and highlights that actresses especially do not age because '[k]eeping young is an art' (Camelline iii). In an advertisement for her own Diaphane powder in an 1891 edition of the *Queen*, the 56-year-old Bernhardt appears clearly middle aged and in her endorsement she describes herself as 'the godmother' of the brand (Diaphane xlvi). *Woman* published an article in the same year expressing amazement that Bernhardt was 'looking fatter and fairer, but absolutely younger, than she did ten years ago' ('How Sarah Bernhardt' 13). This was understood to be especially remarkable because of her age, but also because she had experienced 'unusual stress of work, dissipation, and fatiguing travel' but nevertheless was 'left free from the footprints of time' ('How Sarah Bernhardt' 13). This observation represents a transformation in early Victorian beliefs in which negative thoughts and stresses would be understood as inevitably rendering themselves visible on the ageing woman's

Figure 4.3 Pears' Soap advertisement. *Myra's Journal of Dress and Fashion* 1 June 1888: 325.

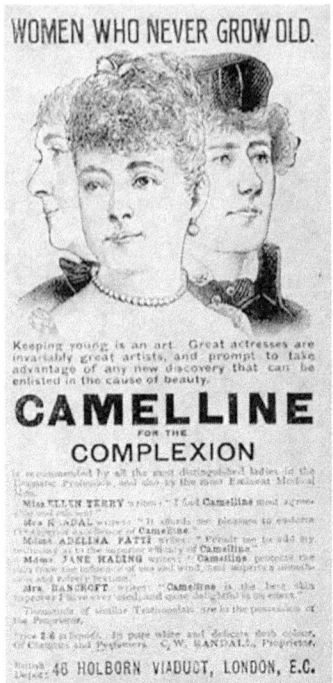

Figure 4.4 Camelline advertisement. *Woman* 15 April 1896: iii. Bodleian Library.

face. Contrary to Bernhardt's prolific advertisements for soap and rice-based face powder, the article suggests that the actual secret of her youthful appearance is bathing in a home-made undiluted Eau Sedative comprised of ammonia, camphor and salt when she is tired. This process keeps the skin firm and prevents wrinkles, providing an example of acceptable preserving or preventative beauty treatments for older women and of editorial emphasis on 'natural' methods of beautification.

In contrast with later advertisements, articles and advice that advocated for the use of soaps and conservative remedies to aid the ageing woman, the services and treatments of the infamous cosmetician Madame Rachel, Sarah Rachel Levison, provided well-publicised examples of older women who were imagined as foolish and vain for seeking to improve their appearances as they aged. The slogan of Rachel's business, 'Beautiful for ever', became a catchphrase that stood for inflated claims in the Victorian period: the criticism implicit in its wider usage is that the quest for beauty into old age is obviously futile. Among the products provided at her salon was Circassian Beauty Wash at one pound and one shilling, Magnetic Rock Dew Water of Sahara for removing wrinkles and Youth and Beauty Cream, both priced at two pounds and two shillings. In 1863, Madame Rachel published a 24-page pamphlet, entitled *Beautiful For Ever!*, which explained her outlay of significant money to purchase the sole right to sell 'the Magnetic Rock Dew Water of Sahara, which possesses the extraordinary property of increasing the vital energies – restores the colour of grey hair – gives the appearance of youth to persons far advanced in years, and removes wrinkle, defect, and blemishes, from whatever cause they may arise' (n.p.).

The treatments for which Madame Rachel was most famous, known as 'enamelling', was primarily sought by older women to mask aged skin. There is nary a kind word about enamelling to be found in Victorian beauty manuals and women's magazines, indicative of the particular discomfort associated with older women's beautification efforts, especially those that were deemed unsuccessful or artless. Yet in Madame Rachel's pamphlet, she claims to avoid dangerous cosmetics in favour of the use of 'the Arabian Bath, composed of pure extracts of the liquid of flowers, choice and rare herbs, and other preparations equally harmless and efficacious' (17). Rachel goes to dramatic lengths to explain the naturalness of her process which keeps 'the pores of the skin from corrosive perspiration', even likening the lack of understanding of the practice to the initial disbelief in Edward Jenner's smallpox vaccine (17).

Older women were indoctrinated by these discourses that reminded them of their ageing bodies and some were persuaded by these advertising claims. The imagined gullibility of older women in chasing the fountain of youth through cosmetics was amply illustrated in Madame Rachel's first trial for fraud in 1868, in which her victim 50-year-old Mary Tucker Borradaile was described as an object of pity.[1] One of the prosecutors, Montagu Williams, found it hard to accept that Borradaile could have believed she could be made beautiful forever. He later recalled her to be a pathetic figure in her attempts to be attractive despite her years: 'She was a spare, thin, scraggy-looking woman, wholly devoid of figure; her hair was dyed a bright yellow; her face was ruddled with paint; and the darkness of her eyebrows was strongly suggestive of meretricious art' (qtd in Roughead 109). Borradaile had been beautiful in her youth and was particularly renowned for her long golden hair, but in court it was observed to be unnaturally dyed or artificial. Fellow prosecutor William Ballantine described Borradaile as 'a skeleton encased apparently in plaster of Paris, painted pink and white, and surmounted with a juvenile wig' (Ballantine 79). According to Helen Rappaport, when Borradaile entered the courtroom to give evidence, there were audible gasps at her made-up face (124–5).

Horror at the cosmetically enhanced older woman continues to be expressed into the early twentieth century. In *The Art of Being Beautiful* (1902), the supposedly 50-year-old Baroness advises:

> For a woman to try and knock more than ten years off her age is an arrogance for which she is punished by every glance of the passers by. When she tries as a brunette to make herself into a blonde by the use of unlimited white chalk, she also makes herself grotesque – as unpleasing as a fly that had dropped into a honey-pot. When, as a blonde, she adorns herself with black eyebrows like croquet hoops, frankly she becomes alarming, if not detestable. (S.G. 58)

The latter description recalls the 'meretricious art' observed in Lady Borradaile's dark eyebrows in contrast with her unnaturally yellow hair. S.G. also remarks that dyed hair does not complement 'wrinkled cheeks, especially when the dye chosen is of a infantine yellow tint' (73), signalling that older women should not attempt to recapture certain signs of youth.

With the shift in the understanding of beauty as God-given and natural, as women aged, they were confronted with three choices: accept the gradual fading of their looks; attract criticism if they attempted to visibly ameliorate signs of age; or pursue the difficult task of staving off wrinkles and grey hair through 'invisible' and 'natural' preventative methods. Beauty manuals, the periodical press and advertisements exhibited a movement away from the acceptance of women's visible ageing, as consumer products promised to extend the span of youthful beauty. However, with the acknowledgement of this possibility came a strategy through which older women could be held personally responsible for their physical ageing if they failed to assiduously adhere to the right kind of beauty regimen.

'The past is a story told': beauty manuals

This section will consider how ageing women are advised to confront their physical decline in a selection of beauty manuals published in the final decades of the nineteenth century and into the early twentieth century, a period in which a large number of manuals were published. These books of beauty advice were sometimes associated with established magazines, and were occasionally authored by public figures, but more commonly published anonymously or pseudonymously. The various prohibitions on visible means of ameliorating looks for older women produced a common narrative in advice literature that depended on a logic of neglect. Older women could be blamed for the natural effects of ageing, or for worsening them, through their habits (such as inappropriate cosmetic use) or for failing to engage in the right preventative behaviours. The failure to maintain a beauty regimen connected visible ageing with personal neglect and laziness for failing to perform the work required. As *The Woman Beautiful* (1899) by Ella Adelia Fletcher suggests, none of the 'charms' of beauty (such as a graceful figure, fine-textured skin, glossy hair and 'delicate, small ears') necessarily 'reach their maximum in youth' and 'none of them need fade with maturity' (21). Fletcher acknowledges that experience can positively influence the growth of a woman's character and 'soul', which, in turn, can draw out the full beauty potential of features such as the eyes (21). As I illustrate in the following section, there are positive assessments of women and ageing, such as Fletcher's, to be found in beauty manuals in the final decades of the nineteenth century, which take account of women's experience and the pleasures still to be enjoyed in old age. Nevertheless, these sentiments co-exist with those found in other manuals that categorise old age as a serious problem, and one for which women can be blamed.

Nevertheless, while beauty manuals may have imagined a way to navigate ageing that did not mean decay and the loss of beauty, the older woman faced numerous dangers in her use of cosmetics and in her clothing choices. A short 1885 advice manual *Beauty: How to Get It and How to Keep It*, which was published by the popular weekly magazine *Tit-Bits*, warns against dyes for grey hair, noting that the colour is only temporary, and that they are 'sometimes injurious to the health; those that contain lead or mercury are especially so, and have been known to cause serious illness' (16). The second caution comes in relation to clothing style: a young girl 'may wear almost anything' while 'A matron who has lost the first plump charm and indefinable beauty of youth has to be very careful how she dresses' (7). This warning in part surrounds the aesthetic perceptions and feelings of spectators and the embarrassment this generates for the 'matron', rather than any concern for an older woman's health and comfort. With its logic of danger and the threat of older women transgressing beauty expectations for their life stage, the manual finds a way to blame women's mental outlook as contributing to the waning of their looks. The author claims that 'a great [male] authority' suggests that

> the majority of women acquire a dull, vacant expression towards middle life, which makes them positively plain. He attributes it to their neglect of all mental culture, their lives having settled down to a monotonous routine of housekeeping, visiting, gossip, and shopping; their thoughts become monotonous too; for, though these things are all good enough in their way, they are powerless to keep up any mental life or any activity of thought. (7)

Though nonsensical, this suggestion reinforces the evolving sense that women who look old have prompted their own decline and a shift in ideas about beauty being bestowed by nature rather than achieved or maintained through various kinds of physical and psychological discipline practised daily.

Today women who have aged 'poorly' might be blamed for their physical behaviours (e.g. smoking, excessive time in the sun, or failure to eat well and exercise). In the Victorian period, various women's thoughts and attitudes were isolated as responsible for their physical appearance in older age. In a section on wrinkles in *Beauty as a Fine Art* (1885), Lady Jean pinpoints 'worry' as '[t]he most determined slayer of feminine beauty' (126). Worry stamps the face with

> its ugly marks, the eyes become lack-lustre, and their pretty colour fades, the complexion soon yellows in sallowness, and the mouth loses its curves and contour, straightening itself into hard lines. The hair, too, becomes full and limp, and the wrinkles –oh! those dreadful wrinkles – furrow their insinuating way over the smooth skin. (Lady Jean 126)

The title of this manual, which refers to beauty as a 'fine art', points toward the significance of tastefulness. For older women, there is a greater requirement to age gracefully than for men. Primarily the notion of grace and care related to ensuring that a woman kept to the degree of naturalness and mode of dress deemed acceptable for her age group; she must not stray into replicating features or wearing clothing that was indicative of youth because it would only magnify her appearance of age. Lady Jean quotes Max O'Rell[2] that:

> an old woman [who] makes to hide her age only helps to advertise it louder. So she feels that her best days are to come, she accepts the inevitable, looks the facts in the face, takes physical help when needed, and has the evident feeling that
> The past is as a story told,
> The future may be paved with gold. (Lady Jean 112)

The quotation from O'Rell insists that older women accept the unavoidable reality of their loss of physical competence and mobility (being prepared to take help) and their loss of youth (looking 'facts in the face'), failing to entertain ideas that are evident in other manuals about the potential to naturally prevent an aged appearance in the first place. O'Rell, as a male author, discounts the rhetoric of self-preservation that is more typical of women's magazines and beauty manuals, instead, perhaps progressively, suggesting that a woman might find greater pleasures in her old age, regardless of the loss of her youthful charm.

H. Ellen Browning's *Beauty Culture* (1897) took a particularly positive attitude toward ageing. Browning maintained that several markers of ageing need not ever be reached with careful attention to self-care. In the case of grey hair, for example, Browning maintains that it is 'caused by a want of tone in the hair-producing organs', which can be 'restored by hygienic treatment' (108). She points to the existence of women in their sixties who have not yet gone grey 'and dozens of charming old ladies over fourscore with luxuriant white hair' but chides those aged in their mid-twenties 'whose locks are turning grey and becoming scanty before they have well reached maturity' (109). In Browning's understanding, health, hair and skin could be lost by failure 'to retain or restore whatever beauties may have been bestowed on them' (109). The responsibility lies with each individual woman not to 'waste any scrap or chance of beauty' (109). In the case of hair, Browning advises that the causes of greying and hair loss are 'want of nourishment to the roots, want of stimulant to the roots, want of cleanliness to the scalp, or want of ventilation to the hair' (112). Elsewhere, she recommends daily routines for toning up '[l]ong or flabby skins' with daily soaping, health salts, cucumber, melon and iris-root added to washing water, skin tonics, twice-weekly baths, good food, exercise, well-ventilated rooms and 'a good wrinkle-lotion' (130–1).[3] Attention to these concerns could all be grounded in notions of health and hygiene, bypassing anxieties about artifice and cosmetics.

Browning takes up the idea of beauty as an art that is evident in other beauty manuals such as Lady Jean's. Her disapproval of hair dyes, for instance, stems not from the dyed hair itself, which can look appealing, but because it can look 'unreal' set against the face, showing up complexion flaws, which then require the application of make-up to mask (119). Both tasks must be performed with skill, otherwise they are 'inartistic' and not beautiful (119). This specific word is used multiple times, as Browning similarly finds dry powder 'inartistic' on older faces because 'it frequently hangs in the wrinkles' (131). In accord with the predominant sense that older women should be more particular about their grooming and use of cosmetics because of their potential to repulse, Browning quotes the Marquise of Blocquville who says aged coquetry is 'sacred': 'it commands us to take more pains with ourselves *not to displease*, than we took in our youth to "please"' (29).

As girlhood beauty was yoked with character and health, so too were women entering middle age encouraged to understand that scrupulous attention to their mental and physical health, as well as feminine behaviour, might prevent a sharp decline in their appearance as they aged. While Browning advocates for 'naked truth' rather than an 'artful lie', she clarifies that a truthful appearance does not equate with physical decay and unattractiveness for older women:

> There is absolutely no reason why we should go down to our graves, 'sans teeth, sans eyes, sans taste, sans everything,' with 'wrinkled brow, bald pate, and rheumy eyes 'of age, peaked chin and parchment chap,' providing that we will only pay attention to our own physical condition. A sound mind in a sound body is the great secret of perpetual

youth. There is nothing that robs us of our youthfulness like ill-health, and there is no species of ill-health that turns our hair grey or ploughs deeper furrows in our brows than that tragic list of functional derangements and nervous ailments set down in medical text-books under the comprehensive heading of: Women's Diseases. (27)

There is much to register in this rallying cry for the retention of all body parts until death, with its quotations from Shakespeare's famous monologue from *As You Like It* and Robert Browning's poem 'Fifine at the Fair'. The first is that H. Ellen Browning rejects the premise that ageing necessarily involves severe physical degradation, noting a shift in the acceptance of sharp physical decline as inevitable. The mention of 'Women's Diseases' coupled with the discussion of a 'sound mind' raises the idea of mental illness as a driver of visible signs of ageing. If not mental illness, then simply being pessimistic, and translating emotions into physical expressions, such as pouting and frowning, are also pinpointed as the cause of wrinkles (33). Like *Beauty: How to Get It and How to Keep It*, Browning maintains that a woman's mindset and attitude to life strongly influences her appearance, which has the effect of demanding pleasant feminine behaviour and beautiful looks. Optimism, she argues, can 'keep the sunshine in our eyes and the dimples in our cheeks long, long after our gloomy pessimistic contemporaries have sunk into miserable faded old women, without a single spark of feminine charm left in them' (33).

Nevertheless, there are contradictions, or perhaps subtleties, to Browning's logic. While in the long passage quoted above furrowed brows steal youth, on the same page Browning praises facial wrinkles as 'visible tokens of character, rather than the mere fleeting loveliness, which is always, more or less, dependent on youth and circumstances' (27). Browning elaborates on the magnetic appeal of older women throughout history. Moreover, she repeatedly suggests that older women can conjure a greater fascination than a younger woman because the passing time have fostered their physical and mental development: 'The fact proclaims itself aloud, that a healthy, well-preserved woman of mature years, is likely to have a firmer hold on a man's heart than a raw girl' (29). The difficulty seemingly rests in shifting attitudes about long-term 'preservation' to understand it as tasteful, with Lady Jean observing that some people regard an 'old lady' who focuses on her appearance as 'a sort of modern Jezebel' (28).

A beauty manual from 1902, entitled *The Art of Being Beautiful: A Series of Interviews with a Society Beauty* by S.G., is constructed as an interview with a baroness who appears 'middle aged' but is 'at least 50' (61). The baroness is depicted as an authority on looking younger without transgressing age expectations for women. As in numerous beauty manuals, women are cautioned against attempting to cover wrinkles with powder, with the baroness noting that it 'marks out every crease' (61). Instead, she proposes 'feeding' wrinkled skin 'by the use of fats nearly imitating the human fat' (61). The ostensibly simple solutions offered by certain cosmetics are consistently downplayed in order to support a logic of blame and neglect regarding the ageing women's face and body. The author notes that the healthy middle-aged woman who has become 'gross and ungainly, can only be explained by imagining that persistent neglect has brought it to the sorry pass' (34). This mirrors the way young girl are blamed for bringing about wrinkles through physical exertion when cycling. S.G. notes 'the hard-drawn mouths and foxy eyes' seen regularly in London as a result of 'the anxiety of cycling' (34).

Entwined with the logic of blame for physical activities, or even mental habits such as worry or boredom *causing* declining looks, was the notion of beauty as something to be preserved through evasive action before degradation occurred. *The Art of Being Beautiful* uses the strongest language possible to emphasise the value of beauty to a woman and to figure the loss of her charms as a loss of power that must motivate her to battle the enemy of time: 'A woman who is ageing knows she has enemies all around her: demons in the form of fat, ossification, wrinkles, despondency, failing health' (108). Women must think preventatively about their behaviour given that the fading of looks 'means the absolute loss of empire' (113). Ageing is imagined as destructive in the same manner as a natural disaster: 'Time works ravages the same as fire, or war, or disease. Look at the fire brigade, the army, the medical profession. Those in authority are unceasing in active preparations to meet and combat the enemy!' (113). The wrinkled hag therefore only has herself to blame for her neglect of her appearance, rather than her genetics or the lot she has been dealt in life. In place of acceptance, the late nineteenth and early twentieth centuries saw the encouragement of beauty regimens for older women that were understood to be preventative rather than artificially masking. S. G., for example, clarifies that powders might be acceptably used

'For those who have lost their bloom', reinforcing both the idea that only older women benefit from the application of such products and that their usage of them is not as problematic as it might be for younger women (52). However, as I will suggest in the following section, Victorian fiction, with its orientation toward youthful female protagonists, contains few positive representations of older women, and often explores the loss of power associated with women's entry into old age. It retains a more pessimistic view of the possibilities of ageing with beauty and dignity.

'The painted object shrivelled underneath her hand': older women in Victorian fiction

In her study of ageing in fiction, Jeanette King points out that '[i]t is almost impossible to find any heroines of Victorian literature who are older than 40' (xvi). Women who have passed the age of marriageability, reproduction and sexual desirability rarely occupy the narrative centre of Victorian novels. However, at the fringes are examples of older women who are characterised as ageing comically in attempts to retain the markers of youthful beauty, or who are painfully aware of the relationship between the loss of their beauty and declining power and significance. In this section, I consider how two older women, Cleopatra Skewton in Dickens's *Dombey and Son* (1848) and Mrs Transome in Eliot's *Felix Holt, The Radical* (1866), serve as contrasting depictions of the comic and tragic nature of ageing and its transformation of physical appearance for women. Given the relative scarceness of fiction with significant focus on older women and their appearance, these two examples were published earlier than the magazines and beauty manuals discussed in this chapter. Nevertheless, their depiction of older women – both artificial and 'natural' – as having the power to physically repulse others continues to manifest into the twentieth century, as this chapter's examination of beauty manuals has already suggested.

Cleopatra Skewton in *Dombey and Son* is ambitious in her aspirations for her widowed daughter to be married to the eponymous Mr Paul Dombey. Mrs Skewton is the Victorian epitome of the saying 'mutton dressed as lamb', a phrase that encodes a sense of displeasure in the 'consumption' of the aged body as much as the futility of attempting to recapture youth. As a woman of 'about seventy', who is transported in a wheeled chair, she

Figure 4.5 Illustration of Mrs Skewton, 'Phiz'. *Dombey and Son*, 1848.

dresses in a way that 'would have been youthful for twenty-seven' (319). Not only does Mrs Skewton dress youthfully and extravagantly, she uses artificial means in a bid to cling to the beauty that inspired 'bucks' to throw 'wine-glasses over their heads by dozens in her honour' (319). She has 'false curls and false eyebrows' and 'false teeth', all of which are 'set off by her false complexion' (317). Her cosmetic artifice is most heavily critiqued, above her attempts to recapture youthful behaviours and mannerisms. When glimpsed in the sun, the 'patched colour' on her 'wrinkled face' is 'made infinitely more haggard and dismal than any want of colour could have been' (321). While her recourse to artifice to reproduce youthful skin, hair and teeth are evident to all who see her in public, Dickens's most grotesque depiction of Mrs Skewton is reserved for the removal of her cosmetics, hairpiece and clothing at her home in the evening. Her maid is likened to a skeleton, or Angel of Death with 'dart and hour-glass' in hand, as the process of readying Mrs Skewton mirrors the actual 'touch of Death', in that the removal of her beautifying aids effectively reduces her to the status of a corpse (431). The language used in the description of the removal of her cosmetics mirrors the abject process of bodily decay and decomposition:

> The painted object shrivelled underneath her hand; the form collapsed, the hair dropped off, the arched dark eyebrows changed to scanty tufts of grey; the pale lips shrunk, the skin became cadaverous and loose; an old, worn, yellow, nodding woman, with red eyes, alone remained in Cleopatra's place, huddled up, like a slovenly bundle, in a greasy flannel gown. (431)

Dickens scholar Michael Slater attempts to explain why the level of disgust in this passage is so heightened in comparison with comparable male characters in Dickens's fiction. Slater proposes that '[t]he source of the extra venom . . . lies in the basic hostility towards women asserting themselves as sexual beings' (362–3). But there is a difference in what this assertion means for younger women in comparison with older women like Mrs Skewton, where the anxiety stems not from the potential tainting of virginal innocence but discomfort in her perception that she might retain any of the sexual attractiveness of her youth. Moreover, in such depictions that draw heavily on connections with death and corpses, older women also lose their femininity along with any sense of sexuality, something that an excess of cosmetics and elaborate clothing might only serve to cruelly highlight. As Amanda Vickery notes in a discussion of spinsters in the eighteenth century: 'Old maids were often depicted with a dizzying array of accoutrements, but underneath the frills they were androgynous, even monstrous. Age had stolen their femininity and the grave beckons' (863). The older woman's use of clothing and accessories associated with young women, and thereby, sexual appeal, provokes discomfort in the viewer, which is only compounded by associations with death.

Dickens is not replicating the kind of arguments that authors of beauty advice such as H. Ellen Browning forged about the potential appeal of a 'well-preserved woman of mature years' who has, with greater experience, had the opportunity to develop 'physically and mentally' (29–30). Cleopatra is not Mrs Skewton's true first name, which we never learn. She acquired the sobriquet in her youth, after a 'then fashionable artist' had sketched her and labelled it 'Cleopatra: in consequence of a discovery made by the critics of the time, that it bore an exact resemblance to that Princess as she reclined on board her galley' (319). Cleopatra was known for her beauty, but as Browning points out – in a section on the largely middle-aged women 'who have fascinated men most powerfully, and influenced the destinies of nations' – she is 'said to have been nearly fifty when she enthralled Antony' (29). Mrs Skewton's first name functions ironically, a comment on her loss of aesthetic appeal in comparison with that of her beautiful widowed daughter, whose cause she seeks to advance. At one point, she is 'arranged, as Cleopatra, among the cushions of a sofa', but the only similarity is the arrangement itself, as she was 'certainly not resembling Shakespeare's Cleopatra, whom age could not wither' (324). One of the ways in which the ironic comparison of the ageless beauty Cleopatra and Mrs Skewton occurs is through her conveyance in the wheeled chair. Her 'attitude' while being so transported was the same 'one in which she had been taken in a barouche' when being sketched by the artist in her youth (319). Dickens makes the comparison with Cleopatra reclining on her ship, while Lucy Hughes-Hallett notes that this reclining posture – which Mrs Skewton emulates through her 'false invalidism' – was one of the historical Cleopatra's 'seductive attributes' (n.p.).

The grotesque aspects of Mrs Skewton's appearance stem from the merger of physical qualities associated with sexual appeal to those of decay, death and decrepitude (such as a mention of her 'shrivelled ear' (424)). Kay Heath points out that women were viewed within the context of their status as potential, actual or retired mothers, and that at the final stage they were expected 'to become sexless and focused only on fostering the younger generation's search for a mate' (15). Yet the juxtaposition of these signs of aged decay are also rendered repulsive in their clash with markers of youth. Both Mrs Skewton's 'dress and attitude were perfectly juvenile' (316); she appears 'in a very youthful costume with short sleeves' (542). Most significantly, she wields her fan with 'juvenile dexterity' to stave off a kiss from the major on her 'exceedingly red lips', perhaps in 'apprehension of some danger to their bloom' (406). As with the repeated comparisons to Cleopatra's reclining pose, the irony is that Mrs Skewton clearly has no authentic 'bloom' left to protect, with her artificially red lips no equivalent to the natural blush on a young girl's cheek. Mrs Skewton's friends similarly awkwardly juxtapose youthful behaviours and aged appearance. They wear 'very precious necklaces on very withered necks', but in particular one friend of 65, who exposes her back and shoulders in her dress has manners that 'had that indefinable charm which so frequently attaches to the giddiness of youth' (556). The decline from the 'plump' or 'full' body to one which can be described as 'withered', like Mrs Skewton's acquaintances, signals decay and death, escalating the sense of disgust in relation to any attempt to emulate the markers of beauty and hence sexual attractiveness. As I suggested earlier in this chapter, beauty advice of the period encouraged routines for older women that were framed as preventative rather than artificially masking like the heavy use of powders, dyes or enamelling. Mrs Skewton is a prime literary example of the repulsion that the wrong approach evoked at mid-century, prior to more relaxed attitudes towards cosmetic usage and greater acknowledgement of the potential for women to retain a pleasing appearance into older age.

In contrast, George Eliot's *Felix Holt, The Radical* is more sympathetic in its depiction of 56-year-old Mrs Transome, who confronts a variety of losses as her son, Harold, returns home to resume control of the family estate that she has long managed. As Jeanette King suggests, Mrs Transome demonstrates that it is not simply a woman's appearance that declines with ageing: 'Age makes ironic the power that younger women are perceived to have over their lovers and their importance in the eyes of their children, both destined to fade' (24). Yet her perception of her lack of power, reflected in her need to relinquish control of the estate and loss of appeal to her former lover Matthew Jermyn, is only magnified by her conscious awareness of her loss of beauty. While Mrs Transome receives reassurance from her son that she has not become 'clumsy and shapeless' (17), and her servant, Denner, points to her health and that she has 'such a face and figure, and will have if you live to be eighty, that everybody is cap in hand to you before they know who you are' (28). Nevertheless, despite these positive observations about her appearance, the reflection of her aged face as she inspects it in the mirror is disturbing to her and imbricated with her returned son's lack of feeling: 'No elderly face can be handsome, looked at in that way; every little detail is startlingly prominent, and the effect of the whole is lost. She saw the dried-up complexion, and the deep lines of bitter discontent about the mouth. "I am a hag!" she said to herself . . . "an ugly old woman who happens to be his mother"' (22).

Though she dresses richly in furs and velvet, Mrs Transome does not commit the sartorial sins of Dickens's Mrs Skewton in attempting to look younger or wear clothing marked out as for young women, which affords her a greater dignity and less comedic representation. Mrs Transome's body is slim, but 'finely formed', she has allowed her full head of hair to grey, and wears a well-worn black dress with fine lace cuffs or elegant sables and velvet (13). Her only signs of excess are the 'rare jewels' that adorn her fingers (13). Despite the significant differences between the two women, Mrs Transome still comes under similar criticisms; she is described by her neighbour Sir Maximus Debarry as riding 'about like a girl of twenty', but promptly marked as 'so thin that she makes me shudder' by his wife, Lady Debarry (92). The combination of youth and the aged decaying body again prompts physical disgust.

The scene in which Mrs Skewton is stripped of her cosmetic layers to reveal her grotesque natural self is also echoed in a rare moment when Mrs Transome unfastens her own hair before a mirror instead of waiting for her ladies' maid. Clothed in a dressing gown, she releases her hair, and stares into the mirror, perhaps no longer looking at her image as she enters a state of reverie: 'Motionless in that way, her clear-cut features keeping distinct record of past beauty, she looked like an image faded, dried, and bleached by uncounted suns, rather than a breathing woman who had numbered the years as they passed, and had a consciousness within her which was the slow deposit of those ceaseless rolling years' (371–2). Though Eliot is infinitely more sympathetic to Mrs Transome's ageing and the disappointments she has suffered, she utilises similar language that implies a loss of colour, desiccation and death. Mrs Transome tells Denner that she undid her own hair to see 'what an old hag' she is, suggesting her 'fine clothes . . . are only a smart shroud' (371). Her self-assessment of her appearance draws both on associations of aged women with witches and dead bodies. Although she is not a figure of mockery, the idea that the older woman's body as akin to a withered corpse is evident, with smart clothing and careful grooming still only ever a mask for the aged body. While Mrs Transome does appear 'majestic' when in her costume, without her external aids, such as her clothing, she appears an entirely different woman in her 'dishevelled' state (375). Though Eliot acknowledges the possibility of an older woman overcoming the physical markers of her age, Mrs Transome's true appearance is always there underneath the costume.

The view of elderly women's appearance in these two fictional examples published at mid-century is relatively pessimistic and preoccupied with the disgusting qualities of ageing female bodies and distinguishing them from youthfulness and sexuality. The efforts of Mrs Skewton to look younger are ridiculed, which represents a stark contrast with ideas found in women's magazines and beauty manuals in the final decades of the century that entertained the idea that a woman need never look old, regardless of her age. Arguably a fear of death might lie at the heart of both perspectives, with a cultural preference for the older woman withdrawing from attempts to cultivate beauty and appear younger than her years, replaced by an array of strategies and advice for staving off an aged face and body.

What is striking about the beauty manuals, advertisements and magazines discussed in this chapter is the diverse range of recommendations and judgements they make for and about older women while largely upholding similar anxieties about the wrong way to age and promoting a reasonably consistent idea of how appropriate behaviours could forestall the most undesirable physical changes before they set in irrevocably. The sexual resonances of beauty for women were clearly implicated in the distaste provoked by the heavily made-up older woman. Indeed, this response of disgust in relation to the older woman who presents herself as sexy, or even simply beautiful or youthfully fashionable, remains powerful in contemporary culture, with the ageing of sex-symbol Madonna into her sixties prompting innumerable declarations of revulsion on social media. As Amanda Vickery observes, women only deserved the visual spotlight 'when the dew was on the peach', and older women who attempted public display 'ran the risk of shudders, not applause' (861). Along with a decline in the minimal sexual power afforded by beauty, women also lost value as people as they aged beyond their reproductive usefulness. While men might suffer some losses in older age, the absence of an equivalent body of print directing their appearance and behaviour suggests that were not scrutinised as carefully, nor judged as harshly, for ageing.

Notes

1 After a retrial, Madame Rachel was convicted and sentenced to imprisonment for five years. Nevertheless, her business practices did not change, and her second trial (also leading to a five-year sentence) was conducted in 1878.
2 Pseudonym of the French author Léon Paul Blouet.
3 The book includes a recipe for '*Wrinkle-lotion* to be painted on thrice daily' comprised of the following ingredients: 1½ oz. tannin, 7 oz. rose-water, 3 oz. glycerine, ½ oz. eau-de-cologne. Or, 1 oz. lemon-juice. 1 oz. eau-de-cologne' (211).

Part III: Reshaping Female Beauty

5

The Celebrity as Beauty Icon

The periodical press circulated visual ideals of beauty, especially through the representation of girls and women in photographs and illustrations, fashion plates and advertisements. While illustrations and plates provided models for emulation of the latest styles of dress, there was little continuity provided by these largely anonymous images because they were not intended to represent particular women. At the same time, the growth of celebrity culture in the late nineteenth century corresponded with developments in printing and advertising, as well as shifts in magazine types and content. The combination of these factors meant that a select subset of women could serve as models of ideal beauty across time and fashion trends, and consequently could become linked with the promotion and consumption of beauty products. This chapter considers the idealised appearances of imagined figures of beauty as constructed through magazine and advertising illustration and pinpoints how the consumerist impulses of the period in print were imbricated with developing models of female celebrity. These women were primarily drawn from the stage, as actresses and singers, and their association with glamour and spectacle contributed to the slowly won acceptance of cosmetics and challenged the impossible natural ideal.

In the 1880s and 1890s, performers who appeared with prominence in articles and advertising in the *Sketch* (1893–1959) and *Myra's Journal of Dress and Fashion* (1875–1912), included Italian opera singer Adelina Patti, English actress Ellen Terry and British-American socialite and actress Lillie Langtry. In this chapter I elaborate on the representation of the female celebrity in both magazines in the late nineteenth century in order to demonstrate how the celebrity becomes an important part of the beauty ideal and its transformation. I discuss how the publicity surrounding glamorous female stage celebrities and their integration within advertisements for beauty products helped to ease some of the sensitivities surrounding cosmetic usage. Finally, I consider how, at the turn of the century, cosmeticians such as Eugène Rimmel and Madame Pomeroy worked to establish themselves as trusted, recognised names in the periodical press to establish the validity of their businesses and legitimise the purchase of commercial beauty products.

The actress celebrity in late-Victorian periodicals

The growth in the number of women's magazines and increase in the presence of periodical advertising also coincided with the popularisation of celebrities as figures of public interest. As Alexis Easley observes, from the 1870s 'celebrity news became a ubiquitous feature of the popular press', with the term 'celebrity' commonly used in the periodical press by the 1880s and 1890s, especially in illustrated monthly magazines and weeklies, including *Truth* and the *Sketch* (137). These popular periodicals constructed 'beauty as "news"' through '[t]he proliferation of images of famous women' (Easley 149). The *Sketch* was a weekly society publication targeted at a readership of both men and women that was rich in photographic content and regularly included features about society ladies and royalty, as well as stage performers. In this section, I first consider how female celebrities become models for emulation with respect to beauty and style in several magazines. I then move into a focused analysis of how the *Sketch* – given its emphasis on the stage performer – constructs actresses and singers as celebrities through its covers, articles and photo features, a status which is then channelled into the magazine's advertisements for a range of beauty and hygiene products.

The female celebrity could be differentiated from the anonymous, pretty illustrated face in advertising by the coverage of the celebrity women's lives in magazine profiles, as well as in news about forthcoming productions and appearances. Mary Luckhurst and Jane Moody describe the way that actresses also utilised memoirs to construct public intimacy through linking themselves with their characters and revealing aspects of their private lives (8). Periodicals capitalised on this connection between stage and personal lives in their construction of celebrity. Both Adelina Patti and Lillie Langtry cultivated their personas through their own publications, as well as through magazine features; in 1888, *Myra's Journal of Dress and Fashion* reported on Patti's memoir publication, as well as Langtry's 'somewhat similar literary work, and a Society novel to boot' ('Society' 462).

Actresses were viewed as 'socially problematic' throughout much of the century for their transgression of gender roles through public performance (R. Miller 17). The birth of celebrity transformed the negative connotations and enabled these women to market their personas. The most extreme self-promoter was French actress Sarah Bernhardt, who was known for her flamboyant life offstage – including her acquisition of pet leopards and tigers – that helped to generate 'extravagant rumours about her behaviour' (Eltis 169). While generating intrigue about their lives could contribute to celebrities' public profile through editorial coverage and interviews, product endorsements and testimonials also played a part in self-advertisement, ensuring repeated presence by name and sometimes photographic or illustrative image in the pages of periodicals. Sarah Bernhardt's rice powder 'Diaphane', for example, was repeatedly advertised in the *Queen* and *Myra's Journal of Dress and Fashion* throughout the early 1890s. As I will discuss in Chapter 6, reference to the naturalness of cosmetics became a commonplace method for counteracting the opposition that had previously dogged such products. However, associations with celebrity also became a byway for acceptability, trustworthiness *and* fashionability. In one of several 1891 advertisements from *Myra's Journal*, Bernhardt's association with the powder forges a clear link with its use by respectable and stylish women: 'This Beautiful Preparation, named after the celebrated Actress who has commended it so highly, now occupies the place of honour on the Toilet Table of every *dame elegante* in Paris' (La Diaphane n.p.). A line illustration of Bernhardt applying the powder while wearing gloves and a feather boa ensures the glamorous associations of the actress celebrity visually balance the textual exhortations of the product's undetectability and harmlessness. In Bernhardt's testimonial in an advertisement published in *Queen* in 1892 (Fig. 5.1), she describes herself as accepting 'the role of "godmother"' in allowing the product to use her name, raising the idea of Bernhardt as a guide for the female consumer, as well as evoking the transformative connotations of the 'fairy godmother' (xxx).

Figure 5.1 Diaphane advertisement. *Queen* 4 June 1892: xxx. Bodleian Library.

Bernhardt is also an example of how beauty was increasingly influenced by the circulation of ideas about beauty and celebrity from Europe and the United States given the fame of international singers and actresses in Britain. In 1899, the *Sketch* included an article about an unnamed actress, 'La Belle El Derido'. She is 'The Newest Beauty in Paris', who performs at the Folies-Bergère and Nouveau Cirque, and is the 'rage of Paris ... whose beauty had put all rivals into the shade' according to the awestruck author ('The Newest Beauty in Paris' 471). Accompanied by two portrait photographs, one full-length image displaying her gown and the other a headshot, the performer, who appears to be unidentifiable,[1] offers her opinions on issues such as riding side-saddle, which she declares 'unsafe and frightfully ugly' ('The Newest Beauty in Paris' 471). Though this actress's career seemingly did not prosper, the publicity surrounding her beauty and publication of her opinions in the *Sketch* indicate how the periodical press actively attempted to cultivate the female celebrity. Irish-born American actress Ada Rehan, however, did obtain lasting fame in the United States and Europe. An 'Appreciation' of Rehan published in the *Sketch* in 1893 identifies the way in which the artistic abilities of the actress or singer magnified her physical appeal. The author suggests that Rehan belongs 'both by nature and art, to the sphere of the absolutely beautiful' in her ability to evoke both sorrow and happiness in the spectator ('Miss Ada Rehan' 1). The stage performer's natural beauty can be successfully complemented by her 'art' as a performer.

Not all – and indeed many – of the celebrity women who were regularly discussed and prominent in numerous advertisements were youthful. Patti, Terry and Langtry were aged from their late thirties to fifties during this period, and their fame was strongly tied to their renown as performers. In 1894, for example, 51-year-old Patti is discussed in the *Sketch* via rumour about when she would return to the stage and in another issue that year she appears in a full-page photograph. The movement from career news and visual appearance, into the realm of personal life and relationships, helps to construct interest in the celebrity beyond the engagement of the theatrical spectator. In 1899, Patti's marriage to a 'young Swedish nobleman, Baron Cederstrom' was the subject of an article in which she also recounted the story of her career beginning with her 1861 London debut ('The Marriage of Madame Patti' 2). The adulation of older celebrity women, particularly in terms of their continued physical beauty, contributed to a shift in perceptions of older women's appearance and their capacity to not only remain attractive, but also to command romantic and public attention.

The world of the celebrity woman was framed as one with alluring connections to high society and wealth, as well as beauty and glamour. Ellen Terry, for example, was earning the highest salary of any British woman by the time she was aged 36 (Eltis 180). Other women's celebrity rested more heavily upon their beauty than their talent. In her biography, Ellen Terry alludes to the importance of Lillie Langtry's physical appearance: 'I am aware that the professional critics and the public did not transfer to Mrs Langtry the actress the homage that they had paid to Mrs. Langtry the beauty' (14). As a beauty commonly known as 'The "Jersey Lily"', Langtry could not go out in public around the 1880s without a crowd gathering, according to Terry (14). Langtry was the subject of several profiles and tributes in the *Sketch* throughout the 1890s and into the early twentieth century. In 'Mrs Langtry. The Happy Possessor of Imperial Beauty and the Imperial Theatre', the author ponders the specific nature of Langtry's visual appeal. Langtry is unique in that her stage makeup detracts from her natural beauty, and her appearance – which conforms to the natural ideal – benefits from being away from stage lighting: 'for then one can better appreciate the delicacy of

Figure 5.2 Pears' Soap advertisement. *Sketch* 3 January 1894: 552.

the pure Greek profile and the wonderful poise of her head, set on her shoulders like nothing in art so much as the Venus de Milo' (330).[2] Langtry's face is recognised far beyond those who attend the theatre because 'her photographs have gone to the uttermost ends of the world, and probably the only way in which they could be compute would be by the ton' (330). The celebrity beauty through the reproduction of her image (Fig. 5.2) could become an object of international admiration: Langtry holds visual command over theatre audiences and throughout the British Empire and beyond.

Indeed, the development of photographic and reproduction techniques in the second half of the nineteenth century enabled periodicals to commonly include photographic portraits of women. On some occasions this could entail the precursor of what would become the 'cover girl', with the cover of the 16 May 1894 issue of the *Sketch* featuring a photograph of Ellen Terry in costume as 'Marguerite' in *Faust* ('Mrs Ellen Terry' 1). In a pose commonly adopted in advertisements, Terry contemplates her own image in the mirror, as she considers how she will be viewed by the spectator. Lori Anne Loeb suggests that advertisements with the mirror pose 'reinforced a commercial ideal of the Victorian woman as an ornament' (42). The foundation for this perception is built in other magazine content, such as photographic portraits of society women, in which beauty is celebrated and the female subject's consciousness of her visual appeal is evident.

The celebrity cover was not the only way that beauty was displayed within the *Sketch* via photography, but also through compilations of photographs of various beauty 'types' based on ethnicity ('Types of Dalmation Beauty' (261), 'French Beauties' (63), 'Beauties of the French Stage' (443)) and individual portraits of young society women including 'The Misses Hathaway' and 'The Countess Clancarty' (music-hall entertainer 'Belle Bilton').[3] The images compiled within 'Types of English Beauty' were photographed by Alexander Bassano, a royal and high-society portrait photographer, suggesting a degree to which these spheres of influence conferred, or overlapped with, a degree of celebrity. The wide circulation of photographs of beautiful women through the periodical press invited the girl or woman reader to consider her own appearance, and the initiation of beauty competitions offered her the chance to take her place alongside them. *The Happy Home*, an illustrated women's magazine, for example, ran a beauty competition in 1895, in which sixty-four women's photographs would be published, to be voted on by readers (*The Happy Home* 119).

The *Sketch* forged the connection between the beautiful celebrity woman and fashionable consumer goods for her home and dress for her body. Langtry's much lauded physical beauty is shown to extend to her home in 'A Chat with Mrs Langtry' in 1895, in which her 'discerning taste' in the decoration of her home is recounted (590). Her 'Eastern love of colour' echoes her own performances as Cleopatra, who apparently would not feel out of place in Langtry's drawing room (590). She is likened to fellow actress Sarah Bernhardt in her attempts to wear authentic costume on stage, and her cabinet of jewels includes 'a necklace of real Scarabei, and the quaint silver amulet, containing a few drops of a lion's blood, which was worn by her when she impersonated "The Serpent of Old Nile"' (590). The grandeur and excess of the stage filters through to the actress's home, along with the decorative beauty of costume that is transferred to interior decoration.

Unsurprisingly, discussions of fashion in the *Sketch*'s ladies' pages reported on the clothing that these and other celebrity

Figure 5.3 'Our Ladies Pages'. *Sketch* 16 January 1895: 590.

women wore on stage or in daily life. Illustrations of Terry, Lena Ashwell and Genevieve Ward in their costumes for 'King Arthur' at the Lyceum (Fig. 5.3), for example, connect stage costume with everyday fashions, with particular items of costume, such as the Olivia cap inspiring a trend in women's hats, as I will discuss later in this chapter ('Our Ladies' Pages' 1895, 590). In 'A Chat with Sarah Bernhardt', she is pictured in photographs in costume for performance as 'La Tosca' and in her off-stage persona wearing a fur coat (458). Part of the work that the female stage celebrity would come to bear was appearing glamorous, trendsetting or excessive in her dress off the stage, maintaining her beauty and spectacle in daily life. In 1894, Ellen Terry was reported to be 'the centre of attraction' at a party at which she wore a white brocade gown with a deep yellow design, a skirt trimmed with pearls, rubies, diamonds, and 'red-velvet geraniums, the same flowers nestling in the fluffy masses of her fair hair" ('Our Ladies' Pages' 1894, 610). The adornments and grooming associated with the performance move with the beautiful celebrity woman into the public sphere and provide a model for other women to emulate. These connections, forged through profiles, theatre news, gossip, ladies' and fashion pages in magazines such as the *Sketch* as well as women's magazines, supported a new type of advertising endorsement.

The Celebrity as Beauty Icon   143

Reporting on actresses' costumes and personal lives was not only confined to high society journals like the *Sketch*, but was becoming integral to women's magazines fashionable content. By the 1870s, affordable fashion journals emerged that replaced expensive fashion plates with a more practical focus on dressmaking through the inclusion of clothing illustrations and patterns (Aindow 44). Rosy Aindow suggests that these magazines, such as *Myra's Journal of Dress and Fashion*, presented 'fashion in a cheap and readily available manner for the first time' (44). *Myra's Journal* also included coverage of theatrical toilettes, with Sarah Bernhardt's Paris costumes, and those of other French actresses, subject to description and evaluation ('Theatrical Toilettes' 329). Opera singer Marie Roze appeared on the cover of the 1 June 1891 issue, being the subject of a poem in honour of her beauty and voice

MADAME MARIE ROZE.

Figure 5.4 Frederick Dolman. 'Madame Marie Roze at Home'. *Myra's Journal of Dress and Fashion* 1 June 1891: 1.

and an interview (Fig. 5.4). Roze casts a 'double spell' with her singing, combined with her 'radiant eyes' and 'dainty chin where dimples play' (Dolman 1). Interviewer Frederick Dolman asks Roze about her opera performances, but also offers up assessments of her appearance, clothing and home: her 'dinner dress of rich red plush', her house near Regent's Park that conveys 'English exclusiveness', and her maintenance of her French identity 'from the tresses of her raven hair, sparkling with diamonds, to the tips of her pearly white, richly bejewelled fingers' (1). Whether society magazine or middle-class publication like *Myra's Journal of Dress and Fashion*, the life of the female celebrity and the details of her dress, jewellery and hair provided inspiration for women reader's own appearance.

In 'Society' from 1888, *Myra's Journal* refers to both Adelina Patti and Lillie Langtry's intended memoirs and discusses a far-fetched account of Langtry's beauty secret for living in the dry climate of the United States. The 'Lily', the article proclaims, learned of the 'mystic virtue' of a treatment used by Persian women, in which she reclines on a sofa with her face 'covered with thin strips of uncooked veal' (462). While the article acknowledges the distasteful aspect of the purported remedy, the author also appreciates that the declaration of such a method by a celebrity could encourage emulation by readers: 'It is also possible that the price of veal may go up in response to the extraordinary demand' ('Society' 462). Another instance of celebrity beauty treatments was published almost ten years earlier in December 1879 under the title of 'Health and Personal Attention' and includes a recipe for a home-made egg-white and alum paste for treating loose skin and wrinkle prevention purportedly used by late actress and opera singer Madame Vestris (283). Another deceased female celebrity, Lola Montez, whose *The Arts of Beauty* (1858) I discussed in Chapter 2, figures in this article with the reproduction of her recipe for increasing the suppleness of dancer's limbs; it would have had a striking smell with eight ounces of deer or stag fat and musk among the ingredients. These various examples from two very different magazines evidence an increasing turn towards the female stage performer for models of emulation when it came to clothing, beauty regimens and styling of the self and the home from the 1880s in particular. In the following section I examine how the increasing depiction of female celebrity bodies in periodicals became, as Easley terms it, 'the focus of heightened, if ephemeral, consumer interest' (138) through magazine advertising.

Advertising, celebrity endorsement and shifting authority

Though advertising was relatively common in women's magazines, as Margaret Beetham and Kay Boardman note, it was not until the 1880s that advertisements began to occupy a greater proportion of each issue and to break out from endpapers and supplements to be interspersed with editorial content (5). This change was significant because it situated advertising alongside other content, contributing to mutually reinforcing ideas about celebrity, beauty and consumer culture. Advertising also became more visually spectacular in the late Victorian period, with increasing depictions of products and illustrations of idealised women serving as models to entice the reader to purchase a growing number of brand-name beauty products. Periodical advertising for health and beauty products had typically called on the authority of medical practitioners, or the seal of approval provided by royalty. From the 1880s, the birth of the beautiful female celebrity fostered a new type of authority that largely subsumed these other forms of endorsement. The promotion of the celebrity stage performer as the model of the feminine ideal – and, in turn, her promotion of beauty and hygiene products – contributed to cumulative acceptance of some measure of cosmetic usage.

Occasionally celebrity endorsements or testimonials emerged for products for which an individual may have had expertise. In the realm of emerging celebrity relating to society and the stage, opera stars, for example, might endorse products relating to the voice, such as Adelina Patti's illustration holding the 'Ammoniaphone' and accompanying testimonial in *Myra's Journal of Dress and Fashion* in 1887 (45). For other products, stage performers were presented as putting products through their most extreme paces, confirming their efficacy for ordinary women's use. Frizzetta curling fluid promised to keep hair curly in the heat and damp. Singer Constance Sims Reeves's testimonial in a *Myra's Journal of Dress and Fashion* advertisement advised that she had 'given it severe trials in the theatre and also in the rain and found it to be a marvellous invention, retaining all its efficacy, despite every drawback' (584). With the assurance of the stage performer, the woman reader could be assured that her hair would retain its shape in the ballroom, a space that would not put the hair through the 'severe trials' of the stage (584).

Most commonly, celebrity endorsements relied on the qualifications of beauty and fame. Connections between the magazine editorial and its advertising cumulatively granted the female celebrity beauty 'authority', or the impression of a status worthy of emulation. Advertisements for clothing in the 1880s, for example, described actresses and singers as 'leaders of fashion' (Nonpareil Velveteen 607). The infiltration – and eventual overtaking – of medical endorsements by celebrity testimonials is evident in an advertisement for Ivorine dentrifrice and complexion cream, for example, which includes a combination of supportive statements from the *Lancet,* a skin specialist and actress Ellen Terry (Ivorine Complexion Cream n.p.). The significance of the developing relationship between editorial content and advertising is evident in a full-page advertisement in the *Sketch* from 28 November 1894 (Fig. 5.5). In its design, it resembles a typical magazine article, with its heading 'The Theatrical Season in London' disguising the true focus on Géraudel's Pastilles, which were frequently advertised in the magazine. The paragraph of editorial refers to 'some of the favourite artistes appearing at the present time, or who will shortly appear, on the boards of our principal lyric and dramatic stages' ('The Theatrical Season' 243), all of whom are illustrated below with their signatures and testimonials about the product.[4] The images of each of the six women opera singers and actresses depict them in elaborate clothing, hair and jewellery, as if ready for a stage performance, and highlighting their striking appearances. The absences of any depiction of the product and even the product name from the heading leaves it to the images of the women themselves to invite attention and the interest in reading about stage performers' lives that the magazine cultivates in each issue. This allowed for the future update of such a piece with new endorsements, as in the case of a similar pastilles advertisement that was published one year prior including other performers such as Marie Roze (Géraudel's Pastilles 328).

Many advertisements found in the dedicated advertising pages in magazines furthered the connections that were being forged in the periodical press between beauty and fame, wealth, and celebrity, as is evident in the ads discussed in the following section. These associations were made possible by changes to beauty and clothing advertisements that saw them increase in size and level of illustration. Loeb notes that by the 1890s fashion ads looked more like fashion plates and were 'among the most visually arresting'

THE THEATRICAL SEASON IN LONDON.

At a time when the theatrical season is in full swing it may be interesting to reproduce the portraits of some of the favourite artistes appearing at the present time, or who will shortly appear, on the boards of our principal lyric and dramatic stages. Among others may be mentioned Madame Albani, whose great talent is daily more and more appreciated at the important concerts; Madame Melba, the London favourite, who holds out the hope of a speedy return; Madame Sigrid Arnoldson, the popular prima donna of the Covent Garden Opera; Madame Sarah Bernhardt, whose new piece, "Gismonda," by Victorien Sardou, is very shortly to be produced in this country; Miss Florence St. John, now appearing so successfully in "Mirette," at the Savoy; Mrs. Langtry, the "Jersey Lily"; Mademoiselle Yvette Guilbert, whose ever-increasing success in Paris affords hope of a not far-distant visit to London. A not uninteresting subject at the commencement of this winter season is to gather the ideas and the advice of these famous artistes as to the means they employ to preserve their voice and to prevent colds, so easily caught at the theatre, especially behind the scenes. With this object in view M. Géraudel, the inventor of the celebrated pastilles which bear his name, has been invited to make known the opinion of these artistes, and here, together with their portraits and signatures, are extracts from some of the letters which have been sent to him. These pastilles, as everyone knows, can be had of all chemists.

I find your Pastilles excellent for the throat. I very often use them when I am hoarse, and they do me a great deal of good.
Yours faithfully,

I have been using Géraudel's Pastilles for some time, and can testify to their being most efficacious for cough or irritation of the throat. There is no doubt of their being of great service to singers.
I am, yours very faithfully,
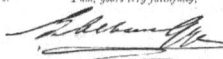

The cold weather is upon us, so be kind enough to send me a further supply of Géraudel's Pastilles.— Compliments.
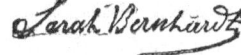

My dear Sir,—At one time it was a trouble to me to sing one or two songs, now I am happy to tell you that, thanks to your Pastilles, my voice is so much strengthened that I can sing eight or ten without feeling any fatigue. You have my permission to publish this.

I have pleasure in informing you that I have tried your Pastilles with great success, and although suffering from a very bad cold, they gave me such relief that I was enabled to continue my performance without interruption. I can thoroughly recommend them for strengthening and clearing the voice.
Yours very truly,

Your Pastilles for the throat and voice have been tried by me, and I am happy to testify to their beneficial results.
Yours faithfully,

Figure 5.5 Géraudel's Pastilles advertisement. *Sketch* 28 November 1894: 243.

(28). The emergence of brand-name competition in clothing and increasingly in beauty products from the 1880s created the need to foster brand identity and distinguish a particular cream from its competitors. Endorsements by female celebrities, which often included illustrations or photographs of these women, were a favoured method for capturing the reader's eye and generating trust in the efficacy of a brand's products. Wakelee's Camelline, for instance, was a liquid preparation for 'softening and beautifying the complexion', according to the bottle. It was sold and advertised in both Britain and the United States, and illustrations of actresses and opera singers who endorsed the product were regularly featured in these ads. An 1895 advertisement from the *Sketch* includes images of and endorsements from Ellen Terry, Adelina Patti, Mrs Kendal and Mme Jane Hading. While the text mentions the recommendation of 'the most eminent physicians in the medical profession', their anonymously merged voice is subordinate to the individualised voices of '[t]he most distinguished ladies in the dramatic profession' (Camelline, *Sketch* 99). The advertisement begins with a line from the nursey rhyme 'Where are you Going my Pretty Maid': '"My face is my fortune, Sir", she said.' This line speaks to the importance of beauty for the female stage performer/celebrity, but also opens up the possibility that the woman reader can buy products that will transform her own face.

As the next section of this chapter explores, most of the products endorsed by female celebrities were of the restorative or natural kind that invited less critique. However, while the use of coloured cosmetics was subject to an array of prohibitions and judgements, and few advertisements in women's magazines made reference to them, the idealisation of the celebrity stage performer initiated some degree of acceptance for cosmetics application. *Myra's Journal of Dress and Fashion* gave advice to 'amateur actresses' on 'the gentle art of making-up' ('Tips for Amateur Actresses' 12). The number of amateur actresses reading the publication were surely minimal, and the premise perhaps provided a neat camouflage for advice to women about the application of make-up. Readers are advised to keep rouge 'well up on the cheek-bones' to lend sparkle to the eyes and add small touches under the brows and on the chin; they are also instructed in how to line the lower lashes with pencil and apply 'black cosmetic' to the lashes themselves ('Tips for Amateur Actresses' 12). While the author briefly mentions the application of 'an immense amount of blue greasepaint on the eye lids' as a technique for highlighting the eyes, the emphasis is on maximum effect from minimal intervention ('the gentle art'). The article proposes a method for conforming with expectations of natural beauty while crossing the once-firm line that prohibited the use of coloured cosmetics, signalling the wider embrace of less controversial beauty techniques and products. The advertising pages of women's magazines and society journals were the most visible location for this transformation, as places where the celebrity identities forged in the magazines' editorial content were put into the service of establishing new norms of hygiene and appearance.

With the growth in branding, celebrity was mobilised in the naming of particular products and styles of clothing. Lori Ann Loeb notes that competition emerged between brand names goods between 1880 and the turn of the century in the area of clothing, with corsets particularly marketed by name (32). While Sarah Bernhardt loaned her name to face powder, Lillie Langtry became associated with a variety of products and even a style of hat. The 'Langtry' invisible hair curler produced by J. S. Foot & Son was advertised in *Myra's Journal of Dress and Fashion* in 1884 as having been 'Adopted by the Queen of Fashion, and acknowledged by all to be the best' (Langtry Invisible Hair Curler 48). These associations were usually formally evident through the presence of testimonials and endorsements from the celebrity women in question. However, in the same way as a celebrity's hairstyle or item of clothing might today become popularised through being associated with them and the world of glamour and style, so too did Victorian stage actresses inspire numerous products named in their honour. Rimmel, for example, marketed a new perfume, 'the "Jersey Lily"' in 1886, dedicated to Langtry and sold along with her autograph and photograph (Rimmel's Fashionable Season Novelties n.p.). Langtry's biographer observes that 'Langtry accessories were all the rage. The Langtry bonnet, the Langtry shawl, the Langtry knot, even a mysterious article called the Langtry dress-improver, were everywhere on sale. Where Lillie went the world of fashion followed' (Beatty 100). Advertisements in *Myra's Journal* from the late 1870s to early 1880s included those of Shetland lace shawls 'as supplied to Mrs. Langtry and many of the nobility', as well as 'Dyer's Registered Silver "Langtry" Necklette' (Shanks, Matheson and Semple 625; Dyer's London Watches n.p.). An advertisement for Hilder and Godbold in *Myra's Journal*

 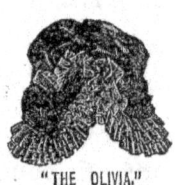

Figure 5.6 Hilder and Godbold advertisement. *Myra's Journal of Dress and Fashion*. 1 July 1879: n.p.

in 1879 depicted 'The Langtry' French cap 'composed of India Muslin, and trimmed with the New Bretonne Lace, in White, Pink, and Pale Blue' (Fig. 5.6) (n.p.) The same advertisement features the eighteenth-century styled, ruffled 'Olivia Cap' popularised by Ellen Terry in the play *Olivia* (1879), which was based on the *The Vicar of Wakefield*. Terry later commented on the way that the Olivia cap 'shared public favour with the Langtry bonnet' in a moment in which the public was '"Olivia" mad' (14). The potential movement of items of stage costume into women's wardrobes is alluded to in an article on theatrical toilettes in *Myra's Journal of Dress and Fashion*, in which the author fears that 'the small serpent brought into vogue by the play of *Cleopatra*, in which Sarah Bernhardt is now acting', though not 'graceful . . . is likely to become fashionable' ('Theatrical Toilettes' 329).

Individual celebrities might become closely associated with a particular product through repeated endorsement, though many major brands, such as Pears' Soap, included multiple celebrity endorsements in each advertisement, and the most popular actresses endorsed multiple brands simultaneously. Adelina Patti, for example, provided endorsements for numerous magazine advertisements for Aspinall's Neigeline skin lotion throughout 1894 and 1895 (Fig. 5.7). Yet she also provided endorsements for other products in this period including Odontobaph, Géraudel's Pastilles, Pears' Soap and Crème Simon – the latter two brands are still sold today. The cumulative power of particular endorsements and advertisements was fostered by the same advertisements being published across multiple magazines. A Géraudel's Pastilles advertisement including endorsements from Adelina Patti, Marie Roze,

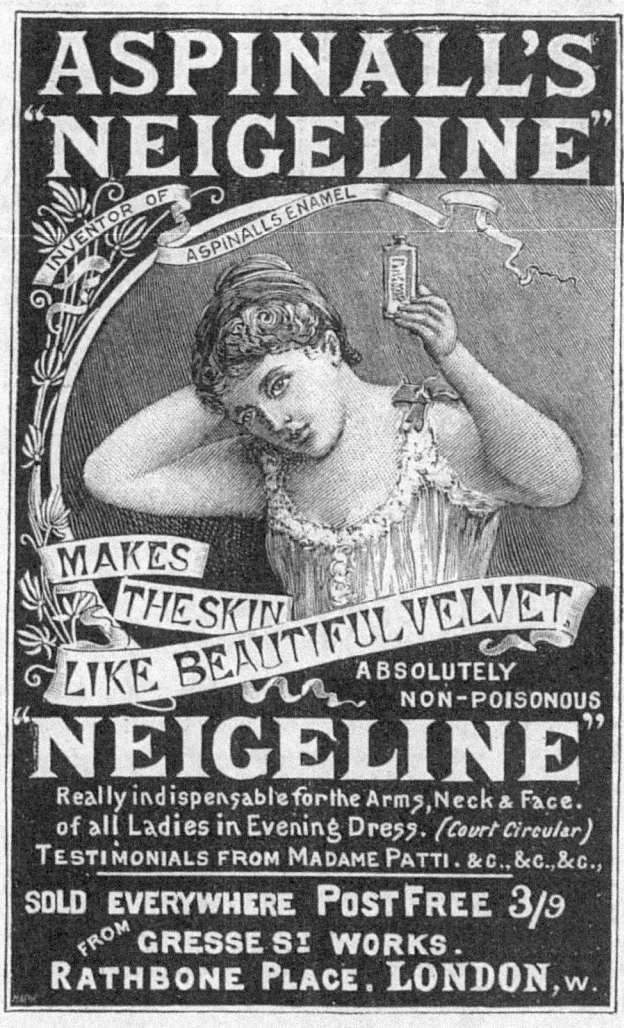

Figure 5.7 Neigeline advertisement. *Sketch* 10 October 1894: 611.

Nellie Melba and Sigrid Arnoldson among others, appeared in both the *Sketch* and *Myra's Journal of Dress and Fashion* in 1893, for instance. The scope of this celebrity was international, as these names of Italian, French, Australian and Swedish singers just noted suggests. An 1893 advertisement for Géraudel's Pastilles used the word celebrity in yoking together the testimonials of Florence St John and Lillie Langtry, with mentions of the endorsement of Roze, Bernhardt, and others: 'Our English celebrities join their fellow artistes of the Continent in the chorus of praise' (Géraudel's Pastilles n.p). As the world of the stage was internationalised, so too was the early celebrity and the early culture of celebrity beauty endorsements. In Chapter 6, I examine how the circulation of beauty culture worked in transatlantic print culture, but first, in the following section, the celebrity that surrounded the purveyors of cosmeticians or beauty culturists themselves is discussed to show how the success of brand-name beauty products relied on a similar cultivation of celebrity in their marketing.

Building beauty brands: Eugène Rimmel and Mrs Pomeroy

As stage performers developed personae that made them the subject of magazine articles about their home lives and appearance, contributing to their capacity to endorse products in advertising, so too did cosmetics brands become known by name, often that of their founder. The cosmeticians who attached their names to their salons and products not only had to promote their brand, but also needed to ensure that their name and reputation were never tarnished. Advertisements by Eugène Rimmel in the 1880s show the developing connection between the identity of the cosmetician and trust in both the brand and respectability of its products. While, as I go on to discuss in this section, from the 1890s, Madame Pomeroy adopted various methods of circulating her own image and establishing trust in her brand and salon treatments.

Eugène Rimmel was an integral figure in the shift from women making their own toilet items; he helped to demonstrate that technological developments and the commercial cosmetics industry in London 'trumped the material resources and technologies available to women's self-production' (J. Clark 121). Rimmel traded on his status as a perfumer to the Princess of Wales and was one of a number of cosmeticians who came to market a variety of

Rimmel's Specialities for the Complexion.

RIMMEL'S BLANC MARIMON, a new and perfectly innocuous white, equally suitable for the stage or the drawing-room. Madlle. Marimon, for whom it was at first prepared, writes, "It produces a marvellous effect, and I find it besides cooling and softening," Price 2s. 6d. per bottle. (Cannot be sent by post.)
RIMMEL'S HEBE BLOOM, a splendid and harmless rouge, 1s. per packet, by post for 13 stps. PERLINE, a pure white, same price.
RIMMEL'S EYE-BROW PENCILS, black, brown, or blonde, 1s., by post for 13 stamps.
RIMMEL'S EGYPTIAN KOHL, to increase the brilliancy of the eyes. 3s. 6d., by post for 43 stamps.
RIMMEL'S VELVETINE, a refined, adherent, imperceptible Toilet Powder (Blanc, Blanc-rosé, or Rachel), 1s. 6d., with puff, 2s. 6d.
RIMMEL'S NEW TRANSPARENT COAL-TAR SOAP unites the purifying action of tar to the emollient properties of transparent soap. 6d. per cake.
RIMMEL'S NEW PERFUMES.—Emma Bouquet, Stéphanie Bouquet, Sarah Bernhardt Bouquet, 2s. 6d. per bottle; the three in a neat box, 7s.
RIMMEL'S TILIA PERFUMERY, a new set of Toilet articles delightfully scented with the flowers of the Lime Tree (Tilia Europea.)

EUGENE RIMMEL,
Perfumer by appointment to H.R.H. the Princess of Wales,
96, Strand; 128, Regent Street; and 24, Cornhill, London. 76, King's Road, Brighton.
17, Boulevard des Italiens, Paris.

Figure 5.8 Rimmel's Specialties for the Complexion advertisement. *Myra's Journal of Dress and Fashion* 1 July 1880: 222.

cosmetics, including coloured cosmetics, through frequent advertising in women's magazines. In the advertisement shown in Figure 5.8 each of the eight product names is prefaced by Rimmel's name, including a rouge, eyebrow pencils, Egyptian kohl, Velvetine toilet powder (in three shades, including Rachel – named for the scandalous cosmetician), and bottles of Blanc Marimon, 'a new and perfectly innocuous white, equally suitable for the stage or the drawing-room' (Rimmel's Specialties for the Complexion 222). Marie Marimon, a French opera singer, provides a written endorsement of the product's efficacy, and the association is readily made between celebrity ('the stage') and women's performance of beauty in settings where she wishes to impress.

In her important history of cosmetics manufacture and marketing, Jessica P. Clark notes that some beauty culturists and cosmeticians, such as American-born Mrs Pomeroy (Jeanette Scalé) mobilised celebrity by 'situating themselves as the subject of emulation while offering unprecedented degrees of intimacy and connection' (151). Pomeroy's seven physical locations, in London's Bond Street, Liverpool, Birmingham, Glasgow, Dublin, Sheffield

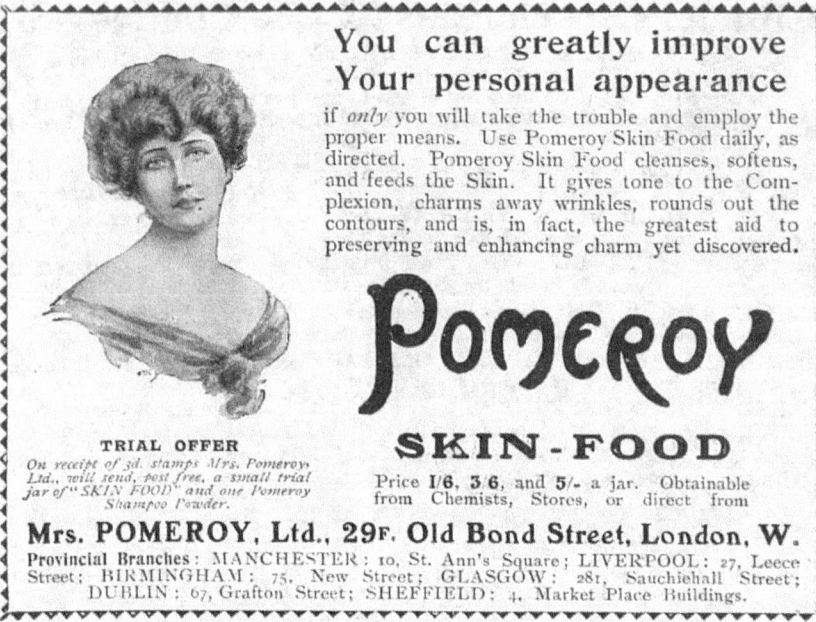

Figure 5.9 Pomeroy Skin Food advertisement. *Sketch* 12 January 1910: vi.

and Manchester, enabled in-person treatments, complementing a range of products that any woman could apply at home. Her advertisements appeared regularly in the *Sketch* and other publications in the early 1900s, and Pomeroy's image was often featured (Fig. 5.9). These included conventional ads promoting services available at her salon (such as electrolysis) and products that would need to be purchased on a regular basis to attain and retain beauty, such as jars of Pomeroy Skin Food, the name of which reconfigures the beauty cream as a nutrient rather than a cosmetic. The frequency of her advertisements may have played a role in her treatments also being detailed in the magazine's ladies' pages, in addition to softening attitudes to beauty treatments. The *Sketch*, in which her advertisements usually appeared on at least a monthly basis, enthusiastically endorses Madame Pomeroy's methods as luxurious, efficacious and natural, describing Pomeroy herself as playing the part of 'Nature's sweet restorer' ('Our Ladies' Pages. Abroad and at Home' 503). The treatments are described in hallowed terms that frame them in terms of 'art' and labour, and in uncovering the beautiful skin that lies below the damaged exterior:

an attendant ministering angel in the person of a white-aproned, soft-voiced, gentle-fingered girl, who kneads, steams, soothes, electrolises the recalcitrant cuticle until wrinkles and roughness are coaxed away and replace by the softness and bloom which Nature, doubtless, intends for each one of us, but that so often get lost *en route*. ('Our Ladies' Pages. Abroad and at Home' 503)

Pomeroy's on-site chemist enables the medicalisation of her treatments as 'restorative', returning women's skin to its ideal state. The debutante 'sighing for rose-petalled complexion' and the woman with 'the wrinkled, crow-footed remainder of a thousand-and-one late nights' can both transform their skin to be as nature intended: soft and blooming (503). The recourse to rhetoric of restoration, art and health is integral to the establishment of Pomeroy's techniques and products as acceptable and the Pomeroy brand as trustworthy. Intriguingly, Pomeroy's celebrity supersedes that of the actress celebrity in her advertising, particularly through contrast of her preparations with the deleterious treatments they purportedly use; for instance, she claims that many actresses use 'Lanoline', which promotes the growth of facial hair, a clearly undesirable consequence given Pomeroy's electrolysis service ('Our Ladies' Pages. Abroad and at Home' 503).

Pomeroy also fostered further connection and exchange with readers that heightened the importance of her persona as a knowledgeable and trusted figure. From the late 1890s, her advertisements often promoted the booklet 'Beauty Rules', which would be posted to the reader at no cost and promised to 'enable every Woman at a small cost to carry out her Treatment at Home in any part of the World' ('Mrs Pomeroy's Hygienic Treatment' vii). The relationship she sought to develop with women was not necessarily one way, with some Pomeroy advertisements inviting readers to consult Mrs Pomeroy for advice about their own personal flaws. A 'Free Offer to Readers of "The Sketch"' includes a series of checkboxes to enable readers to mark off the blemishes, hair woes and skin defects from which they suffer. In return readers will receive a response from Mrs Pomeroy about the optimal form of 'treatment': 'For superfluous hairs you will receive particulars of the only real cure for this annoying disfigurement, as also for warts, prominent veins, or birthmarks' (viii). This invitation to magazine readers to correspond is an example of how Pomeroy cultivated what Clark calls a 'mode of public intimacy' through her advertisements that 'encouraged a demure feminine sociability, marketing a respectable space for women to exchange bodily secrets' (151).

Pomeroy also sought to build the recognition of her brand into the twentieth century through other methods of public engagement in the periodical press. A large 1914 advertisement in the *Sketch* drew attention to an 'Independent Investigation' conducted by *Truth* into the treatments available at Pomeroy Beauty Salons, and the editor's subsequent endorsement ('"Truth" and Beauty Culture' x). *Truth* practised investigative journalism, looking 'to uncover irregularities or illegalities that might be present' in various social institutions including, for instance, building societies (Weber 41). However, the paper also included society journalism and the discussion of personalities (Weber 39). The use of one magazine's scrutiny to support advertisements in other periodicals shows the way in which beauty brands actively engaged with print culture to build and promote a trusted name. In addition, it also alludes to the continued existence of occasional unscrupulous operators, such as the self-promoting American beauty culturalist Anna Ruppert, who figures in the following chapter. Nevertheless, the use of various forms of print – including the beauty manual, advertisement and editorial – by beauty culturalists and cosmetics manufacturers helped to build recognisable brand names. The work of these men and women, in turn, as Clark suggests, played a significant part in instilling the belief that beauty could be made and in 'legitimating the pursuit of beauty as a worthy task of self-improvement and feminine duty' (143).

Conclusion

The growth of female celebrities as icons of beauty and style in turn fostered their relationship to beauty products in magazine endorsements. The celebrity editorial content of magazines such as the *Sketch* was locked in mutually reinforcing relationship with its beauty advertising. Insight into the actresses' home life and personal style increased the power of the celebrity endorsements found in magazine advertisements. However, this is not to suggest that the scepticism surrounding cosmetic usage and other beauty and dress practices was entirely eliminated in print culture in the latter decades of the nineteenth century. Exhortations towards natural appearance and minimal usage of artificial aids and products continued to be found in occasional editorial content. 'The Ladies' Gallery' column in *Myra's Journal of Dress and Fashion* in March 1890, for example, made reference to celebrity women to encourage women to eschew corsets: 'It is certain that no healthy girl or woman requires stays if she is content to let nature alone, and the example of such comely ladies as Mrs. Brown Potter, Miss Ellen Terry, Mrs. Bernard-Beere, and Miss Mary Anderson, proves that those who do so, choose the better way' (10). The 'unnatural waist' is linked with ill health and pain, especially for fashion conscious young women, and the celebrity is used as an example of the preferability of the 'natural'.

Nevertheless, the periodical press was thoroughly enmeshed with the developing beauty industry by the turn of the century, and such overt cautions became less common and less prominent. This shift was not only driven by the evolution of brand-name beauty advertising, and changing attitudes towards the beauty regimen, but also because the women celebrities who became pivotal to the editorial content of women's and society magazines were idols of beauty culture and consumption. The beautiful celebrity's image was reproduced on a mass scale in illustrations, but also increasingly in photographs that offered models of ideal appearance that could be emulated as both the reader and the celebrity aged. The reader who did not match up to these images when she looked into the glass now could attempt to do so through following trends in hair, style and maintenance of the skin and body. Easley's identification of '[t]he desire to gaze and be gazed upon' as a specific feature of magazine celebrity profiles can be extended to the readers of women's periodicals more generally (149).

The images of beauty to be consumed in women's magazines are often described as sites of fantasy, and the greatest source of this fantasy in the late nineteenth century was the female celebrity who yoked together the fame of the stage, with the glamour of her personal and domestic life, and the repeated visibility of her image. Most importantly, the widespread acceptance and even valorisation of these women in the periodical press aided in the cultural embrace of beauty products and the daily beauty regimen, as they endorsed various products and reported on their own beauty practices. In addition, beauty culturists themselves, such as Eugène Rimmel and Mrs Pomeroy, became trusted figures and well known through their widespread advertising, constituting a marked comparison with earlier figures with scandalous reputations such as

Madame Rachel and comparatively faceless brands that sold products of dubious origin and safety. These changes make possible a shift to an understanding, and practice, of female beauty that more closely resembles the norms of the international beauty industry from the twentieth century to the present.

Notes

1. In November 1899, the *Oakland Tribune* also reported on 'La Belle El Derido', declaring that the '[n]ew stage beauty is all the rage in France' (4). As in reports on other actresses in the British press, this actress is declared to be more beautiful off the stage as '[h]er clear skin and rich complexion seem to lose much in the false lights' ('La Belle El Derido' 4).
2. Ellen Terry similarly suggested that Langtry was 'not a showy beauty', given that her hair colour and skin were natural, and that she displayed less of her neck and arms than 'was the vogue, yet they outshone all other necks and arms through their own perfection' (14).
3. The *Queen* also included exoticised portraits of anonymous women of various ethnic types on its covers such as 'An Iberian Beauty' (1 October 1892), and 'An Eastern Beauty' (21 May 1892), who had a veil pulled across the lower half of her face. These images helped to reinforce that the beautiful women who featured occupied another realm, whether through celebrity or geographically.
4. The women pictured are Emma Albani, Nellie Melba, Sigrid Arnoldson 'the popular prima donna of the Covent Garden Opera', Sarah Bernhardt, Florence St. John, Mrs Langtry the 'Jersey Lily', and Madame Yvette Guilbert ('The Theatrical Season' 243).

6

Embracing the Beauty Regimen in British and American Women's Magazines

A brief text-based advertisement for the skin lotion Rowland's Kalydor in *Myra's Journal of Dress and Fashion* in 1880 begins with two words in capital letters: 'WOMAN'S RIGHTS' (198). It goes on to propose that 'One of the chief rights of woman is to look as beautiful as she can, and to use all legitimate means to this end.' While the advertisement suggests that 'art has seconded nature's efforts by supplying such an elegant preparation as ROWLAND'S KALYDOR' (198), there were distinct limits to the acceptable use of beauty products and procedures. This reference to art supporting nature did not mean a broad acceptance of cosmetics as we know them today, specifically in relation to 'make-up' such as lipstick, eyeshadow and mascara. As the previous chapter argued, the birth of the stage celebrity and the publicity that surrounded the images and lives of these women played a critical role in transforming beauty norms and practices. Kathy Peiss proposes that in the American context, photographic and stage techniques surrounding make-up and posing 'introduced external and standardized models of beauty that challenged the "natural" ideal' (49). The lingering power of the natural ideal, combined with the growing abundance of brand-name products and visual models of beautiful women for emulation, required a decades-long process of negotiation in the pages of women's magazines.

Margaret Beetham has likened women's magazines to corsets in that each can serve as an 'instrument of control and source of pleasure' ('Natural' 163). This sense of competing ideologies – between demarcating the bounds of acceptable femininity and enabling a range of fantasies – is especially visible in women's fashion magazines in the late nineteenth century. Such a tension between oppression and emancipation, as Elizabeth Carolyn Miller puts it, can also be extended to beauty consumerism in the late nineteenth century (318). For Miller, femininity in the Victorian period became increasingly tied to 'self-imposed regimens of healthy, beauty, fashion, and appearance', shifting women's status as the property of individual men to that of 'social property, in need of constant maintenance to meet the new cultural standards of femininity' (318). This chapter focuses on the embrace of these new beauty standards in two British women's magazines, the *Queen* (1861–1958) and *Woman* (1890–1912), and the American women's magazine the *Delineator* (1873–1937, from the 1890s to the first decade of the twentieth century, exploring the complicated ways in which commercial beauty products and methods came to occupy more advertising space and how related daily tasks to maintain the face and body were incorporated within editorial content and advice columns. It considers the promotion and adoption of the daily beauty regimen – a phenomenon that signals the acceptance, and necessity of, certain kinds of beauty practices and products – within both British and American women's magazines. Despite the British focus in this monograph, the consideration of an American magazine is important in order to examine the remarkably similar ideas about beauty and beauty culture evident on both sides of the Atlantic at the turn of the twentieth century. In previous chapters, I have drawn from articles and advertising in girls' and women's magazines, situating them alongside examples from fiction and beauty manuals in order to make broader arguments about cultural norms surrounding beauty with respect to health, artifice, age and celebrity. However, this chapter concentrates on three magazines in their entirety in order to demonstrate how the beauty regimen was normalised on a transatlantic basis through women's periodicals.

In the late nineteenth century, women's magazines transformed substantially: first, because there was a 'great increase' (Fraser et al. 171) in the number of magazines published; and second, because of the increased prominence and visual appeal of the advertisements they contained. Though advertising was relatively common in women's magazines, as Beetham and Kay Boardman note, it was not until the 1880s that advertisements began to occupy a greater proportion of each issue and to break out from endpapers and supplements to be interspersed with editorial content (5). The *Queen*, for example, which is one of the two British periodicals considered in this chapter, gave up half of its pages to advertising by the mid-1880s. Advertising also became more visually spectacular in the late-Victorian period, with increasing depictions of products and illustrations of idealised women serving as models to entice the reader to purchase a growing number of brand-name beauty products.

Hilary Fraser, Stephanie Green and Judith Johnston point out that women's magazines hosted 'important debates about class and gender', but that these 'were often displaced into discussions relating to the apparently trivial and ephemeral world of fashion' (1). In the late-Victorian period, the work of femininity, as it was constructed in many illustrated women's magazines, became increasingly tied to knowledge about, purchase and correct usage of a variety of consumer goods that might be broadly termed beauty products. Nevertheless, women's fashion magazines were infused with contradictory impulses. In their editorial content, women's magazines often maintained traditional views about the subjects of beauty, cosmetics and women's dress, frequently advocating 'natural' beauty and home-made cosmetics, yet at the same time these magazines relied upon promotion of an extensive variety of beauty commodities and introduced the notion of the beauty regimen. This chapter first explores two very different illustrated women's magazines, the *Queen* and *Woman*, and the ways in which the practical beauty advice provided in their editorial content largely conforms with ideas about the attainment of beauty in the advertisements contained within them. It focuses on period of the 1890s to enable contemporaneous comparison of the two periodicals and because the 1890s saw a rapid growth in the quantity and spectacle of advertising in British women's magazines. This section of the chapter aims to demonstrate how beauty ideologies remained consistent across these publications aimed at distinct audiences, showing that prescriptions and limits relating to women's beauty largely transcended class differences. The centrality of advertising to women's magazines in the 1890s was integral to transformations in the way women consumed beauty products and to the reframing of their purchase and use within pre-existing ideals relating to health and appearance.

Women's magazines and changing patterns of consumption

The growth of women's magazines in the second half of the nineteenth century had a profound and practical impact on how goods were purchased and by sparking the initial desire to buy them. Rachel Bowlby describes the corresponding transformation in consumer patterns, in which goods no longer came to buyers but 'it is the buyers who have taken themselves to the products' (1). Women's magazines played a critical role in this process of looking upon consumer goods relating to the home, clothing and beauty in a way that did not require a special visit to a store, and which could be repeatedly revisited on the page. Much as department stores became a 'fantasy world of escape from dull domesticity', the fashion magazine transformed 'merchandise into a spectacle' (Bowlby 4, 6). Beauty products, which were not as readily browsed in stores given that creams and elixirs were encased in glass jars and tins, were ideally suited to display in advertising through images of what girls and young women could become if they used them.

Young women's bodies were imbricated in creating the spectacle associated with merchandise, as symbols of consumption and objects of desire for the reader. Thomas Richards suggests that the initial transformation of the female body 'into a specific site of advertised spectacle' took place in patent medicine advertising (206). In addition, fashion plates were already in use throughout the century in quality women's magazines, utilising beautiful colour illustrations of women to sell both a physical product in the form of patterns that readers could purchase by mail and a particular image of femininity. Crucially, in the final decades of the century, these discrete uses of women as image and commodity became universalised in women's magazines: women's bodies and faces infused both descriptions and depictions of idealised femininity, and advertisements came to sell these idealised selves as much as the products that sponsored them. As I discussed in the previous chapter, one form of ideal female self that rose to prominence in women's magazines was the celebrity, who served as a model of idealised beauty, especially in demarcating how to retain youthful looks into middle age. This chapter argues that women's magazines construct a fluid dialogue between editorial and advertising in the commodification and construction of the self in response to these idealised femininities.

As consumer objects, cosmetics and other beauty products worked differently to other goods in that they require an ongoing – even lifelong – pattern of consumption. In 1899, in *The Theory of the Leisure Class*, Thorstein Veblen proposed that the motivation to own consumer objects is 'emulation' (25). When 'popular esteem' is based on the ownership of property 'it becomes also a requisite to that complacency which we call self-respect' (31). Here Veblen refers to the need to accumulate as many goods as others of a person's same social class and the satisfaction inherent in possessing more items than others. In addition, material goods, once obtained, had a degree of permanence (financial ruin notwithstanding) through which the self-respect that they conferred might be largely permanent. As the promise of beauty products was the almost immeasurable attainment or preservation of youthful features, the same equivalencies of accumulation or possession did not apply. Moreover, emulation of female beauty ideals required a continuous process of consumption and the maintenance of a beauty regimen. 'Complacency' was not an option when emulation required repeated consumption, and it is the ongoing work of beauty that magazine advertising sought to promote and editorial content to regulate.

Health and the beauty regimen

While I am arguing for a shift in acceptable beauty practices propelled by print culture and the growth of consumerism surrounding women's appearance, a wide range of late-Victorian publications for girls and women still did not generally advocate for the unlimited use of cosmetics. Instead, the key to true beauty was tied to the acquisition of health – a long-standing requirement, as I detailed in Chapter 1 – and a daily regimen of cleanliness. *Woman*'s beauty advice column is entitled 'Health and Appearance', showing the presumption of a close link between the two. The combination of health and cleanliness may superficially reproduce beauty expectations from mid-century; however, the subtle but important change lies in the way that *beauty products and regimens* are reframed as part of a quest for 'health', which avoided the negative connotations associated with potentially harmful cosmetics comprised of dangerous ingredients. Health rhetoric also became a means to disassociate the quest for beauty from undesirable personal characteristics such as vanity and being 'fast'. Indeed, *Woman*'s slogan, 'Forward! But not too fast', extrapolated from the specific idea of 'forward', or modern, fashion that avoided the pejorative meaning of 'fast' regarding women to its general approach to all topics.

The emphasis on health in the cultivation of beauty through the purchase of beauty products is present in advertising in both *Queen* and *Woman*. A Pears' Soap ad published in *Queen* in 1891 declares: 'Health is always beautiful. Other beauty there is none' ('Look in the Glass!' xxv). The implicit suggestion in this motto, which was reflected in advice manuals of the period, is that beauty without health – such as any attempt to obtain beauty by artifice – was an impossibility. An ad for Bovril beef tea from *Woman* in 1896 adds a further link to the causal chain to tie food consumption to beauty: 'Beauty depends upon health, and health depends largely on proper food' (Bovril 17).[1] The Pears ad is underpinned by a revised ideology of beauty as something that can be cultivated, imploring the reader not to tolerate skin faults that are 'directly within our control' ('Look in the Glass!' xxv). The text calls on the reader to look into a mirror because most people 'do not know how ugly' they are, placing responsibility on women to actively assess their faces for flaws (xxv). On contemplating their reflection in the glass, women must ask the following question: 'Can you see no use for a soap that purges the skin of pallor and pimples and oil, that softens and smooths it, brings out the rose and alabaster?' (xxv). Adopting a nutritious diet, regularly seeking out fresh air and exercise, taking baths, and keeping the face and body clean were all acceptable methods for the maintenance of health and therefore the production of beauty. The Pears ad calls on women to adopt a routine of cleansing the face with soap to suppress indicators of ill health like pallor and pimples and bring out idealised pale skin with a healthy blush – the promised result mimics that of powder and rouge, but without the lingering threads of transgression.

The beauty regimen that would merely allow a woman's inborn qualities to shine, or which would diminish their degradation through the ageing process, mandated continual labour in the pursuit of beauty and demanded the woman reader's keen attention to practices and products that conformed to and transgressed the 'natural', healthy ideal. Quick-fix solutions or attempts to artificially mask flaws in appearance or signs of ageing were generally not advocated in either magazine editorials or advertising. As Paula Black observes, the scepticism surrounding cosmetics fed into the selling of the daily beauty routine as 'a duty to women in order to preserve their own natural assets' (29). An advertisement for Saunders's Face Powder or 'Bloom of Ninon' that appeared in *Queen* tellingly uses the language of preservation, promising that the product 'preserves the Beauty and Freshness of Youth to extreme age' (xxxiii). In their editorial and advertising, women's magazines continued to provide judgements about beauty and health, but their reflection of changing norms and commercial imperatives to support the products meant that commercial beauty products were not only no longer discouraged, but actively promoted through editorial content.

Slippage between advertising and editorial

Women's magazines were arbiters of acceptable behaviour through the advice and instructions provided in their editorial content and as their endorsement carried a degree of reputability. This authority was mobilised in these advertisements with magazine endorsements elevating the products to which they gave their approval above those that they were published alongside. Moreover, this value translated across publications with the seal of any magazine bringing some weight with it to wherever it appeared. An ad for Beetham's Glycerine and Cucumber published in *Queen* in 1892 includes multiple endorsements from both the *Queen* ('is at all times safe, as we have found from personal experience') and the *Gentlewoman* (14 May 1892: n.p.). The product was mentioned in brief notes sections of the magazines that were interspersed with advice and responses to correspondents, but these endorsements were marked with a relatively unintrusive '[ADVT]'. A note in *Queen* in 1891 gave an 'IMPORTANT CAUTION!' for readers to specifically ask for Beetham's product and goes on to warn of imitations that 'are often poisonous preparations of lead and other minerals', lending weight to the case for seeking out branded products as featured in the magazine ('IMPORTANT CAUTION!' 629).

The slippage between the designated areas of editorial and advertisement was also evident in the way in which some advertisements took on the appearance of informational articles, with extensive copy. This was another way in which the legitimacy carried by the women's magazine could be imparted onto the products being advertised. For instance, throughout 1891 and 1892, advertisements for Anna Ruppert, whose toxic skin tonic I discussed in Chapter 2, often appeared in the *Queen* (Ruppert n.p.), some of which included a substantial amount of copy. The ads also made mention of her book on 'natural beauty', as well as various products including a skin tonic. The example of Ruppert also demonstrates how the authority of a women's magazine like *Queen* and the adoption of the features of editorial content could convey an air of legitimacy for beauty products and services, even those as dubious as Ruppert's tonic.

In contrast with *Queen*, *Woman*'s name was not commonly used as an endorsement within the advertisements it published, perhaps owing to the fact it was not an upscale magazine; however, *Woman*'s advice columns regularly named specific branded products. The frequent naming of certain brands indicates a paid arrangement with the companies who produced health and beauty products, perhaps tied to the regular placement of advertising within the magazine. In 'Medica's' short article on the treatment of sunburnt skin, she recommends the application of Rowland's Kalydor and the use of Pasta Mack Tablets dissolved in a bath ('Sunburnt Skin' 11). In the 'Health and Appearance' column in the same issue, she recommends Pasta Mack Tablets for the second time. Both products appear in the magazine, with Kalydor advertised regularly, including on the cover. Other products such as Beetham's Glycerine and Cucumber and Broux's Mixture, to give a few examples, are products both advertised in the magazine and recommended by Medica. Boardman and Beetham note a 'strong relationship' between advertising and editorial advice in magazines of the period (5), and this is extremely evident in the recommendation of products in *Woman*'s editorial content. Medica also, however, frequently recommends home-made treatments in each issue, such as hair washes composed of ingredients including rose water and diluted sulphuric acid ('Health and Appearance' 18). The connection of advertised cosmetic products with medicine and health was nevertheless critical in establishing their acceptability. While readers may have discerned the commercial relationships between advertisers and magazines, given the decades of criticism that had surrounded cosmetic use and regular warnings about dangerous products, women's magazines constructed themselves as trusted sources of advice about beauty culture and cosmetics.

In addition to magazine endorsement through columns such as Medica's, magazine advertisements for beauty products frequently sought legitimacy as healthful through supporting statements obtained from doctors and chemists. The frequently advertised product Koko for the Hair in 1891 in *Queen*, for example, included 'An Authoritative Analysis' from a laboratory that verified the product did not contain any 'injurious' elements nor any 'colouring matter or dye' (xxxviii). Unlike Ruppert's potentially harmful product, Koko was sold well into the twentieth century and subsequent analysis by the British Medical Association in 1912 showed that it contained 94 per cent water, 3 per cent alcohol, 2 per cent glycerine, as well as smaller amounts of borax and formaldehyde, which in large quantities can be carcinogenic (*More Secret Remedies* 25). It is likely, however, that the 'Authoritative Analysis' to which the advertisement in *Queen* referred was merely advertising bluster. The medicalisation of cosmetics, as is evident in the language used to advertise Koko, gave one framework for designating certain products as not only free from injurious components, but as acceptable to use, and even beneficial for a woman's health. Guided by the advice provided in advice columns and articles, the woman reader could gradually negotiate acceptable use of branded products in tandem with home-made methods and daily attention a beauty regimen grounded in hygiene.

Beauty as daily work in the *Delineator*

The embrace – and normalisation – of the daily beauty regimen occurred on both sides of the Atlantic, with certain products and magazines – and beauty norms with them – promoted in both Britain and the United States. Among wealthy consumers, there was also a 'substantial growth in sustained transatlantic travel between London and New York', reinforcing the traffic in both beauty products and ideals (J. Clark 166). While this monograph concentrates on British print culture, in the following section I elaborate on how the daily beauty regimen is detailed in the American magazine the *Delineator* to highlight the transnational nature of this shift at the turn of the twentieth century. I have chosen this magazine because it was one of the 'Big Six' American women's periodicals published from the 1870s, with a circulation of close to half a million by 1900, by which point each monthly issue ran to between 150 and 200 pages at a cost of 15 cents (Heberling 59).[2] In addition to Spanish, German and French editions, by 1912 the magazine was also sold in England and Canada, with foreign offices located in London, Toronto and Winnipeg (Heberling 59). One of the key differences between British women's magazines and American women's magazines such as the *Delineator*, *McCall's* and *Pictorial Review* is that they were initiated to promote and sell paper clothing patterns. As a tool to advertise Ebenezer Butterick's patterns nationwide, the *Delineator*'s editorial content focused on the home sewing of practical clothing for middle-class women in a way that most British women's magazines did not. Mary Ellen Zuckerman estimates that two-thirds of the magazine content focused on fashions, with the remainder on women's role and relations between the sexes (13). While the original magazine subtitle from 1873 suggested that it illustrated 'European and American Fashions', the clothing designs were not highly elaborate, and by the turn of the twentieth century the magazine was squarely aimed at a middle-class readership (Zuckerman 14).

In this section, I focus largely on advertising and beauty advice in the *Delineator*, as the very design of the magazine – in which individual articles were broken up to require readers to view the back pages of advertisements – fostered consumerism (Peiss 122). From the 1890s, advertisements increased in number and expanded well beyond those for Butterick patterns and products, such as the company's own manicure equipment (Zuckerman 15). The kinds of beauty products advertised in British and American women's magazines in this period were largely consistent, with an emphasis on products for cleansing and moisturising the skin, and minimal visibility of coloured cosmetics in small text-based ads. Soap brands, such as Pears, for example, were advertised prominently in women's magazines in both locations. Very specific and less enduring products also appear in periodicals on both sides of the Atlantic. Madame Rowley's Toilet Mask, invented by an Ohio woman in 1875 and also marketed as a 'face glove', was one of the most striking products to be advertised in both countries (Madame Rowley's v). The contraption was similar to a modern sheet mask that adheres to the face and required thrice-weekly application. Lesser-known Cuticura soap and ointments were also sold and advertised in both Britain and the United States, and evidence the transatlantic circulation of particular products, brands and their advertisements. Remarkably, the brand – founded in 1865 – is still manufactured today and is exemplary of the normalisation of the beauty routine. The visualisation of clogged pores as masses of dark spots across the face that are poised to erupt into pimples, blackheads and oily skin manufactures the need for daily preventative treatment through the use of Cuticura soap (Cuticura n.p.). The birth of the beauty regimen required several shifts in thought

Figure 6.1 'Beth'. 'The Diary of an Ugly Duckling'. *Delineator* January 1908: 117.

about women's appearance, specifically regarding the ability for any woman to remake herself to eliminate undesirable physical qualities, including those with which she was born.

In 1908, a series of *Delineator* articles by 'Beth' was entitled 'The Diary of an Ugly Duckling: The Story of a Girl who Wasn't Attractive, but Became So, and How She Did It' (Fig. 6.1). The very premise of the series encapsulates transformations in attitudes toward female beauty from the mid-nineteenth century to the turn of the twentieth century. Beauty was no longer a quality bestowed by God or nature, but something that the unattractive girl could work towards through following a series of regular actions and behaviours. This embrace of a daily regimen as the route to beauty or youthful appearance is also evident in the titles of manuals at the turn of the century, such as Mrs Humphry's (C. E. Humphrey) *How to be Pretty though Plain* (1899), published in London, and *The Fountain of Youth* and *Beauty: Its*

Attainment and Preservation, an American manual first serialised in the *Delineator* that I discuss below. Moreover, there was now acknowledgement that individual women of varying appearance might require differing advice. Ugly Duckling 'Beth' learns that particular hairstyles are not flattering to her high forehead and straight hair, and receives instruction to instead part her hair, roll it over her ears and fasten it at the back of her head 'like something like that of the Venus de Milo' ('Beth' 117). Both of these factors were integral to the rise of the beauty advice column, such as the *Delineator*'s which was instituted in 1907, much later than in comparable British magazines; however, prior to this, advertisements served as the key source of direction about 'improving' women's faces and bodies.

Advertisements increasingly used photographic images of women to add to the appeal of their products, rather than illustrations, providing actual models of beauty for emulation, in the same manner as the celebrity women discussed in the previous chapter. The woman looking into the mirror also became a 'recurrent motif' in advertisements, which, as Lori Ann Loeb suggests, served to amplify the 'commercial ideal' of the leisured woman focused on her own pleasure (42). In an advertisement for La Blanche face powder in 1905 (Fig. 6.2), a photographic image of a woman glances out from a hand mirror accompanied by the heading 'Pleasant Reflections' (La Blanche 42). The significance of observing one's own facial reflection daily was an integral part of the new beauty regimen, and the mirror image in the advertisement provides a stand-in for the ideal reflection the woman reader would wish to see. The mirror itself had become a more reliable tool for assessing personal appearance during the course of the nineteenth century. Kathy Peiss suggests that people 'had only a hazy apprehension of their facial qualities' earlier in the century given that mirrors varied wildly in quality, each producing a different reflected image (44–5). Women were now regularly confronted with detailed photographs of beautiful women's faces and had the facility to know their own faces intimately, as well as the various ways in which they may have fallen short of the ideal. Beauty advertising seized on this discrepancy, offering methods to 'correct' flaws.

New York dermatologist John H. Woodbury's facial soap was the most prominent of the products sold by his company from 1870. The title of an 1892 advertisement for the soap in the *Delineator*

Embracing the Beauty Regimen 171

Figure 6.2 La Blanche face powder advertisement. *Delineator* August 1905: 297.

implores the reader: 'LET ME MAKE YOU A NEW FACE. I can do it. I have been doing it for 20 years' (Woodbury's vi). A beautiful face and beautiful hair are made possible through daily use of a soap that brings with it the expertise of a doctor. While this ad is reflective of the promotion and acceptance of the daily beauty regimen and the common way in which products were made acceptable through medical authority, it is also striking for the potential beauty 'problems' it creates and to which it draws attention. Over fifty skin, facial, body and hair flaws are named, with reference made to the solutions and cures offered at Woodbury's offices and in his 145-page book. These range from procedures commonly offered by British beauty culturists, such as electrolysis – which was developed in the 1880s (Banner 214) – and the treatment of minor skin afflictions such as warts and pimples, to more ambiguous references to improving 'an ugly nose', 'ill-shaped' ears and tattoo removal (Woodbury's vi). The dozens of potential flaws in hygiene ('your breath is terrible'), grooming and appearance create a rigorous series of obligations to be performed with regularity at home and to attend specialist treatment to remedy long-term flaws such as pits, veins and bald spots.

The relationship between beauty and health, as discussed in Chapter 1, included some consideration of bodily well-being and exercise, aligning with the importance of self-discipline and 'natural' methods for improving the character and appearance. More prominent attention to a daily exercise routine accompanied the promotion of daily care for the face and hair, and various systems of physical culture were detailed in books with excerpts published in women's magazines. The *Delineator* included nine different articles or 'papers' on the Delsarte system of physical culture from a book by Eleanor Georgen. The system was derived in the late nineteenth century from the methods pioneered by Francois Delsarte for use in the performing arts to fine-tune their bodily expression of emotions. In the sixth paper, exercises for the relaxation of the facial muscles are recounted, with twelve actions for correcting 'crooked mouths, set lips, stiff jaws, blinking eyes, crow's feet, wrinkled and frowning brows and innumerable other faults' (Georgen 163). Avoiding or remedying faults, or even 'the ravages of time', requires daily or nightly practice, creating yet another beauty obligation. As Lois Banner points out, there were anti-feminist elements to these and other ideas inherent in beauty literature, such as the idea that wrinkling and ageing were brought on by 'mental and emotional exertion', requiring women to 'remain calm and serene' (207).

Grace Peckham Murray's 'The Fountain of Youth, or Personal Appearance and Personal Hygiene' was published in 1905 based on a series of articles published in the *Delineator* in the year prior (Fig. 6.3). Medical doctor Murray's first article on the face resembled the Delsarte system, outlining an elaborate series of facial exercises that could influence fat distribution and skin texture and tone (Murray 92). The premise of the article is that the tension and relaxation of the facial muscles can produce wrinkles and distortions, as well as creating the appearance of undesirable features such as a receding chin or hollow cheeks. Just as these movements can be deleterious, exercise, massage and applying electricity to the skin are identified as a way to preserve the appearance through promoting blood flow and therefore skin 'nourish[ment]' (94). The mention of massage is important here, as by the 1890s in the US it had become an important part of the services offered by cos-

Figure 6.3 Grace Peckham Murray. 'The Fountain of Youth. First Paper: The Face'. *Delineator* January 1904: 92.

Figure 6.4 Grace Peckham Murray. 'The Fountain of Youth. First Paper: The Face'. *Delineator* January 1904: 95.

meticians; Banner explains that because make-up remained out of favour, potential services were limited 'thus they added massage to make their beautification rituals more attractive to their clients' (214).

In Murray's article and subsequent book, a series of instructions turn the daily washing of the face into an elaborate and time-consuming ritual (Fig. 6.4). This involves massage of the forehead, the eyelids, cheeks and chin, scrubbing the nose ('the pulpy part of the middle finger should be searching in its work around the nostrils' (Murray 95), and the lifting of excess flesh in order to smooth it.

The medicalisation of the beauty regimen through methods such as physical culture and massage also aided in the normalisation of regular consumption of beauty products. Some scepticism about the efficacy of products without an established reputation no doubt still remained. The Sylvan system, incorporating the Massageo facial tool and soap is one of many products that offered a significant reward – in this case $500 – if the consumer experienced any harm, clearly distancing the brand from disreputable products (Massageo xvii). Massageo is also an example of the daily exercise regimen being drawn into advertising for skin treatments in the 1890s: 'The facial skin needs food; the facial muscles require exercise' (xvii). Associating the system with both nutrition and exercise placed it on the right side of acceptability, legitimating the promise that daily use 'brings back the youthful bloom' (xvii). The lingering belief in the superiority of naturalness is incorporated into the product description, which 'supplies Nature's needs, nourishes and soothes, invigorates and restore tissues: feeds wasted skin' (xvii). Where once 'natural' more closely referred to the state of the skin and body without the application of any external treatments, nature is reconfigured as in an inevitable process of decay and to require assistance in order to rejuvenate. Advertisements for Pompeian Massage Cream – the name of which recalls classical beauty ideals – likewise connect the medical and health benefits of massage and facial exercise, exhorting *Delineator* readers to 'be your own Beauty Doctor' (Pompeian Massage Cream 285). The cream not only promises to clean and nourish the skin, but to 'build [. . .] up and round [. . .] out the contour of the face and form by cleansing, exercising and feeding the skin, *through* and *through* and strengthening the muscles' (285). Familiar language about the facial muscles found in the systems described above is combined with co-option of historical discourse about natural beauty, with Pompeian promising to impart a healthful glow 'that only nature at her best can give' (285). The sanctity of 'natural' beauty is dismantled, while ideas related to health and medicine merely take on new forms. For instance, by the 1890s, it was more common to admit that natural looks did not equal perfection, and indeed that nature often cursed women with unappealing aesthetic features. In 1896, Henry Tetlow's Gossamer Powder made references to lightening the skin or making the fair face even 'fairer' (Tetlow's Gossamer Powder xxxiii). The shifting sense of beauty as no longer innate, but the product of regular work and care is evident in the following description of the powder's 'corrective' function: 'It corrects the little mistakes of nature – imparts a delightful softness and a delicate beauty to the skin without becoming visible to the eye' (xxxiii). This is a distinct change from language about the correction of flaws produced by exposure to the elements, ageing, or ill health, as it suggests that most girls and women will *require* powder to conceal the flaws that are inherent on most faces, even young faces.

Despite the relative consistency of the kinds of beauty products marketed on both sides of the Atlantic, several types of advertisement were more common in American women's magazines, presumably owing to more relaxed expectations about the public acknowledgement of problematic aspects of the body that could either be construed as embarrassing or sexual in nature. Depilatory products, such as the Modene solution manufactured in Cincinnati, were more visibly advertised in American magazines such as the *Delineator*, while they tended to be part of the range of services offered in-person at salons in Britain. In addition, the magazine was less circumspect about weight-loss commodities, with treatments for fatness advertised frequently and occupying half and full pages. Dr Edison's obesity products – pills, salt, compound, and waist bands – were advertised regularly in the *Delineator* in the 1890s. There is significant emphasis on health in Dr Edison's advertisements (Fig. 6.5), with the use of 'Dr' in the product title potentially a marketing device, along with claims that the products will 'cure chronic diseases' (Dr Edison's Obesity Pills 12). References to getting 'thin before the hot season advances' and the testimonial provided by Mrs Caroline Parker Storey – who had become 'fifty pounds too heavy, either for comeliness or good health' – point to clear concerns about the aesthetics of fatness. Couching desires for comeliness within those of health performs the same deflection as many ads for products intended for the skin that I discuss below.

Obesity had clear medical implications, yet health also remained one of the most pervasive ways to market beauty products for the face. Madame Ruppert's formulation in its original American incarnation as 'Face Bleach' was promoted in the *Delineator* as removing 'all diseases the skin is heir to' including tan, freckles, pimples, eczema and 'moth' (Madame Ruppert's Face Bleach

Figure 6.5 Dr Edison's Obesity Pills advertisement. *Delineator* July 1896: 12.

n.p.). The theatricality of the beauty culturist delivering lectures and building her reputation through the publication of a beauty manual or guide – as Ruppert did – is elevated to sensational display: a young woman named Hattie Trainor is advertised as a spectacle to be viewed at Ruppert's Parlors in New York, with one side of her face treated with the bleach and blemish-free and the other in its original state with 'dark deep-set skin freckles'.

While coloured cosmetics remained at the margins of advertising in women's magazines in the late nineteenth century, somewhat indelicate items such as breast enhancers did begin to appear, but were more visibly advertised in American publications. The prominence of such advertisements in American magazines is indicative of bolder advertising for beauty products more broadly. The first American patent for a breast prosthesis was issued in 1874 for a cosmetic 'breast pad' with a cotton cushion casing and inflatable India-rubber interior intended to create the appearance of larger breasts (Gardner 103–4). H. & H. pneumatic bust forms were advertised regularly in the *Delineator* in the early twentieth century and they show the application of two of the central tenets of the daily beauty regimen to a device external to the body. First, the breast forms accord with the ongoing importance of perceived naturalness. One woman's testimonial for the forms claims that her attempts to recommend the forms are brushed off, as admirers refuse to 'believe my bust is not real' (H. & H. Pneumatic Bust Forms 152). Not only do the forms create the *appearance* of naturalness, but the product spiel asserts that they '**create natural development** and may be worn small at first and gradually increased in size; then decreased as natural bust develops' [emphasis in original] (152). The importance of secrecy surrounding the use of artificial aids is evident in the advertisement's reassurance that all correspondence and products will be sent in plain packaging, such that neighbours or even other household members need not know that a woman is wearing the forms. Second, this procedure also replicates the repetitive and long-term daily work required for the cultivation of beauty, with the promise of incremental daily progress that will transform the body itself.

Beauty advice and the daily work of beauty

The previous chapter observed that some beauty culturists published books to foster their public profile and cement their position as the reader's regular source of advice on all matters of appearance. The *Delineator*'s publisher, Butterick, produced a substantial advice manual, *Beauty: Its Attainment and Preservation*, in 1890. Though it featured a substantial amount of advertising for beauty and hygiene products in every issue, the magazine did not regularly include beauty advice – as was common in British women's periodicals – until the early twentieth century, though it gave prominence to the advertising of the Butterick beauty manual. The large 528-page book aimed to be a complete guide for 'Those Who Desire to Beautiful in *Mind, Manner, Feature and Form*' and went into multiple editions. While the book was distanced from the *Delineator* itself, which gave greater emphasis to housekeeping and dressmaking in particular, it provided a surrogate form of advice for the magazine's readers. The 'innumerable remedies' must coexist with training of the mind and character 'in order that natural or acquired physical beauty may rest on an imperishable foundation' (xxxii). The regular beauty regimen develops into an acceptable expectation in conjunction with the remnants of beliefs about the relationship between character and external appearance.

Advice columns in girls' and women's magazines responded to readers' letters about health and appearance, among other personal issues, throughout the nineteenth century. Columns with a specific focus on dress and appearance queries largely emerged in fashion magazines late in the century and in the early twentieth century, with the increasing acceptance of the daily work of beauty (Beetham and Boardman 166). Precursor columns in girls' and women's magazines devoted to more general health and well-being dilemmas, such as Medicus's long-running column in the *Girl's Own Paper*, generally did not accept the pursuit of an 'improved' appearance as valid. Kristine Moruzi notes, for instance, that Medicus believed that 'the health of the female body is much more important than its shape or appearance' (95). The hangover of such beliefs meant that, as Peiss notes, American women's magazines from the 1890s 'took an ambiguous position on the traffic in beauty aids and advice' (50) – related to the fact that cosmetics apart from skin creams and lotions were not widely advertised – and were 'reluctant advisers' despite readers' demands (122). The beauty advice columnist emerged to help the girl or woman reader negotiate the difficult balancing act of developing her appearance acceptably, through making products at home or selecting reliable cosmetics.

While magazines may have frequently advised readers to concoct their own beauty preparations at home, they were 'unable to stanch the flood of readers' queries about beauty aids and makeup' (Peiss 51). In the September 1907 issue of the *Delineator*, Mrs Prescott invited 'beauty seekers' to send queries to the magazine. Within two months, the volume of letters had reached hundreds each day and the content was 'of such complicated character, requiring time and research' that a beauty specialist, Mme Millicent Marvin, was appointed to prepare responses for the 'Asked by Beauty-Seekers' column (Marvin 775). Readers wrote to ask for advice on preventing grey hair and remedying dark circles under the eyes. The column developed in 1908 to also include lengthy articles by Marvin on topics such as 'Avoiding the Complexion Ills of Winter' and 'How to Look Younger than You Are'.

What was significant about the embrace of the beauty regimen was the regularity and continuity of the tasks required. Marvin emphasises that improvements in the skin and treatments of problems such as acne, blackheads, blocked pores and sallowness, require a long-term commitment: 'One hears a great deal about ugly ducklings being transformed into swans in a week, but that is only fiction' ('Avoiding the Complexion Ills' 302). The most vital component of the daily regimen was washing the face with soap, a task that cohered with historically acceptable beauty practices and emphasis on hygiene. Marvin went as far to say that 'cleanliness is personal beauty' (302). Washing the face, however, did not merely involve a quick lather of soap and splash of water. With the embrace of the beauty regimen, cleansing the face became a multi-step, complex process, with complexion brushes, for example, lauded for their capacity to 'freshen' skin tissue and maintain the strength of the facial muscles (302).

As the column took shape, it began to share a page with beauty advertisements, linking Marvin's advice and answers to correspondents with products such as powder, skin food and corsets that were detailed and recommended to readers in broad terms. For example, Marvin advised that rubbing powder into the skin was 'a good thing' that would preserve the skin from the effects of winter winds; however, the prohibition of 'visible' usage remained, with Marvin deeming it to be 'a hideous thing' ('Avoiding the Complexion Ills' 303). The aforementioned column was placed on a page that included an advertisement for La Blanche face powder and Sempre Giovine skin food. However, as a rule, Marvin did not name particular products in her answers, instead opting for routines that could be practised at home, or inviting the reader to send a stamped envelope to obtain a recipe for a home-made concoction. The decision not to publish recipes in a regular column is unusual given their frequent appearance in other magazines and beauty manuals, but might stem from the necessity of magazine's cultivating trusted relationships with beauty culturists and advisers, as was evident in the advertising techniques of Mrs Pomeroy discussed in the previous chapter.

Weight loss through the daily work of dieting and exercise would come to define the quest for a slim figure in the twentieth century. However, as with the time-consuming and all-encompassing nature of theories about facial expression, exercises and massage, Marvin proposes methods that require conscious management of bodily elements on a continual basis, such as posture and breathing. Exercise and diet are named as prerequisites for slenderness, but Marvin describes 'proper sitting' as the third requirement ('How to Gain a Graceful Figure' 844). She refers not only to the effects of posture on the prominence of the belly, but to the subsquent 'develop[ment]' of the abdomen through poor posture (844). For an ideal figure, women are therefore required to think about the way they sit, stand and move; in addition, they must also conduct 'regular breathing exercises' – which can be obtained by writing to Marvin – to develop their chest if they have 'a flat chest, or an undeveloped bust' (845). While not explicitly linked with health, as in the advertisements for fatness, the advice that Marvin provides about maintaining an ideal weight are firmly connected with the overarching change in beauty discourse that required a significant amount of each day to be devoted to maintaining or improving the face and body.

These women's magazines at the end of the nineteenth and into the early twentieth centuries demonstrate how a subtle, but significant, shift normalised the work of beauty for women by the twentieth century, departing from earlier beliefs in beauty as inborn, natural and a by-product of ideal character. This does not mean that opposition to the new norms did not exist, even within the same publications that advertised products that were integral to the beauty routine. An article in the *Delineator* from 1908, 'The Making of an American Beauty' drew a distinction between different kinds of American girls and women, denigrating the cultivated beauty. Author Martha Gale Gates describes girls and women who merely seek to be 'beauties in their own circle or city', but who are unable to attend a finishing school (777). Instead, these girls and women seek out courses in 'Physical Culture' and 'The Art of Expression' in order to enhance the appearance of their faces and bodies. Gates delivers one of the more biting lines of the article when she observes that if instructions for facial massage, hair brushing and 'deep breathing and gymnastics for plumpness or thinness, hollowness and crookedness' were followed they 'would consume ten hours of the day' (777). This American Beauty can be made, but the clear insinuation is that the process requires an excessive focus on the external self, and the contravention of long-established expectations for being useful and of benefit to family and children. The majority of Gates's critique focuses on the 'Millionaire Princess' type of American Beauty who is 'trained by babyhood to fulfil her destiny' (777). Her 'profession' is the work of becoming an American beauty, rather than intellectual development: 'An American Beauty must not only have a lovely face and graceful carriage and a musical voice; she must have personality, charm, presence, poise; she must have cultivation, discrimination and tact, if she is to hold her own in the world' (778). The difficult work entailed in becoming a beauty involves restricting her intake of food, sitting on 'straight chairs', lying on 'a hard bed', and exercising for five hours a day in activities such as walking, basketball, dancing and riding (779). Gates criticises the self-consciousness and affectations associated with this type of beauty, who does not take pleasure in looking at the world, but in attracting the gaze of passers-by:

> As she trots through Central Park, head up, eyes looking straight ahead, with a half-dozen other girls under the escort of the riding master, she misses the beauty of the green about her, but she is aware of the attention she is attracting. Distinguished simplicity of the young American girl; her simplicity must be of the sort that people will turn to look at. To be looked at, but to act as though she does not know she is being looked at – that is her ideal. (779)

The Millionaire Princess Beauty's superficiality means she neglects her education and awareness of current events. Gates tellingly describes this beauty as 'an artificial American beauty – a hothouse growth' (880). The hothouse metaphor is a new development of the old opposition between artifice and nature, with its connotations of exotic and potentially fragile and temperamental plants, valued only for fleeting moments in bloom. While Gates despairs that the 'false ideals' the American beauty represents are present across the country, she takes comfort that this type 'does not overlie all America' (880). Better types of American girl who are 'simple, pretty, unaffected' can be found, and the article calls out to the *Delineator* reader who 'may be reading longingly in the magazine about the American beauty, not knowing that they are the best hope of the future and are themselves the rarer flower' (880).

'The Making of an American Beauty' is a reminder that the transformation of long-held beliefs about femininity, appearance and ideal behaviour could never be straightforward nor absolute. Moreover, generational change perennially attracts the ire of parents and elders, with some women who were raised with the strong association between beauty and character outlined in Chapter 3 unforgiving of the superficiality associated with the self-conscious, cultivated beauty. Where the pursuit of beauty would once have been flagged as a fruitless errand and a waste of time that could be spent on productive, improving activities, by the turn of the century, the potential for daily beauty work to produce and maintain an improved appearance was largely accepted, along with the interest of girls and women in doing so, as is evident in the flourishing of the beauty advice column and the extensive advertising of beauty products.

Another unique aspect of beauty advertising in the *Delineator* was appeals to women readers to join the beauty culture 'profession' by founding their own beauty parlours at home, or by visiting customers. Beauty culturists, Peiss notes, devised and 'taught their systems of cleansing, face massage, and cosmetic application' (85). The Elizabeth King System of 'Beauty Culture by Mail' was widely advertised in various American periodicals in the early twentieth century, training women in only eight weeks to perform manicures, hairdressing, facial massage, scalp treatment and cosmetics manufacture (Elizabeth King System 163). Jessica Clark's account of British beauty culturists in the late nineteenth century describes women who were small-scale entrepreneurs like King who were able to capitalise on 'twentieth-century ideas about femininity, beauty, and mass consumption to irrefutable success' (163). British firms would, however, lose their status in comparison with the rise of American companies in the twentieth century, echoing 'the shifting fashionability of London versus Paris and New York' (J. Clark 191) and perhaps a warmer embrace of the commercialised aspects of beauty culture. The Elizabeth King System, as regularly advertised in the *Delineator*, highlights how the embrace of beauty procedures as routine practice supported women's small business and income generation, a possibility that would develop throughout the twentieth century in the United States through multi-level marketing cosmetic businesses such as Avon and Mary Kay.

Conclusion

In her study of beauty and poetry in women's periodicals, Kathryn Ledbetter highlights how the periodical might be purchased for the reader's 'imaginative use as fantasy or for practical use in enhancing their own physical and spiritual beauty' (117). This practical function is, as I have argued in this chapter, central to how beauty is presented in women's magazines such as *Queen* and *Woman*, despite their different implied readerships. While figures such as celebrities might have provided exotic glimpses into the glamourous world of the stage, for instance, beauty advice and advertising were often grounded in the production of 'ordinary' beauty or the preservation of youth. Disgraced skin specialist Anna Ruppert wrote in *A Book of Beauty* (1892) that if a woman wanted a happy home, the worst thing she could neglect after marriage was her appearance. As she reminded the reader, even '[t]he most noble beauty, if unattended, will soon lose its charm' (Ruppert n.p.). In the 1890s and early twentieth century, through revised rhetoric surrounding beauty culture and a related increase in the visibility of beauty advertising in women's magazines in both Britain and the United States, beauty was transformed into a process of daily work. It was work that required the woman's magazine as a supervisor and arbiter of what role products like cosmetics should play in the production of acceptable models of beauty and ideal femininity that were increasingly standardised through the transatlantic circulation of women's magazines, beauty manuals, brand-name beauty products and celebrities. Moreover, the ideologies these magazines reproduced about the essential place of naturalness and health within this ideal contributed to the content of the beauty advertisements they contained, which reproduced accepted beliefs about cosmetics as undesirable at the same time as heralding the imminent arrival of an internationalised beauty industry.

Notes

1 There are several different Bovril advertisements published throughout 1896 in *Woman* that repeat this precise line about the relationship of health to beauty.
2 The other five American magazines that comprise the 'Big Six' are *Ladies Home Journal*, *Good Housekeeping*, *McCall's*, *Pictorial Review* and *Woman's Home Companion*.

Conclusion

> For behold! The Victorian era comes to its end and the day of sancta simplicitas is quite ended. The old signs are here and the portents to warn the seer of life that we are ripe for a new epoch of artifice. Are not men rattling the dice-box and ladies dipping their fingers in the rouge-pot?
>
> Max Beerbohm, 'In Defence of Cosmetics' (1894) (2)

In the twenty-first century, girls and women are undergoing cosmetic surgery to remodel their bodies or facial features, reduce the markers of ageing and lighten their skin, so the question of how the female beauty ideals that hold today came to be standardised and disseminated in the nineteenth century is especially significant. Western beauty and fashion industries still grapple with an overwhelming promotion of whiteness and creation of products designed for white skin. Ideas about 'natural' beauty as superior to 'artificial' beauty continue to underwrite modern cosmetic advertisements and plastic surgery procedures, with a 'natural' or 'undetectable' look to any product, facelift or implant being the desired outcome for most women. Most of all, the idea that beauty is of prime importance to girls and women remains predominant in an era of social media and Instagram 'influencers', even as the cultural conditions surrounding marriage, employment and family have substantially transformed.

What it was to be feminine was transformed by the significant changes wrought in relation to women's appearance through print culture in the Victorian period. Elizabeth Carolyn Miller contends that since the nineteenth century, femininity 'has been constituted more and more by self-administered regimens of healthy, beauty, fashion, and appearance' (83). Everyone from Victorian beauty and style experts such as Eliza Haweis to contemporary feminist writers have argued that women take pleasure in, and make subversive use of, beauty culture. More common, however, is the suggestion that beauty norms – and their extreme manifestations, such as beauty contests – limit women. Robyn Cooper, for example, suggests that patriarchal culture 'assigned beauty to woman' in order to control women's bodies and secure their 'subordination' (51). The continued figuration of beauty as women's preserve and a form of social power that must be fought to be retained into middle and old age is indicative of the ongoing subordination of women through their physical appearance. Indeed, real harm was caused by some beauty treatments and products throughout the nineteenth century, which contributed to the critique of cosmetics in print culture. While the medical men who were publishing treatises on beauty at mid-century can be understood as enacting a form of control over women's bodies, they were also providing a relatively reliable source of information about the dangers of some beauty products and practices.

The double-edged sword of female beauty in a patriarchal culture ensured that women's pursuit of the ideal was frequently ridiculed and demeaned in the Victorian period. The narrator of Mary Elizabeth Braddon's sensation novel *Lady Audley's Secret* (1862), for example, asks the reader to 'imagine all the women of England elevated to the high level of masculine intellectuality; superior to crinoline; above pearl powder and Mrs Rachel Levison' (153). It is women alone who are preoccupied with fripperies such as elaborate clothing and cosmetics, and who lack the sense that would keep them away from the doors of those who peddle false promises and snake oil. Young women were frequent targets for criticism for vanity and for openly enhancing their sexuality while older women were lampooned as objects of repulsion for attempting to retain or regain beautiful features, which were equated with youth. Victorian fiction offers an insight into how both young and older women attempted to navigate the complexities associated with being beautiful and its gradual dissipation over time. The challenges that faced older women as they aged, with the loss of the limited feminine power of beauty, or pity if they attempted to retain a youthful appearance, remain true today. The impossibility of the beauty ideal lies at the core of these judgements. Despite the sheer volume of beauty guidance contained in advice manuals and women's magazines, even the most conscientious girl or woman could not avoid transgressing these often conflicting instructions *and* remain 'beautiful for ever'.

Nevertheless, as this monograph has argued, there is a marked transformation between Alexander Walker's assertion in *Beauty* in 1845 that paint is only used by 'meretricious persons and by those harridans of higher rank who resemble them in every respect' (333) and attitudes towards – and the use of – cosmetics by the end of the nineteenth century. Max Beerbohm's essay 'A Defence of Cosmetics' (1894) was published in the first edition of *The Yellow Book*, an aesthetic literary journal, and registers easing of the critique of artifice. He observes an increase in the trade of cosmeticians in preceding years and asserts that a walk down 'any modish street' or glance under any woman's bonnet will attest to 'over how wide a kingdom rouge reigns' (4). Likewise, Beerbohm comments on a change in attitudes towards women who use 'brush and pigment' to combat the effects of ageing, with the response no longer one of public 'anger' (4). Beerbohm was not representative of commonplace viewpoints in his welcoming of the disassociation of the face and beauty as 'a mere vulgar index of character of emotion' (10). However, his essay does register a variation in the prevalence of visible cosmetic use and a decrease in hostile attitudes toward cosmetics.

The opinions of these two male commentators on beauty bookend changing understandings of cosmetic use across the second half of the nineteenth century. The contrast illuminates the way in which beauty shifted from being viewed through medically informed advice to the perspectives found in magazine editorials, advice columns and celebrity endorsements, which reframed women's beauty through the consumption of the products advertised and discussed in the pages of women's magazines. As Lyn Pykett clarifies, Victorian periodicals are not simply mirrors of Victorian culture but 'have come to be seen as a central component of that culture' (102). Print culture became the central method for informing and moulding how girls and women thought about beauty. From affordable weekly magazines to expensive monthly magazines and beauty manuals, women were overwhelmed with information that shaped their perception of beauty ideals. As the chapters in this study have sought to demonstrate, periodicals responded to transformations in the market for beauty products and the changing views of their readers in order to keep pace with the shifting nature of beauty ideals and retain their readerships.

Regardless of shifting levels of cultural acceptance or condemnation, the reality is that women have always used artificial methods to improve their appearance. The cosmetics industry that grew from the late nineteenth century, and especially in the early twentieth century, simply 'translat[ed] such perennial desires into brands, factory production, and ultimately, multinational enterprises' (Jones 5). The 'natural' aesthetic that was widely endorsed in print culture in tandem with the relaxation of prohibitions on cosmetic use nevertheless became a challenge for the British beauty industry in the twentieth century when 'tastes for overt beautification ramped up' (J. Clark 14). The bold advertising campaigns and novel colour cosmetics sold by American cosmetics companies evident in the pages of magazines such as the *Delineator*, and elegant products offered by French perfumers made it harder for the British industry – which had been shaped and grounded in ideas surrounding 'natural' beauty for decades – to prosper on an international scale (J. Clark 14).

Ideas about natural beauty were not entirely superseded when negative perceptions of artifice relaxed, and cosmetics were more openly consumed. Underneath an image of a woman who is heavily made up (complete with beauty spots), the cover of *The Lady Beauty Book* (1900)[1] includes two lines from Thomas Campion's poem 'Cherry-Ripe' (1617): 'There is a garden in her face/Where roses and white lilies grow'. The poem compares a woman's beauty to 'pleasant fruits', lips of 'cherries' or alternatively of 'rose-buds fill'd with snow' when she laughs. The use of the seventeenth-century poem at the beginning of the twentieth shows the enduring connection of female beauty with what springs forth from nature, an idea that heavily informed suspicions about, and prohibitions on, the use of coloured cosmetics.

This monograph focuses on the promotion of an ideal in print culture and its gradual refinement over the course of many decades. Nevertheless, girls and women clearly made conscious choices to both follow and ignore the predominant ideal and the prevailing advice. The consistent presence of small advertisements for certain coloured cosmetics during periods in which their use was discouraged or condemned alone tells us that some women placed the desire to improve their looks first above any moral or aesthetic judgement to which they might be subject. Today we see similar rejections of the beauty ideal in the fat positivity movement, for example. However, traces of Victorian beauty ideals undoubtedly linger in contemporary culture, combined with new expectations and judgements imposed by the vast expansion and embedding of beauty consumption into girls' and women's lives, from 'pamper parties' for pre-teens through to Botox injections and facial fillers.

Note

1 The book was comprised of material that had been published in the magazine *The Lady* (1885–present).

Bibliography

Primary sources

'A Chat with Sarah Bernhardt'. *Sketch* 27 June 1894: 458.
'A Chat with Mrs Langtry'. *Sketch* 10 July 1895: 590.
Alex Ross Nose Machine, advertisement. *The Examiner* 3 February 1872: 138.
Ammoniaphone advertisement. *Myra's Journal of Dress and Fashion* 1 January 1887: 45.
'An Eastern Beauty'. Front cover. *Queen* 21 May 1892: 1.
'An Iberian Beauty'. Front cover. *Queen* 1 October 1892: 1.
Ballantine, Mr Serjeant. *Some Experiences of a Barrister's Life*. Vol. 2. London: Richard Bentley and Son, 1882.
Bayard, Madame. *Toilet Hints; or, How to Preserve Beauty, and How to Acquire It*. London: Weldon & Co. [1883].
'Beauties of the French Stage'. *Sketch* 7 April 1897: 443.
Beauty: How to Get It and How to Keep It. London: *Tit-Bits* Office, 1885.
Beauty: Its Attainment and Preservation. New York: Butterick, 1890.
Beerbohm, Max. *In Defence of Cosmetics*. 1894. New York: Dodd, Mead & Co., 1922.
Beetham's Glycerine and Cucumber advertisement. *Girl's Own Paper* 'Evergreen' Christmas number, 1887: n.p.
Beetham's Glycerine and Cucumber advertisement. *Queen* 14 May 1892: n.p.
'Beth'. 'The Diary of an Ugly Duckling'. *Delineator* January 1908: 117–19.
Blackham's hair products, pamphlet. John Johnson Collection of Printed Ephemera, Bodleian Library, 1895.

Bovril advertisement. *Woman* 30 September 1896: 17.
Braddon, M. E. *Lady Audley's Secret*. Mobile, AL: S. H. Goetzel, 1864.
Brinton, D. G. and Geo. H. Napheys. *Personal Beauty: How to Cultivate and Preserve it in Accordance with the Laws of Health*. Springfield, MA: W. J. Holland, 1870.
Browne, M. Hedderwick. 'To the Girls'. *The Girl's Own Paper* 22 October 1892: 55.
Browning, H. Ellen. *Beauty Culture*. London: Hutchinson and Co., 1898.
Burnett, Frances Hodgson. *The Secret Garden*. New York: Frederick A. Stokes, 1911.
Camelline for the Complexion advertisement. *Sketch* 6 February 1895: 99.
Camelline for the Complexion advertisement. *Woman* 15 April 1896: iii.
Caplin, Roxey A. *Health and Beauty, or, Corsets and Clothing Constructed in Accordance with the Physiological Laws of the Human Body*. London: Darton and Co., 1856.
C. Bond and Son's advertisement. *Woman* 2 April 1892: xx.
Collins, Wilkie. *The Law and the Lady*. 1875. London: Penguin, 1998.
Cowell, Sydney. 'They Had the Beauty of Youth and Health'. (Illust.) *Girl's Own Paper* 4 July 1896: 632.
Cuticura soap advertisement. *Delineator* September 1896: n. p.
Dale, Darley. 'The Face of an Angel'. *Girl's Own Paper* 10 October 1885: 28.
Diaphane advertisement. *Queen* 11 July 1891: xlvi.
Diaphane advertisement. *Queen* 4 June 1892: xxx.
Dickens, Charles. *Dombey and Son*. 1848. London: Penguin, 2002.
Dolman, Frederick. 'Madame Marie Roze at Home'. *Myra's Journal* 1 June 1891: 1.
Dr Edison's Obesity Pills advertisement. *Delineator* July 1896: 12.
Dyer, Reverend T. F. Thiselton. 'Beauty Lore'. *Girl's Own Paper* 19 May 1894: 521–2.
Dyer's London Watches advertisement. *Myra's Journal of Dress and Fashion* 2 December 1878, n.p.
'Editor of "Health News"'. *Exposures of Quackery: Being a Series of Articles upon, and Analysis of, Various Patent Medicines*. London: Savoy, 1897.
Eliot, George. *Adam Bede*. 1859. London: Penguin, 2008.
—. *Felix Holt, the Radical*. 1866. London: Penguin, 1995.
Elizabeth King System advertisement. *Delineator* June 1908: 163.
Ewing, Juliana Horatia. *Six to Sixteen: A Story for Girls*. London: George Bell and Sons, 1886.

Fletcher, Ella Adelia. *The Woman Beautiful*. 1899. New York: Brentano's, 1901.
'French Beauties'. *Sketch* 4 May 1898: 63.
Frizzetta advertisement. *Myra's Journal of Dress and Fashion* 1 December 1886: 584.
Gates, Martha Gale. 'The Making of an American Beauty'. *Delineator* May 1908: 777–9, 880.
Georgen, Eleanor. 'The Delsarte System of Physical Culture. Sixth Paper'. *Delineator* August 1892: 163–4.
Géraudel's Pastilles advertisement. *Sketch* 6 December 1893: 328.
H. & H. Pneumatic Bust Forms advertisement. *Delineator* January 1904: 152.
Haweis, Mrs H. R. *The Art of Beauty*. 1878. London: Chatto & Windus, 1883.
'Health and Personal Attention'. *Myra's Journal of Dress and Fashion* 1 August 1879: 187.
'Health and Personal Attention'. *Myra's Journal of Dress and Fashion*. 1 December 1879: 283.
Hilder and Godbold advertisement, *Myra's Journal of Dress and Fashion* 1 July 1879: n.p.
'How Sarah Bernhardt Preserves Her Youth'. *Woman* 12 August 1891: 13.
Humphry, Mrs (Madge of 'Truth'). *How to be Pretty Though Plain*. London: James Bowden, 1899.
'IMPORTANT CAUTION!' *Queen* 18 April 1891: 629.
Ivorine Complexion Cream advertisement. *Myra's Journal of Dress and Fashion* 1 December 1893: n.p.
Jean Stehr's Vegetable Hair Colouring advertisement. *Woman* 9 December 1896: 7.
Koko for the Hair advertisement. *Queen* 27 June 1891: xxxviii.
'La Belle El Derido Captures the Parisians'. *Oakland Tribune* 4 November 1899: 4.
La Blanche face powder advertisement. *Delineator* August 1905: 297.
La Diaphane advertisement. *Myra's Journal* 1 July 1891: n.p.
Lady Jean. *Beauty as a Fine Art*. 2nd ed. Applied Physiology Series, 1904.
Langtry Invisible Hair Curler advertisement. *Myra's Journal of Dress and Fashion*. 1 January 1884: 48.
Linton, Eliza Lynn. *The Girl of the Period and Other Social Essays*. Vol. 1. London: Richard Bentley and Son, 1883.
'Look in the Glass!' Pears' Soap advertisement. *Queen* 17 October 1891: xxv.

Madame Rachel. *Beautiful For Ever!* London: Madam Rachel, 1863.

Madame Rowley's Face Mask advertisement. *Delineator* December 1899: v.

Madame Ruppert's Face Bleach advertisement. *Delineator* August 1896: n.p.

Madame Ruppert advertisement. *Queen* 31 October 1891: xl.

Marvin, Millicent. 'Asked by Beauty-Seekers'. *Delineator* November 1907: 775–6.

—. 'Avoiding the Complexion Ills of Winter'. *Delineator* February 1908: 302–4.

—. 'How to Gain a Graceful Figure: Slenderness Depends Largely on a Correct Fit of Clothes and Corset'. *Delineator* May 1908: 844–6.

Mason, Nanette. 'Plain Looks and Good Looks'. *Girl's Own Paper* 14 March 1891: 374–5.

Massageo advertisement. *Delineator* November 1892: xvii.

Meade, L. T. *The Sorceress of the Strand and Other Stories*. Ed. Janis Dawson. Peterborough, ON: Broadview Press, 2016.

'Medica'. 'Health and Appearance'. *Woman* 11 January 1893: 18.

—. 'Sunburnt Skin'. *Woman* 1 July 1896: 11.

Medicus. 'A Bundle of Hints on Beauty'. *Girl's Own Paper* 26 June 1897: 612–13.

—. 'Beauty'. *Girl's Own Paper* 4 August 1888: 717–18.

—. 'Beauty in Woman: From a Man's Point of View'. *Girl's Own Paper* 14 January 1899: 246–7.

—. 'Is Beauty Evanescent?' *Girl's Own Paper* 5 July 1890: 631–2.

'Miss Ada Rehan. An Appreciation'. *Sketch* 28 June 1893: cover?

Montez, Madame Lola. *The Arts of Beauty; or, Secrets of a Lady's Toilet. With Hints to Gentlemen on the Art of Fascinating*. New York: Dick & Fitzgerald, 1858.

More Secret Remedies. What they Cost and What they Contain. Based on Analyses made for the British Medical Association. London: British Medical Association, 1912.

Mr Kirkham's Patent Medicine Warehouse pamphlet, Birmingham, 1890. John Johnston Collection of Printed Ephemera, Bodleian Library.

Mrs Anna Ruppert advertisement. *Queen* 21 November 1891: xxxii.

'Mrs Ellen Terry'. *Sketch* 16 May 1894: 1.

'Mrs Langtry. The Happy Possessor of Imperial Beauty and the Imperial Theatre'. *Sketch* 17 December 1902: 330.

'Mrs. Pomeroy's Hygienic Treatment'. *Sketch* 10 December 1902: vii.

Murray, Grace Peckham. 'The Fountain of Youth. First Paper: The Face'. *Delineator* January 1904: 92–5.

Narubine Blush advertisement. *Woman* 4 March 1896: 21.
Neigeline advertisement. *Sketch* 10 October 1894: 611.
'The Newest Beauty in Paris'. *Sketch* 4 October 1899: 471.
Nonpareil Velveteen advertisement. *Myra's Journal of Dress and Fashion* 1 December 1884: 607.
Odontobaph advertisement. *Myra's Journal of Dress and Fashion* 1 September 1885: n.p.
'Our Ladies' Pages'. *Sketch* 11 July 1894: 610.
'Our Ladies' Pages'. *Sketch* 16 January 1895: 590.
Pears advertisement. *Myra's Journal of Dress and Fashion* 1 April 1887: 165.
Pears advertisement. *Myra's Journal of Dress and Fashion* 1 June 1888: 325.
Pomeroy Skin Food advertisement. *Sketch* 12 January 1910: vi.
Pompeian Massage Cream advertisement. *Delineator* August 1905: 285.
Rimmel's Fashionable Season Novelties advertisement. *Myra's Journal of Dress and Fashion* 1 August 1886: n.p.
Rimmel's Specialties for the Complexion. *Myra's Journal of Dress and Fashion* 1 July 1880: 222.
Rossetter's Hair Restorer advertisement. John Johnson Collection of Printed Ephemera, Bodleian Library, c. 1880.
Roughead, William. *Rascals Revived*. London: Cassell, 1940.
Rowland's Kalydor advertisement. *Myra's Journal of Dress and Fashion* 1 April 1880: 198.
Rowlands' Kalydor advertisement. *Girl's Own Paper* 'Feathery Flakes', Extra Christmas Number, 1886: n.p.
Rowlands' Kalydor advertisement. *Girl's Own Paper*, 'Lily Leaves', Extra Summer Number 1886: n.p.
Ruppert, Mrs Anna. *A Book of Beauty*. London, 1892.
Saunders's Face Powder advertisement. *Queen* 11 April 1891: xxxiii.
S. G. *The Art of Being Beautiful: A Series of Interviews with a Society Beauty*. London: Henry J. Drane, 1902.
Shanks, Matheson and Semple lace shawls advertisement. *Myra's Journal of Dress and Fashion*. 1 December 1883: 625.
'Society'. *Myra's Journal of Dress and Fashion*. 1 August 1888: 462.
Stables, W. Gordon. 'Beauty: A Duty'. *Girl's Own Paper* 1 January 1898: 222–3.
—. *Boys' Book of Health and Strength*. London: Jarrold & Sons, 1892?
—. *The Girl's Own Book of Health and Beauty*. London: Jarrold & Sons, 1891?
Terry, Ellen. *The Story of My Life*. London: Hutchinson, 1908.

Tetlow's Gossamer Powder advertisement. *Delineator* April 1896: xxxiii.
'The Art of "Making-Up"'. *Woman* 22 August 1894: 9.
'The Art of Preserving Beauty'. *World of Fashion and Continental Feuilletons* 1 October 1849: 120.
'Theatrical Toilettes'. *Myra's Journal of Dress and Fashion* 1 July 1886: 329.
The Celebrated American Specialist advertisement. *Queen* 3 December 1892, n.p.
The Happy Home advertisement. *Sketch* 15 May 1895: 119.
'The Ladies' Gallery'. *Myra's Journal* 1 March 1890: 10.
'The New Doctor'. 'Some Practical Hints on Cosmetic Medicine'. *Girl's Own Paper* 1 October 1898: 6.
The Extraordinary Life and Trial of Madame Rachel at the Central Criminal Court, Old Bailey London. London: Diprose and Bateman printers, 1868.
'The Marriage of Madame Patti'. *Sketch* 25 January 1899: 2.
'The Service of Beauty. Personal Beauty'. *Girl's Own Paper* 9 February 1889: 299–300.
'The Theatrical Season in London'. *Sketch* 28 November 1894: 243.
'Tips for Amateur Actresses "On the Gentle Art of Making-up".' *Myra's Journal* 1 August 1900: 12.
'"Truth" and Beauty Culture', Mrs Pomeroy advertisement. *Sketch* 24 June 1914: x.
'Types of Dalmation Beauty'. *Sketch* 27 February 1895: 261.
Veblen, Thorstein. *The Theory of the Leisure Class: An Economic Study of Institutions*. 1899. New York: Macmillan, 1912.
Walker, Alexander. *Beauty; Illustrated Chiefly by an Analysis and Classification of Beauty in Woman*. 1836. New York: Henry G. Langley, 1845.
Walker, Mrs A. [pseud. Alexander Walker?]. *Female Beauty, as Preserved and Improved by Regimen, Cleanliness and Dress*. 1837. New York: Scofield and Voorhies (revised and amended), 1840.
Wilde, Oscar. *The Picture of Dorian Gray*. London: Ward, Lock & Co, 1891.
Wood, Mrs Henry. *East Lynne*. 2nd ed. London: Richard Bentley, 1862.
Woodbury's soap advertisement. *Delineator* August 1892: vi.

Secondary sources

Aindow, Rosy. *Dress and Identity in British Literary Culture, 1870–1914*. Farnham: Ashgate, 2010.

Altick, Richard D. *The Presence of the Present: Topics of the Day in the Victorian Novel*. Columbus: Ohio State UP, 1991.
Auerbach, Nina and U. C. Knoepflmacher. *Forbidden Journeys: Fairy Tales and Fantasies by Victorian Women Writers*. Chicago: U of Chicago P, 1992.
Balfour, Ian. 'Torso: (The) Sublime Sex, Beautiful Bodies, and the Matter of the Text'. *Eighteenth-Century Studies* 39 (2006): 323–36.
Banner, Lois. *American Beauty*. New York: Knopf, 1983.
Beatty, Laura. *Lillie Langtry: Manners, Masks and Morals*. London: Chatto & Windus, 1999.
Beetham, Margaret. *A Magazine of Her Own? Domesticity and Desire in the Woman's Magazine*. Abingdon: Routledge, 1996.
—. '"Natural but firm": The Corset Correspondence in the *Englishwoman's Domestic Magazine*.' *Woman: A Cultural Review* 2.2 (1991): 163–7.
—. 'Periodical Writing'. *The Cambridge Companion to Victorian Women's Writing*. Ed. Linda H. Peterson. Cambridge: Cambridge UP, 2015. 221–35.
Beetham, Margaret and Kay Boardman, eds. *Victorian Women's Magazines*. Manchester: Manchester UP, 2001.
Bellamy, Liz. 'The Uses of Fruit: Literary Symbolism and Technological Change in the Long Eighteenth Century'. *Literature & History* 24.2 (2015): 1–17.
Black, Paula. *The Beauty Industry: Gender, Culture, Pleasure*. London: Routledge, 2004.
Bowlby, Rachel. *Just Looking: Consumer Culture in Dreiser, Gissing and Zola*. New York: Methuen, 1985.
Braun, Heather. *The Rise and Fall of the Femme Fatale in British Literature, 1790–1910*. Madison, NJ: Fairleigh Dickinson UP, 2012.
Briefel, Aviva. 'Cosmetic Tragedies: Failed Masquerade in Wilkie Collins's *The Law and the Lady*'. *Victorian Literature and Culture* 37 (2009): 463–81.
Clark, Beverly Lyon. *Regendering the School Story: Sassy Sissies and Tattling Tomboys*, New York: Routledge, 2001.
Clark, Jessica P. *The Business of Beauty: Gender and the Body in Modern London*. London: Bloomsbury, 2020.
Cooper, Robyn. 'Victorian Discourses on Women and Beauty: The Alexander Walker Texts'. *Gender & History* 5.1 (1993): 34–55.
Dyhouse, Carol. *Glamour: Women, History, Feminism*. London: Zed Books, 2010.

Easley, Alexis. *Literary Celebrity, Gender, and Victorian Authorship, 1850–1914*. Newark: U of Delaware P, 2011.

Eltis, Sos. 'Private Lives and Public Spaces: Reputation, Celebrity and the Late Victorian Actress'. *Theatre and Celebrity in Britain 1660–2000*. Ed. Mary Luckhurst and Jane Moody. Basingstoke: Palgrave, 2005. 169–90.

Fitzgerald, Annarose. '"Following the Fashion": Women, Work, and Class Construction in *East Lynne*'. *Women and Work: The Labors of Self-Fashioning*. Ed. Christine Leiren Mower and Susanne Weil. Newcastle-Upon-Tyne: Cambridge Scholars, 2011. 302–18.

Flint, Kate. *The Victorians and the Visual Imagination*. Cambridge: Cambridge UP, 2000.

Fraser, Hilary, Stephanie Green and Judith Johnston. *Gender and the Victorian Periodical*. Cambridge: Cambridge UP, 2003.

Gardner, Kirsten E. 'From Cotton to Silicone: Breast Prosthesis Before 1950'. *Artificial Parts, Practical Lives: Modern Histories of Prostheses*. Ed. Katherine Ott, David Serlin and Stephen Mihm. New York: New York UP, 2002. 102–18.

Gilbert, Pamela K. *Victorian Skin: Surface, Self, History*. Ithaca: Cornell UP, 2019.

Gilman, Sander L. *Making the Body Beautiful: A Cultural History of Aesthetic Surgery*. Princeton: Princeton UP, 1999.

Gorham, Deborah. *The Victorian Girl and the Feminine Ideal*. 1982. Abingdon: Routledge, 2013.

Halloran, Jennifer A. 'The Ideology Behind *The Sorceress of the Strand*: Gender, Race, and Criminal Witchcraft'. *English Literature in Transition, 1880–1920* 45.2 (2002): 176–94.

Hartley, Lucy. 'A Science of Beauty? Femininity, Fitness and the Nineteenth Century Physiognomic Tradition'. *Women: A Cultural Review* 12.1 (2001): 19–34.

—. *Physiognomy and the Meaning of Expression in Nineteenth-Century Culture*. Cambridge: Cambridge UP, 2001.

Heath, Kay. *Aging by the Book: The Emergence of Midlife in Victorian Britain*. Albany, NY: SUNY, 2009.

Heaton, Sarah. 'Gender and Sexuality: Tresses Adorned and Adored, Locks Coiled and Cut'. *A Cultural History of Hair in the Age of Empire*. Ed. Sarah Heaton. London: Bloomsbury, 2020. 101–16.

Heberling, Lynn O'Neal. 'The Delineator'. *Women's Periodicals in the United States: Consumer Magazines*. Ed. Kathleen L. Endres and Therese L. Lueck. Westport, CT: Greenwood Press, 1995. 58–67.

Horne, Jackie C. 'Empire, Hysteria, and the Healthy Girl: The Deployment of the Body in Juliana Horatia Ewing's *Six to Sixteen*'. *Women's Studies* 33.3 (2004): 249–77.

Hughes-Hallett, Lucy. *Cleopatra: Queen, Lover, Legend*. London: Pimlico, 2006.

Jones, Geoffrey. *Beauty Imagined: A History of the Global Beauty Industry*. Oxford: Oxford UP, 2010.

King, Amy M. *Bloom: The Botanical Vernacular in the English Novel*. Oxford: Oxford UP, 2003.

King, Jeannette. *Discourses of Ageing in Fiction and Feminism: The Invisible Woman*. Basingstoke: Palgrave Macmillan, 2013.

Korstch, Christine Bayles. *Dress Culture in Late Victorian Women's Fiction: Literacy, Textiles and Activism*. Farnham: Ashgate, 2009.

Ledbetter, Kathryn. *British Victorian Women's Periodicals: Beauty, Civilization, and Poetry*. New York: Palgrave Macmillan, 2009.

Lennox, Sarah. 'The Beautified Body: Physiognomy in Victorian Beauty Manuals'. *Victorian Review* 42.1 (2016): 9–14.

Loeb, Lori Anne. *Consuming Angels: Advertising and Victorian Women*. New York: Oxford UP, 1994.

Luckhurst, Mary and Jane Moody. 'Introduction'. *Theatre and Celebrity in Britain, 1660–2000*. Ed. Mary Luckhurst and Jane Moody. Basingstoke: Palgrave, 2005. 1–14.

Mangum, Teresa. 'Growing Old: Age'. *A Companion to Victorian Literature and Culture*. Ed. Herbert F. Tucker. Malden, MA: Blackwell, 1999. 97–109.

Marck, Nancy Anne. 'Narrative Transference and Female Narcissism: The Social Message of *Adam Bede*'. *Studies in the Novel* 35.4 (2003): 447–70.

Marland, Hilary. *Health and Girlhood in Britain, 1874–1920*. Basingstoke: Palgrave Macmillan, 2013.

Martin, Morag. *Selling Beauty: Cosmetics, Commerce, and French Society, 1750–1830*. Baltimore: The Johns Hopkins UP, 2009.

Marwick, Arthur. *It: A History of Human Beauty*, London: Hambledon, 2004.

Matthews David, Alison. *Fashion Victims: The Dangers of Dress Past and Present*. London: Bloomsbury, 2015.

Miller, Elizabeth Carolyn. '"Shrewd Women of Business": Madame Rachel, Victorian Consumerism, and L. T. Meade's *The Sorceress of the Strand*'. *Victorian Literature and Culture* 34 (2006): 311–32.

Miller, Renata Kobetts. *The Victorian Actress in the Novel and on the Stage*. Edinburgh: Edinburgh UP, 2019.

Mills, Claudia. 'Choosing a Way of Life: *Eight Cousins* and *Six to*

Sixteen'. *Children's Literature Association Quarterly* 14.2 (1989): 71–5.

Moruzi, Kristine. *Constructing Girlhood through the Periodical Press, 1850–1915*. Farnham: Ashgate, 2012.

Moruzi, Kristine and Michelle Smith. '"Learning What Real Work . . . Means": Ambiguous Attitudes Towards Employment in the *Girl's Own Paper*'. *Victorian Periodicals Review* 43.4 (2010): 429–45.

Mount, Dana and Susie O'Brien. 'Postcolonialism and the Environment'. *The Oxford Handbook of Postcolonial Studies*. Ed. Graham Huggan. Oxford: Oxford UP, 2013. 521–39.

Newton, Michael, ed. *Victorian Fairy Tales*. Oxford: Oxford UP, 2015.

Nicholas, Jane. *The Modern Girl: Feminine Modernities, the Body, and Commodities in the 1920s*. Toronto: U of Toronto P, 2015.

Ofek, Galia. *Representations of Hair in Victorian Literature and Culture*. Farnham: Ashgate, 2009.

Peiss, Kathy. *Hope in a Jar: The Making of America's Beauty Culture*. New York: Henry Holt, 1998.

Pykett, Lyn. 'Reading the Periodical Press: Text and Context'. *Victorian Periodicals Review* 22.3 (1989): 100–8.

Rappaport, Helen. *Beautiful For Ever: Madame Rachel of Bond Street – Cosmetician, Con-Artist and Blackmailer*. London: Vintage, 2012.

Reis, Pamela Tamarkin. 'Victorian Centerfold: Another Look at Millais's "Cherry Ripe".' *Victorian Studies* 35.2 (1992): 201–5.

Ribeiro, Aileen. *Facing Beauty: Painted Women & Cosmetic Art*. New Haven, CT: Yale UP, 2011.

Richards, Thomas. *The Commodity Culture of Victorian England: Advertising and Spectacle, 1851–1914*. Stanford, CA: Stanford UP, 1990.

Schaffer, Talia. *The Forgotten Female Aesthetes: Literary Culture in Late-Victorian England*. Charlottesville: U of Virginia P, 2000.

Shuttleworth, Sally. *The Mind of the Child: Child Development in Literature, Science, and Medicine, 1840–1900*. Oxford: Oxford UP, 2010.

Slater, Michael. *Dickens and Women*. Stanford, CA: Stanford UP, 1983.

Steele, Valerie. *Fashion and Eroticism: Ideals of Feminine Beauty from the Victorian Era to the Jazz Age*. New York: Oxford UP, 1985.

—. *The Corset: A Cultural History*. New Haven, CT: Yale UP, 2001.

Thesander, Marianne. *The Feminine Ideal*. London: Reaktion, 1997.

Van Remoortel, Marianne. 'Who do you think they were? What Genealogy Databases Can do for Victorian Periodical Studies'. *Researching the*

Nineteenth-Century Periodical Press. Ed. Alexis Easley Andrew King and John Morton. London: Routledge, 2017. 131–44.

Yeazell, Ruth Bernard. *Fictions of Modesty: Women and Courtship in the English Novel.* Chicago: U of Chicago P, 1991.

Vickery, Amanda. 'Mutton Dressed at Lamb? Fashioning Age in Georgian England'. *Journal of British Studies* 52 (2013): 858–86.

Weber, Gary. 'Henry Labouchere, *Truth* and the New Journalism of Late Victorian Britain'. *Victorian Periodicals Review* 26.1 (1993): 36–43.

Zimmerman, Bonnie S. '"Radiant as a Diamond": George Eliot, Jewelry and the Female Role'. *Criticism: A Quarterly for Literature and the Arts* 19.3 (1977): 212–22.

Zuckerman, Mary Ellen. *A History of Popular Women's Magazines in the United States, 1792–1995.* Westport, CT: Greenwood, 1998.

Zweiniger-Bargielowska, Ina. *Managing the Body: Beauty, Health, and Fitness in Britain, 1880–1939.* New York: Oxford UP, 2010.

Index

abortion, 71
actresses, 7, 24, 77, 114, 135, 136–8, 142–3, 146, 148–52, 156, 158n
advertisements, 4–5, 25, 64, 65, 67, 110, 114, 136, 140–1, 145–52, 153, 154, 155–6, 159, 160–1, 162, 164, 165–7, 170–2
aesthetics, 12, 18, 32, 89
ageing, 5, 20, 23–4, 35, 35, 39, 60, 61, 73, 77, 109–32, 172, 185, 186
  disgust, 117–18, 122, 125, 127–9, 130
  premature, 83, 95, 96, 111
  preventative measures, 35–6, 116, 118
artifice, 10, 22, 45, 46, 52, 72–3, 74, 78, 93–4, 113, 126–7, 164, 181

Bayard, Madame
  Toilet Hints, 30, 38–42
beauty
  as art, 20, 31, 34–5, 114, 118, 121, 122, 124, 148–9, 154–5, 159
  biology, 12, 18
  danger, 2, 13, 22, 47, 54, 74, 78–9, 89, 90, 96
  definition, 7–8
  as duty, 2, 3, 11, 20, 39, 61, 94–5, 156, 164
  exotic, 71, 158n

industry, 3, 5, 9, 21, 24, 71, 72–3, 152, 187
  male, 14
  manuals, 3, 11, 17, 18, 19, 21, 22, 30–42, 51, 56–63, 111, 119–25, 169–70
  medicalised, 20, 31–3, 37, 71–2, 145, 155, 167, 171, 174
  natural, 5, 10–11, 19, 21, 29–30, 33, 39, 48, 49, 54–5, 58, 61, 63, 73, 75, 77–8, 83, 85, 105, 121, 157, 174, 184, 187
  power of, 13, 20, 70, 88, 129, 185
  preservation, 66, 91, 155
  regimen, 1, 25, 63, 109, 118, 119, 122, 124–5, 157, 160, 163–5, 167–75
  salon, 153–4
  types, 14, 15–17
Beerbohm, Max, 184, 186
Bernhardt, Sarah, 24, 114, 116, 137–8, 142, 150
blushing, 11, 50, 85
bodies, 8, 15, 32, 36, 37, 41, 162, 185
  ideal measurements, 32, 33
boys, 87
Braddon, Mary Elizabeth
  Lady Audley's Secret, 185
brand names, 4, 24, 148, 149, 152, 161, 166, 168
breasts, 32, 63, 176–7

Brinton, D. G. and George Napheys
  Personal Beauty, 21, 30–8
Burnett, Frances Hodgson
  The Secret Garden, 23, 97, 102–6, 107

celebrities, 2, 7, 24, 109, 114, 135–52, 155
  older, 139
  product endorsement, 149–52
character, 14, 18, 19–20, 21, 43, 49, 62, 83, 89, 93, 101, 103–4, 106, 107, 119, 120
class, 3, 8, 11–12, 16, 49, 96, 161, 163, 168
cleanliness, 58, 59, 65, 88, 90, 94, 163, 179
Collins, Wilkie
  The Law and the Lady, 21, 42–6, 52
complexion, 86, 91–2, 95, 96, 104, 120, 122, 155
  false, 126
consumerism, 2–3, 4–5, 23, 33, 137, 159–60, 161–3, 168
corsets, 33, 41, 51, 157
cosmetics, 9–10, 14, 19, 21, 33–4, 39, 43–4, 56–7, 58, 66, 111, 159, 160, 186
  blush, 64–5
  coloured, 62, 66–7, 73, 77, 93–4, 148–9, 153
  danger, 30, 33, 35, 40–2, 45, 54, 59, 60–1, 63, 66, 68–9, 73, 78, 79, 91, 92, 95, 119–20, 167
  deceptive, 69–70, 74, 85, 93–4
  dyes, 34, 41, 65, 112–13, 118, 119–20
  enamelling, 35, 67, 69, 117
  home-made, 40, 116, 178, 179
  industry, 24, 70–1, 182, 187
  lipstick, 33, 62, 128
  powder, 44, 57, 62, 92, 124, 137, 164–5, 170, 174–5, 179
  recipes, 57, 60, 61, 66, 132n, 144, 166
  secrecy, 40, 42, 45, 177

cosmeticians, 152–6
cosmetic surgery, 8, 35

defects, 38, 39
Delineator, 24, 160, 167–82
Dickens, Charles
  Dombey and Son, 24, 109, 125–9
diet, 17, 164, 95–6, 179
dress, 3, 4, 9, 20, 75–6, 98–9, 120, 130, 141–2
  rational, 94, 108n

Eliot, George
  Adam Bede, 21, 46–51
  Felix Holt, the Radical, 24, 109, 125, 129–31
emotions, 36, 69, 85–6, 90, 93, 101–2, 103, 105–6, 123, 172
Ewing, Juliana Horatia
  Six to Sixteen, 23, 97–102, 106–7
exercise, 36–7, 51, 95, 104, 172, 174

face, the, 9, 102
fashion, 55, 161; see also dress
fashion plates, 6, 135, 162
fiction, 3, 4, 22, 23, 30, 46–7, 51–2, 54–5, 56, 62, 63, 69, 74, 78, 79, 87, 96–7, 125, 185

girlhood, 23, 83–107
'Girl of the Period', 55–6, 85, 97
Girl's Own Paper, 1–2, 23, 83–4, 88–96, 107, 178

hair, 45, 65, 87, 102–3, 104–5, 110, 112–13, 118, 121–2, 145, 170
Haweis, Eliza
  The Art of Beauty, 18–21
health, 1, 21, 29–30, 33, 34, 35, 37, 85–8, 95–6, 101, 102, 104–6, 107, 122, 163–5, 175

illness, 97, 100–1, 102, 103, 106, 123
innocence, 49, 50, 73, 111
intellect, 88–90

jewellery, 47–8, 75

Langtry, Lillie, 24, 137, 139–40, 141, 144, 149–50, 152, 158n
Linton, Eliza Lynn; see also 'Girl of the Period'
lips, 33–4, 77

Madame Rachel, 22, 66, 68–9, 116–17, 153, 158
marriageability, 34–5, 51, 102, 110
massage, 172–4
Meade L. T.
 The Sorceress of the Strand, 22, 54, 69–74
menopause, 110
mirrors, 5, 170
modesty, 47, 48, 51
Montez, Lola, 144
 The Arts of Beauty, 22, 60–3, 69
morality, 51, 55, 88
mothers, 98, 100, 101, 102–3
Myra's Journal of Dress and Fashion, 24, 57, 135, 143–4, 157

patterns (clothing), 3, 24, 143, 162, 168
Patti, Adelina, 114, 135, 137, 139, 144, 145, 148, 150
periodicals, 3–4, 6, 24–5, 63, 135, 142–3, 156–7, 158, 159–62, 182–3, 186–7
 advice columns, 178–80
 endorsement of advertising, 165–7
photographs, 6–7, 140–1, 157, 170
physiognomy, 14, 18–19, 47, 89
Pomeroy, Mrs, 153–6, 157
puberty, 86–7

Queen, 11, 22, 24, 63–4, 114, 137, 160, 161, 164, 165–7

racism, 14, 56
Rimmel, Eugène, 11, 136, 149, 152–3, 157
Ruppert, Anna, 22, 67–8, 73, 156, 165–6, 175–6
 A Book of Beauty, 183

sexuality, 9, 14, 22, 46, 49–51, 54–5, 79, 110, 127, 131, 185
Sketch, 24, 135, 136–43, 146, 154–6
skin, 8, 11–12, 39–40, 59–60, 72, 90–1, 95, 111, 113, 116, 124, 155, 164, 171–2, 174, 178–9
soap, 34, 59, 90–1, 111, 113–14, 164, 170–1
Stables, Gordon ('Medicus'), 91–6
 The Girl's Own Book of Health and Beauty, 85–6, 104–5, 106
sublime, 14

Terry, Ellen, 7, 114, 135, 139, 140–1, 142, 146, 148, 150, 157
transatlantic ideals, 3, 6, 8, 160, 167

ugliness, 19–20, 43, 164
unhealthiness, 23, 41–2, 76–7

vanity, 21, 39, 46, 47, 48–9, 76, 98
visual culture, 6–7, 135

Walker, Alexander
 Beauty, 12–17, 186
 Female Beauty (Mrs A. Walker), 22, 58–60
weight, 104, 175, 179–80
whiteness, 11–12, 34, 59, 61, 71, 184
Wilde, Oscar
 The Picture of Dorian Gray, 22, 55, 74, 77–8
Woman, 4, 22, 24, 63–6, 114, 160, 161, 164, 166
Wood, Mrs Henry (Ellen)
 East Lynne, 22, 74–7
World of Fashion, 19
wrinkles, 39, 59, 111, 118, 120, 123, 124, 126, 155

youth, 22–3, 73, 74, 78, 83, 88
 recapturing, 128–9
 preservation of, 39–40, 90, 110, 111, 123, 124–5, 163, 164–5

EU representative:
Easy Access System Europe
Mustamäe tee 50, 10621 Tallinn, Estonia
Gpsr.requests@easproject.com